The Farm Labor Movement in the Midwest

THE FARM LABOR
IN THE MIDWEST

THE UNIVERSITY OF TEXAS PRESS   AUSTIN

MOVEMENT

W. K. Barger and Ernesto M. Reza

Foreword by Baldemar Velásquez

Social
Change
and
Adaptation
among
Migrant
Farmworkers

Requests for permission to reproduce material from this work
should be sent to Permissions, University of Texas Press, Box 7819,
Austin, TX 78713-7819.

⊗ The paper used in this publication meets the minimum
requirements of American National Standard for Information
Sciences—Permanence of Paper for Printed Library Materials,
ANSI Z39.48-1984.

Library of Congress Cataloging-in-Publication Data

Barger, W. K. (Walter Kenneth), date.
 The farm labor movement in the midwest : social change and adaptation among
migrant farmworkers / W. K. Barger, Ernesto M. Reza.—1st ed.
  p. cm.
 Includes bibliographical references and index.
 ISBN 0-292-70796-7 (cloth : alk. paper). — ISBN 0-292-70797-5 (pbk. ; alk. paper)
  1. Migrant agricultural laborers—Middle West. 2. Mexican Americans—
Middle West. I. Reza, Ernesto M. (Ernesto Mendoza) II. Title.
HD1527.A14B37 1994
331.5′44′0977—dc20
                                                              93-3962
                                                               CIP

This book is dedicated to
Baldemar Velásquez and the staff and members
of the Farm Labor Organizing Committee (FLOC),
who have taught us much about social change and adaptation,
and, most of all, about
human dignity and social justice.

Contents

Foreword

Baldemar Velásquez
President, Farm Labor Organizing Committee

Many years of hard work, debate, and caring activity have yielded six master agreements that presently cover five thousand workers on almost 120 different family farms in Ohio and Michigan, representing a significant change in employment practices and putting thousands of extra dollars in workers' pockets. It is easy to rattle off a long list of accomplishments of the union, some of which are precedent setting and historic. Nevertheless, in this era of union busting, a call needs to be issued to organize for radical changes in the infrastructure of how the agricultural industry does its business. Empowering the farmworker community has been an elusive struggle for twenty-four years. Finally, FLOC has hit on a cornerstone strategy that has culminated in this nation's first multiparty collective bargaining agreements. While many liberal supporters backed the small family farmers' movement, many danced around the fact that these farmers actually exploited the farmworkers who worked for them. In fact, it was the profits from labor-intensive crops such as cucumbers and tomatoes that offset the low and marginal returns from corn, wheat, and soybeans, thereby providing a key asset in helping the family farm. What FLOC did, however, was to bring the food processors to the negotiating table; negotiate a master agreement that applied to their contracted farms; and insist that they bring their growers to the negotiating table and sign one agreement as a third party in a collective manner. Campbell Soup and Vlasic Foods have since allowed associations of their growers to

Baldemar Velásquez, founder and president of the Farm Labor Organizing Committee (FLOC), addresses a rally of supporters in 1982. He and other FLOC leaders were able to mobilize the active support of both midwestern farmworkers and other segments of American society to achieve farm labor reform.

accommodate this process. After five years of collective bargaining, these associations have learned from FLOC the significance of collective action. In fact, some growers now support FLOC's organizing campaigns. The reason is simple: the small family farmers used to think they were of the upper class, when compared to the farmworkers. It was a counterfeit status that was as much emotional as fact, gained by marginalizing an impoverished community of color. They have learned at the bargaining table to look upward at the real decision makers and real conditions that influence industry prices and therefore, their livelihood, along with farmworkers.

It is also our desire to usher in a new era of relationships with the agricultural industry. This is one of the few areas of the country where the industry has accepted the notion that farmworkers have legitimate concerns about their families and their roles in the workplace. We hope to use this opportunity to secure our livelihood and improve the areas that have been overlooked.

Let us continue our prayers for a healthy industry in which all its workers, from top corporate officials to the last of the field workers, can make a living that is decent and conducive to raising a healthy family.

Yet, all that has been achieved has to be attributed to the quality of individuals whose commitments are cornerstones to any successful struggle. If FLOC is to have a long future, much will depend on the continuous acts of love, sacrifice, and unselfish giving that staff, members, and supporters have demonstrated over the years.

Let me be specific. For the first eleven years of FLOC's twenty-four-year history, no one was paid, not even for expenses such as gasoline. Many of us who were the first organizers had to find part-time jobs to support our organizing. Many members donated constantly in many ways, including taking us into their homes for meals. Supporters kept us on the road by helping get us to our next meeting. The spirit of this exciting volunteerism continues, always pressing toward the next history-making breakthrough.

Since the early days, things have changed, and FLOC can now pay travel expenses and offer a modest living budget to its staff. However, FLOC still needs to enlist in the cause individuals whose commitment and character are not unlike those of the people who began the organization. It is these special people that FLOC still needs now and in its future.

We must not forget to build on those relationships that have been keys to the success we have had thus far. For the most part, the thread that has woven staff, members, and supporters together into effective action has been the Church. With the Church there has always been the common point of moral reference that has held us accountable for our actions.

God Moves His People

The powerful words of Jesus calling us to believe in him, to receive and demonstrate the gift of faith, cause us to transcend our puny perceptions of reality and measure the world not within its present parameters but on the promised Kingdom of God.

It has not been unusual to encounter members, staff, and supporters alike whose actions are motivated by what they describe as an "inexplicable impulse." It is encouraging to us to witness God's moving of his people. The many donated hours, dollars, and selfless acts are counted to the Lord's glory, and his grace enables us to lift up humble workers of the fields.

FLOC must continue to encourage the involvement of the Church among staff, members, and supporters alike and seek the next step that God has called us to take together.

There have been rocky times with plenty of problems to frustrate our work, but we all cared enough, not only about the work, but about each other, to hang in and finish what we started. All this reminds me of one hot day when I was a little boy picking cotton in North Texas. I stuffed my cotton bag so full that I could no longer drag it through the rows. My aunt rescued me. She helped me get the bag to the scales, and that night she solved my problem by cutting the bag in half and sewing it so that I could no longer overfill it beyond my strength. She cared, and she helped me do my job. I don't remember anything about how much cotton I picked or how much money I earned, although I am sure that was the focus of my attention then. Now all I remember is that she cared and she helped me. So, as the victories come and the years go by, I will remember less the details of winning and losing and more the acts of caring and love of the many people who have made FLOC possible. This is the stuff that makes life worthwhile. Let us continue to build on this service to one another through this next decade.

Preface

This book is about the Farm Labor Organizing Committee (FLOC), which represents a social reform movement of migrant and seasonal farmworkers in the Midwest. We have two purposes in preparing this book. One is to document the story of FLOC, and the second is to examine those processes in social change that directed the movement and helped FLOC achieve its major goals. FLOC's story began in 1967, when Baldemar Velásquez founded the movement. For eight years, from 1978 to 1986, FLOC farmworkers struggled with Campbell Soup to win a direct voice in their own conditions. They were supported in this struggle by churches, labor unions, and over a million individual Americans. These supporters cast their vote for social justice in the marketplace by boycotting Campbell's products. In 1986 and 1987, three-way contracts were signed by FLOC, Campbell, and Campbell's tomato and cucumber growers in Ohio and Michigan. Similar contracts were signed in 1987 with Heinz and its cucumber growers in Ohio and Michigan and in 1991 with Dean Foods and its cucumber growers in the same states. These contracts instituted significant social reforms in the American socioeconomic system in which farmworkers exist.

Each of our purposes in preparing this book may appeal to different audiences. Some readers will be specifically interested in FLOC, the farm labor movement, and issues such as social justice. Others will be interested in the process of social change, as illustrated by a particular social reform movement. We ask each audience to consider the additional lessons in the other's interests, which will supplement their own learning.

In documenting the FLOC movement, we will review the case of

The symbol of the Farm Labor Organizing Committee (FLOC) is the black Mexican eagle. The FLOC slogan, *Hasta la Victoria*, means "Onward to Victory," signifying the sacrifices and persistence of farmworkers in achieving social justice.

those migrant and seasonal farmworkers in the Midwest whose labor produces the food we eat every day. These workers are at least as important to our personal and national well-being as those who produce our petroleum, educate our children, and provide us with health care. Yet it is still a shock to realize that the people who produce our food are themselves malnourished. They live in poverty and suffer among the most severe health problems of any group in the country. A long series of studies document that these conditions have remained virtually unchanged for almost a century. The deprived conditions experienced by farmworkers reflect America at its worst, the results of displaced priorities in our economic and social systems.

There are a number of options for solving the problems farmworkers face, from enacting new legal standards to providing social welfare services. But the alternative that has historically been the most effective is the farm labor movement, led by the United Farm Workers (UFW) in California. FLOC is a sister group, which has sought similar reforms for farmworkers in the Midwest. This book, then, documents the story of FLOC and its role in achieving farm labor reforms in the Midwest.

For those readers primarily interested in the FLOC case, we would like you to be aware of the organization of this book. We are examining the story of FLOC from a systems perspective of social change. That is, we are looking at two sets of forces that have guided the FLOC movement. One involves those forces that are *internal* to midwestern farmworkers. These factors include their living and working conditions, their motivations for seeking changes, their inherent powerlessness to make meaningful changes on their own, and their support for the FLOC movement. The other set involves *external* forces in the farmworkers' larger societal environment. These include both those who have supported FLOC's efforts and those who have opposed farm labor reforms.

In the first chapter, we explain our systems approach to social change, which we believe will help all readers better understand the FLOC story. We then describe midwestern farmworkers and their living and working conditions in the second chapter. Chapter 3 provides a history of the FLOC movement. In the next two chapters, we review those internal and external forces that have contributed to FLOC's success. Chapter 6 summarizes the impacts of the FLOC movement on farmworkers and on the socioeconomic system in which they exist. In the final chapter, we review the FLOC case in terms of the systems model of social change, which explains the forces that have directed the FLOC movement and enabled it to achieve social reforms. Readers who are primarily interested in the FLOC story will find a full documentation of the movement in Chapters 2 through 6. We urge you to also look at the first and last chapters, which we believe will help you better understand *how* and *why* the FLOC movement has been able to make significant social changes.

Our second purpose in writing this book is to examine the processes of social change in the FLOC case. We wish not only to tell the story of FLOC but to explain why and how FLOC was able to achieve farm labor reforms in the Midwest. Social change is a phenomenon that affects us all. Every day we encounter ideas about "progress," the "good old days," the "stresses of modern life," and new "opportunities." Politicians, teachers, investors, evangelists, revolutionaries, corporate managers, and many others are constantly seeking to change our daily lives. Yet how well do these change agents understand social change itself? How well can they foresee the impacts of the changes they propose, particularly the negative effects? How well do we understand how their changes will affect us? Do either we or they really know why and how changes occur as they do? Do we understand enough to make sure that changes are constructive?

For those readers interested in social change, we have organized a set of ideas about systems change to better understand the FLOC story. We generally look at FLOC as a social reform movement, but we specifically examine the FLOC movement in terms of systems adaptation. FLOC represents a successful attempt by midwestern farmworkers to achieve a more worthwhile life. As already indicated, the perspective of systems adaptation can help us understand the internal and external forces that have guided social change in the FLOC case. In the first chapter, we review those ideas about systems change, which help us understand the FLOC movement. Chapters 2 through 6 document the forces, processes, and outcomes evident in the FLOC movement. And in the last chapter, we summarize those ideas about social adaptation, which are illustrated in the FLOC case. We urge you to consider the ideas about social change presented here. But we also urge you to examine carefully the specifics of the FLOC story, since it is a unique case that has important lessons for understanding social change.

We have used a number of research methods in examining the FLOC case. We have been involved in continuing field work for over ten years with midwestern farmworkers and with the Farm Labor Organizing Committee. On the one hand, we have sought to understand the meaningful experiences and views of farmworkers and others affected by the FLOC movement. We have thus conducted systematic participation-observation in migrant camps and at FLOC activities. We were there when many of the events described in this account occurred. We have interviewed farmworkers and have talked with growers and representatives of agribusinesses. We have informally discussed issues and events with FLOC's leaders and supporters over the years. We have also sought to understand how views and experiences are distributed and how some factors affect other factors. We have thus conducted field surveys among farmworkers and among the public in the Midwest.

We have drawn upon our combined knowledge and skills in presenting the concepts and materials included in this work. Concepts and methods from cultural anthropology, brought to this study by Barger, are supplemented by those from organizational psychology, brought by Reza. Reza has contributed insights from the perspective of a Mexican American, which are complemented by the Anglo American perspectives of Barger. We both have also contributed our personal experiences with the FLOC movement, which include working on the FLOC staff and community organizing in support of FLOC's boycott of Campbell Soup. We have thus drawn upon the breadth and depth of our combined knowledge and experience in understanding and presenting the FLOC story.

In presenting the story of FLOC, we should clarify that our involvement has not been an abstract, detached study. We have both been directly involved in supporting FLOC in its efforts. Barger coordinated a local support group in central Indiana that advocated FLOC and its boycott against Campbell Soup, and Reza served on FLOC's staff, coordinating its boycott activities (Barger and Reza 1985a, 1987). At the same time, we have both operated from an academic base in conducting field surveys, interviewing farmworkers and key people involved in the FLOC struggle, and observing the course of the FLOC movement. Some might feel that academic research and applied involvements are mutually exclusive activities. We disagree.

We argue that holding the highest scientific standards possible in applied activities is an ethical as well as a professional responsibility. Since applied work inherently involves social changes and can therefore make a direct impact in people's lives, we need to assess carefully where we are valid in our understandings and also where we are limited. When pressed, most scientists would agree that there is no such thing as purely "objective" research because the whole research process from beginning to end is influenced by conceptual, methodological, situational, and personal biases. Valid scientific research is therefore based on the control of such biases rather than their absence. Such controls must be consciously included in the conceptualization of the issue, in the collection of data, in the analysis of data, and in making grounded interpretations of findings. In addition, we have tried to clearly state our value positions so the reader will be aware of our perspectives in discussing events and the issues.

We also believe that applied work can make as important theoretical contributions as "pure" research. This is because the validity of concepts and methods are prospectively tested in the real world. Since applied work inherently involves change, we need to be validly grounded in our understandings if those changes are to be predicted and constructive. For example, the model of sociocultural change used in applied projects (or the lack of clear conceptual understandings of change) can be crucial to the constructive achievements of such projects. Our concept of change will be tested in concrete life situations, for better or for worse. That is why we have invested so much effort in developing the model of systems adaptation concept presented here (Barger 1982 and 1977; Barger and Reza

1987). We have felt the need to understand social change in a valid and predictive manner because we have been so invested in applied change.

We argue that because value positions are taken in applied change, the highest scientific standards are needed. We must have valid understandings if our contributions are to be effective and constructive. For example, in the 1983 survey of midwestern farmworkers, it would have been satisfying to find that all farmworkers were solidly behind FLOC, and it would have been easy to invest less effort because we were "sure" this was the case. In order for FLOC to be truly effective in making farm labor reforms, however, we also needed to understand the views and motivations of those workers who were unconcerned about the issues and also of those who were opposed. Because we did have value commitments for effective changes, we had to prove to ourselves what FLOC's actual situation was. If it was to make effective reforms, the farm labor movement could not rely on something that was not there. We are satisfied that our research data, analysis, and conclusions are valid and fulfill scientific standards more than most "pure" social research.

We readily acknowledge that we have several biases in our study of the FLOC case. As some see a glass of water as half-full rather than half-empty, we have been greatly impressed with FLOC's efforts. Having seen firsthand the bitterness of some growers against FLOC, for example, we were amazed to see some of these same farmers address the 1991 convention of FLOC farmworkers, praising them for their achievements. We have also observed over the years a number of farmworkers grow from cautious and defensive individuals to proud, confident, and active FLOC members. Our intimate involvement with the FLOC movement has also provided us with insights into FLOC's reasoning, strengths, and limitations in activities to organize midwestern farmworkers and win social reforms. We believe that our biases are an asset in presenting the FLOC story and that as a result, the reader will gain better understanding of the change process involving the FLOC movement.

There are many people whom we wish to recognize as having contributed to this volume. The 1982 public survey cited in this report was codirected by Ain Haas in the Department of Sociology at Indiana University at Indianapolis. This survey was supported by the Indiana Council of Churches, the Indiana Catholic Conference, and the Project Development Program of Indiana University at Indianapolis. The 1983 field survey of midwestern farmworkers, which is also cited, was supported by the Project Development Program of Indiana University at Indianapolis. In addition, Bill Plater, John Barlow, Susan Sutton, Wendell McBurney, and Anne Kratz of Indiana University at Indianapolis provided both material support and personal encouragement in our field research and manuscript preparation. Their support has made possible our long-term professional involvement with farm labor issues. Mary Qualls Grossman, Vicki Cummings Copenhaven, and Rosío Yaselli assisted in the collection and analysis of research data. Karen Swing helped identify photographs to illustrate the textual materials. Mary Templin, Theo Majka, and Amy Keeler reviewed drafts of the manuscript and provided valuable feedback and input into the accuracy and balance of the contents. Theresa May, executive editor of the University of Texas Press, also provided excellent feedback, advice, and support in preparing this book. In addition, Nancy Warrington helped move the book through the process of publication with efficiency and cheerfulness, and Rebecca Schwartz's technical editing helped make the text more focused and readable. Marnia Kennon, Philip Barger, and Rosa Rivera endured our absences in both mind and body in our work with FLOC and in the preparation of this book, and we are grateful for their moral support.

We also wish to thank those farmworkers who shared with us their experiences and who actively cooperated in our field research. We particularly wish to express our deep appreciation to Baldemar Velásquez and to the staff and members of FLOC. Their struggle for dignity and social justice for midwestern farmworkers has contributed to a society where these values can be better realized for all of us, and it is this ideal that has inspired this book. We therefore dedicate this volume to them, and also to the FLOC kids, Philip, and the next generation of Americans. May those who come after us experience greater justice and dignity as a result of the achievements of FLOC and other social movements that promote the human worth of *all* individuals and groups in our society.

CHAPTER 1

Social Reform and Adaptation

Alfredo, his wife, and five children headed north out of Pharr, Texas, early one June morning in 1977.[1] The old family pickup with a homemade cover was packed with minimal clothes and equipment to last the family for the next five months. Money for the trip had been earned by collecting and selling scrap metal. During the four days' trip to Michigan, repairing a flat tire had drained the family's available cash, and they had to go one day without eating.

In Michigan, the family looked for part-time work to help support themselves until they could link up with their crew leader in a migrant labor camp. A week later, all members of the family were bent over in a field, harvesting cucumbers on a hot and humid day. Over the next three weeks, the family earned $1,600. They then went to Ohio to harvest tomatoes. Since the tomatoes were late in ripening, the family had to wait two weeks, drawing heavily upon their meager earnings. For the next six weeks, the family earned $3,200 harvesting tomatoes. In the last week, they spent more money than they earned, because most of the harvest was completed. But they decided to stay in order to collect their "bonus" of $210. This was part of their earnings held back by the grower until the end of the season. This practice was designed to ensure workers were available at the end of the harvest when there was little left to pick.

After odd jobs and a brief period picking apples, the family had earned most of its annual income of $6,800. They then returned to their home in the lower Rio Grande Valley of Texas. The children entered school four weeks late, already behind in their studies. Within four months, the family's earnings ran out. With no other work available, the family applied for public welfare. Alfredo in

particular felt ashamed at having to ask for help, since this acknowledged that he was not able to provide for his family. A
month later, their daughter Gloria came down with pneumonia,
complicated by malnutrition, and had to be hospitalized. The
family was now in debt, owing the hospital $3,500.

Next June, the family again headed north. But now they owed
$6,000 to the Internal Revenue Service. The cucumber grower for
whom they had worked in Michigan for the last four years had
paid them as independent "sharecroppers" rather than employees. Alfredo had not understood this and did not realize that the
grower had not withheld taxes and Social Security. When the IRS
discovered this, they imposed the back taxes on Alfredo, plus interest. He appealed, asking the IRS to waive the interest and to
take payment on the taxes in small amounts over the next several
years. He was turned down, but he could not make any payments,
so the interest kept increasing. The family, already existing at a
marginal level, was now in debt for years to come.

Alfredo is a quiet man with a warm smile and gentle manner.
He has a deep concern about his children's future and believes
education will improve their situation in life. He worries that they
have been behind in school, but the children's earnings have been
necessary for the family's survival. He has also been ashamed
when he could not provide them with new clothes for school.

In 1978, Alfredo and his family made an important decision
that changed their lives. They joined the Farm Labor Organizing Committee (FLOC), a labor union of farmworkers in the Midwest. At that time, they had met with Baldemar Velásquez, the
young leader of FLOC, because they knew and trusted his father.
They listened to Baldemar's argument that farmworkers would
never have security or dignity as long as others made decisions for
migrants, whether agribusinesses or welfare agencies. The only
meaningful and effective solution, he maintained, was for farmworkers to decide for themselves what conditions were acceptable. FLOC had been seeking collective bargaining rights with
Campbell Soup and its tomato growers. When there was no response, Alfredo and two thousand other farmworkers voted to
strike all Campbell's tomato operations in northwestern Ohio.
The strike was soon followed by a boycott of all Campbell's
products.

Over the next eight years, Alfredo and his family remained
poor, but important changes occurred. Alfredo, his wife, and their
children made many sacrifices in order to organize other farmworkers. Alfredo spent many hours discussing the issues with

workers harvesting Campbell tomatoes and cucumbers. Most were interested and supported the cause, and some joined FLOC. Many were afraid of losing their meager earnings and remained marginal to the conflict. A few like Alfredo made the sacrifices every summer to join the picket lines in Ohio and every winter to organize farmworkers in Texas and Florida. Alfredo and other key FLOC members continually debated the issues and strategies. In the process, Alfredo gained new insights into farmworkers' conditions, FLOC's goals and methods, and human nature. As he developed the depth of his own understandings, he became more skilled in convincing other workers about the rationale and justice of FLOC's cause.

Alfredo became aware that FLOC's cause was supported by many churches, labor unions, and other groups. He sometimes met with such groups, discussed the issues, and asked for their support of the farmworkers' boycott against Campbell. He was encouraged by their support and at times was surprised that Campbell seemed more responsive to FLOC's supporters than to the farmworkers themselves. In the process, he became convinced that their struggle was not just for farmworkers but for a better society for all Americans.

Other changes were also occurring in Alfredo's life. Though he only had a sixth-grade education, he began to read and to talk with others in order to better understand national and world affairs. His family began discussing their plans together, and all members participated in family decisions. Alfredo laughs about this, saying his kids organized their traditional Mexican father. Perhaps one of the greatest benefits of their involvement with FLOC, he says, has been how he and his family have grown. They have learned to respect others, to deal with conflicts, and to have faith in who they are and what they are doing. Alfredo is a devout person, and he thanks God for how he and his family have developed.

In 1986, their commitment and sacrifices were rewarded when FLOC signed a farm labor contract with the Campbell Soup Company and its growers. The next harvest season, Alfredo worked cucumbers and tomatoes under FLOC contracts. The family experienced new conditions that before had only been a dream. They not only earned significantly higher wages, but they also received unemployment insurance, workers compensation for job-related injuries, and other benefits that they had never before enjoyed. Under the contracts, these benefits were available whether they worked pickles in Michigan or tomatoes in Ohio.

Alfredo says that for the first time he feels more secure in life. He notes that he can now come north assured of work and better earnings. He also says that growers and crew leaders cannot treat workers arbitrarily now because the contracts provide a grievance procedure for dealing with problems and workers' complaints. Alfredo says he has gained a new sense of dignity because he now can do something about his children's future. He gives FLOC credit for these changes in their lives. Baldemar Velásquez, on the other hand, states that their cause was successful because of people like Alfredo, who made the personal sacrifices to help all farmworkers. He also acknowledges that millions of other Americans made the farmworkers' cause a success by boycotting Campbell's products.

    The story of Alfredo and his family reflects the story of the farm labor movement in the Midwest. It serves as an example of social changes that have had many adaptive advantages for midwestern farmworkers. These changes have been the results of a social reform movement led by the Farm Labor Organizing Committee. There are many forces that have guided the FLOC movement. Some have been internal to midwestern farmworkers. Alfredo and other farmworkers, for example, were strongly motivated to dedicate so much effort to the FLOC cause. Other forces have been external to the farmworkers' immediate existence. These include the policies of Campbell Soup toward the farm labor issues and the widespread support of church, labor, and other groups for the Campbell boycott. It is the combination of these forces that in the long run enabled FLOC to succeed in reorganizing the socioeconomic system in which midwestern farmworkers exist.

    The FLOC movement has made important internal changes among farmworkers. Midwestern migrants have found a new sense of security and have achieved a new stability for their families. They have formed new views about themselves and about the socioeconomic system in which they work. They have also developed a cohesive organization to promote their cause.

    In addition, FLOC has made significant impacts in a larger social, economic, and political environment in which farmworkers exist. FLOC workers have mobilized allies and supporters among churches, labor organizations, and other segments of society. Agribusinesses and growers now relate differently to the migrants working their crops. They have new legal obligations to their workers, as defined by labor contracts. These changes have provided new opportunities and benefits, and working conditions have been greatly improved for FLOC workers. Perhaps the most important change is that FLOC farmworkers now have a direct role in the decisions about their own life conditions.

These internal and external impacts have changed the agricultural system in the Midwest. The farm labor pool has become more stable, and the farmworkers expect more of themselves and the system. Growers and agribusinesses now treat farmworkers as an integral part of the system. Farmworker conditions have significantly improved. FLOC workers now earn higher wages, receive new benefits, are provided more adequate housing and sanitary facilities, and no longer have to rely on child labor to help their families survive. They also have a new structure for addressing problems, rather than being dependent upon the whims of their crew leaders and growers. In the longer term, FLOC workers now have a realistic hope for better health and for more educational opportunities for their children. They can also make meaningful contributions to the larger American society by being more productive citizens and taxpayers. Taken together, these changes have gone to the root of the system that has caused discrimination against farmworkers and brought about their deprived conditions.

We have two purposes in examining the FLOC movement. The first is to document the FLOC movement. There are several studies of the United Farm Workers (UFW) in California. But there is very little information available on the farm labor movement in the Midwest, which has also achieved creative and important reforms for farmworkers. We will review the events since FLOC's founding in 1967 by Baldemar Velásquez, during its eight-year struggle with Campbell Soup from 1978 to 1986, and through its first two periods of farm labor contracts from 1986 to 1991.

Our second purpose is to explain *why* and *how* FLOC was able to achieve farm labor reforms in the Midwest. We wish not only to tell the story of FLOC but to examine the forces and process of social change as they are evident in the FLOC case. To that end, we pose a set of concepts about social change that can help us better understand the FLOC movement.

First, to consider social change itself, we will review major ideas about social movements and pose a systems concept of social adaptation. These ideas will then be used to guide us through the story of FLOC and analysis of social change in the FLOC case.

Social Change and Social Movements

Social change involves the reorganization of a group's structure and behavior. We are all affected by the many kinds of social change in contemporary history. These include generation gaps, federal policies on environmental pollution, the development of new technologies, and shifts in values and perceived needs. They also include trade imbalances, civil wars in Central America, social dissension in South Africa, and religious conflict in the Mideast. While such cases reflect different types of changes, they all share certain features. Changes in one arena often produce changes in other areas. Changes in women's roles in America, for example, automatically produce changes in men's roles. And new biotechnology in medicine affects the availability of health care for many Americans.

Understanding principles of social change is important, particularly for those who try to make changes happen. Politicians, bureaucrats, revolutionaries, prophets, community groups, and many others continuously try to initiate sociocultural changes. Their ideas about what change is and how it works can have serious implications. Their views influence their goals and methods, and the outcomes of their efforts can have dramatic consequences. In the process of developing new policies and programs, the lives of many people can be affected, for better or worse. In addition, the impacts of such efforts can be experienced at the individual, organizational, community, societal, and even global level.

As the world transforms around us, it is important to note that a wide variety of changes involve similar mechanisms and processes. If we can understand what change is and how it works, we can apply these principles to anticipate events and to help foster productive changes. We can better understand what forces precipitate an act of terrorism, or we can foresee events initiated by a new law on occupational safety, for instance. Also, we will be better able to positively *direct* changes, rather than just react to events.

A number of studies have examined intentional and organized efforts of social change as opportunities to develop our understanding of change itself (Arensberg 1978; Barger and Reza 1987, 1989; Clifton 1970; Holmberg 1958; Kimball 1978; Maquet 1964; Partridge and Eddy 1978; Reining 1962; Schensul 1985, 1987; Schensul and Schensul 1978; Tax 1958; Thompson 1965). Such efforts allow social scientists to test the validity, predictability, and comprehensiveness of ideas about change. In the process, these efforts also provide new ideas and information to expand our understanding of social change.

One dramatic example of social change is a *social movement*, a purposeful and organized effort by a particular group of people to change its sociocultural setting to achieve a more meaningful order (Ash 1972; Killian 1964; McCarthy and Zald 1977; Morrison 1971; Nicholas 1973; Smelser 1963; Wallace 1956; Zald and Ash 1966). Social movements represent a mass effort to achieve a rapid and massive restructuring of a society. They thus provide an excellent opportunity to test our understandings of social change.

Two ideas have been posed to explain what motivates mass protest evident in social movements. One is the Marxist concept of internal inconsistencies in a social system, which lead to conflict (Marx 1904; Dahrendorf 1964). The concept most used to explain the motivational sources of mass change is relative deprivation (Aberle 1967; Geschwender 1968; Katz 1974; Morrison 1971; Murphy and Watson 1971). This involves an increase in the gap between the ideal of what people desire and the realities that they actually experience. The important point here is the *increase* in the gap. There are always discrepancies in any social system. However, it is not just the gap itself that is important but rather a rapid expansion of the discrepancy. An increase in the ideal-real gap can occur in two ways. One is for the ideal to be raised. For example, African Americans have experienced deprived conditions for much of their history in the United States. During the Second World War, many African Americans filled industrial jobs vacated by Anglos who joined the armed forces. Their hopes for occupational opportunities were raised by this event. But when these hopes were unrealized after the war, the motivation for the civil rights movement was triggered. The second way for the ideal-real discrepancy to increase is when the realities dramatically drop. For example, the Depression seriously affected the industrial labor force. The ideal of steady employment and job opportunities remained constant, but many workers were left without jobs and others faced a constant threat of job loss. It is no accident that this was the period of great gains by organized labor and of broad new labor legislation like the National Labor Relations Act of 1932. We will see that midwestern farmworkers have become involved in mass action, and several events suggest that relative deprivation has been a motivating force.

The farm labor movement, like the civil rights and women's rights movements, is a *reform* movement (Katz 1967, 1974; Killian 1964). It seeks to work within legitimate channels of the existing social order, restructuring the system to be more beneficial to a particular group in the society. Such a movement accepts the basic norms and organizational premises of the larger society. In fact, the overall goal is for groups like farmworkers to *share* in the opportunities and benefits enjoyed by other segments of society. They essentially seek to be *included* in the basic norms and structures of the larger society. A revolutionary movement, on the other hand, seeks to replace the existing social order with a different one, like in the American and Russian revolutions. The goal is to do away with the existing political, economic, religious, or other system and substitute a new system that promises to provide new opportunities and greater benefits. It is important to note that revolutionary movements often begin with reform as their primary goal. But when this is blocked, the frustrated participants question the basic norms and structures of their society and look to alternative systems.

FLOC's efforts have reformed the agricultural system in which midwestern farmworkers exist. Because FLOC has been able to use legitimate means to achieve change, including a labor strike and consumer's boycott, there has never been a move to resort to violence or to replace the existing system. In fact, FLOC has had and continues to have a strong commitment to nonviolence.

All social movements are based on a constituent population, the group from which a social movement arises and whose cause it advocates. One question particularly critical for a social movement is the degree to which a constituent group endorses and actively supports its efforts. This has major implications for the credibility, effectiveness, and ultimate success of the movement. One issue we will examine, therefore, is the support for the FLOC movement among farmworkers themselves.

Leadership is an important factor in social movements (Killian 1964; Nicholas 1973; T. Schwartz 1962; Wallace 1956, 1970; Zald and Ash 1966). César Chávez and Martin Luther King, for example, have been instrumental in shaping movement goals and in organizing efforts for mass change. The charisma of leaders is important in mobilizing social movements. Their ability to initiate and direct actions is based on a moral power, where people *choose* to follow them, rather than on formal authority. They are able to tap shared needs and sentiments, thereby inspiring people to follow their lead. As we shall see, creative and effective leadership has been an important force in guiding the FLOC movement.

Another factor in social movements is ideology, the philosophy which explains a group's problems and presents the solution (Mooney 1965; Morrison 1971; Nicholas 1973; and Wallace 1956, 1970). This perspective is included in recent studies concerned with frame alignment (Snow 1986; Scott 1990). During the Depression, for example, the prosperity of industrial leaders was easily interpreted as the exploitation of the workers' labor for their own selfish gain.

With this view of their problems, workers came up with a logical solution of labor organizing and collective bargaining, where workers could negotiate the exchange of their labor for acceptable benefits. The principle of collective bargaining posed a logical solution to the perceived problems of workers. We will see where the FLOC ideology has evolved within particular circumstances, drawing upon this labor philosophy and such ideals as social justice and self-determination.

Social movements must also have organizations that can coordinate activities for change (Killian 1964; Zald and Ash 1966). Both the United Farm Workers (UFW) and the Southern Christian Leadership Conference (SCLC) are examples of such organizations. As we shall see, FLOC has had a rather fluid organization, which has proved important in maximizing its limited resources.

An important factor in the success of any social movement is how it can mobilize resources (Freeman 1979; McCarthy and Zald 1977; Zald and Ash 1966; Zald and McCarthy 1979a, 1979b; also see Wallace 1956). Resource mobilization involves enlisting allies and supporters in other segments of society, initiating and directing the political process concerning the issues, and overcoming opposition and constraints. We will review how the mobilization of external forces has been critical in the FLOC movement. A deprived minority like farmworkers has possessed little socioeconomic power to effect social reforms. The combined power of all those who have supported FLOC, on the other hand, has outweighed the vested interests threatened by farm labor reforms.

Concepts about social movements will help us understand the events involved in the FLOC case. But we believe a key theoretical issue in social change is the process of change. To understand the forces involved in the FLOC movement and how these forces have interacted to initiate and direct social reform toward a particular outcome is essential. To better understand this process, we offer a systems model of change, which we term *social adaptation*.

Social Adaptation

One set of ideas about social change focuses on the content and direction of changes as a *systems* phenomenon (Marx 1904; Dahrendorf 1964; Parsons 1964; Barnett 1953; Wallace 1956; Miller 1978). A system is an organized unit whose interdependent parts are regularly interacting and functioning together as an integrated and balanced whole. The human body, for example, is such a system, composed of muscles, legs, a heart, antibodies, hormones, and many other parts functioning together as a single unit. Such systems strive for a complex equilibrium. In the body's case, this would be a balanced state which controls temperature, disease, and other processes for optimal functioning. But just as a person is more than simply his or her body parts, a system is more than its individual traits. It is, rather, a dynamic and holistic unit with its own unified character.

A society is also a system. It is composed of different subsystems. These include ethnic and social groups, gender and age roles, social institutions like political and religious bodies, social classes, values and sanctions regarding individual behavior, means of production and distribution of material goods, urban and rural settings, and many other components. All the parts of a social system are interrelated and function together. This is seen, for instance, when an economic recession affects jobs and families, which in turn affect politics and government agencies, and so on. A social system is more than the sum of its traits. It also involves a dynamic and holistic unit with its own character. The United States, for example, has many overlaps with Great Britain, Germany, and Japan. But it has its own distinct configuration and identity as well. In examining the FLOC movement, we will be concerned with several levels of the American social system. Our concepts, therefore, have to be able to explain social change in the larger system, as well as specific events.

A systems concept is particularly important in understanding the process involved in sociocultural change. It calls for the identification of those forces actively influencing change. It also calls for examination of how these forces interact in directing the course of change. This in turn provides a basis for predicting the course and outcomes of phenomena, a basic goal in all sciences.

A systems approach to social change is seen in the conflict model of Hegel and Marx (Marx 1904; Dahrendorf 1964). Their dialectical theory poses that social systems have inherent internal contradictions. These imbalances produce a reaction which causes the system to reorganize to produce a better balance between the original forces and the reaction forces. This model, then, focuses on conflicting forces within a society and how this conflict leads to a basic restructuring of that society. The strength in this model is that it calls for consideration of the process of change. We do not believe that Marx's emphasis on economic production and social class is necessarily valid in itself. But we do believe the process functions in all components of a social system. In our view, where the conflict model has led to successful socialist revolutions in modern history, it is due to its emphasis on the process of change, rather than in its focus on social classes and material property.

Talcott Parsons (1964) has also posed a systems perspective in his views of social change. In particular, he considers the interaction of forces that are both internal and external to a group. Ideas involving a broader interaction between a group and its environment are also included in the multilineal models of cultural evolution (Steward 1955; Murphy and Steward 1956). Related ideas which focus on a group's interaction with its environment are evident in concepts of cultural ecology (Geertz 1963, 1972; M. Harris 1966; Moran 1979; Rappaport 1968, 1971). These views, however, focus more on the maintenance of a system than its development and alteration.

Sociocultural Adaptation

The specific systems model of change that we propose to examine the farm labor movement is sociocultural adaptation. *Adaptation* is a process of change made by a population in its interaction with its environment that enhances its survival and continuation. Systems adaptation is essentially an evolutionary model of change, but it is one that emphasizes the process involved rather than particular traits or directions. Significantly, it is the *system* which changes, not just traits. Since the focus here is on sociocultural change, we will be concerned primarily with those behavioral changes made by a social group. This is consistent with our view that culture is the whole, learned, and shared behavior of a group of people. In cultural adaptation, changes can involve the group's morphology, behavioral patterns, material goods, and/or environment, as long as they are initiated by behavioral processes. Physical morphology, for example, can be altered by new medical technology, which is the outcome of a process initiated by behavior, such as a new idea about disease.

The concept calls for a measure of adaptiveness. Change in and of itself is not adaptation. A change makes an impact on the well-being of the group. The ultimate measure of the adaptive success of a change is how much it contributes to the survival and continuation of a group. A change is most adaptive when it fully maximizes the group's continuation as a distinct unit. The most maladaptive change is one that results in a group's demise or extinction. Adaptation is basically a process that continues over many generations, but in social science research, it is usually not feasible to assess the adaptiveness of a change over long time periods. Several intermediate measures of adaptation have therefore been posed, including population growth and health (Alland 1970; Alland and McCay 1973; Barger 1982; Cohen 1971; Dubos 1965; McElroy and Townsend 1979; Mazess 1975, 1978). The rationale is that when a change contributes to the more immediate well-being of a group, it is also enhancing that group's long-term adaptiveness. Better nutrition and reduced psychological distress, for example, would help a group function more completely, and therefore increase its chances for long-term continuation. On the other hand, increased pollution that results in greater rates of illness and mortality can be considered maladaptive, since it reduces the group's ability to function optimally. The definition of adaptation, then, includes empirical measures of the adaptive success.

As used here, adaptation refers to a group process. Similar processes occur within the individual organism and also at biomes and other large-scale living systems (Miller 1978; Alland 1967:119, 1975:59; Alland and McCay 1973:151–156; DiMarco 1974; Pollock 1961; and Mazess 1975, 1978). We use the term "adaptation" for population-scale processes, in sociocultural adaptation, with the unit of analysis a particular social group. We see adaptation as an evolutionary process, and it is a population that evolves rather than individual organisms (Cohen 1971:5; Stini 1975:1; Alland and McCay 1973:143). We do recognize, however, that a population is an aggregate of individuals, and so we offer the term "adjustment" to indicate individual-scale processes.

The Process of Change

As mentioned, a key idea in the concept of adaptation is that it focuses on the *process* of change (Barger 1977, 1982; Alland 1967, 1972, 1975; Alland and McCay 1973; Parsons 1964; Mazess 1975, 1978; Dubos 1965; Moran 1979; Stini 1975; Cohen 1971). "Process" usually has two meanings. One is the sequence of events involved in change. The second meaning focuses on how forces interact and direct events toward a particular outcome. It is this second meaning in which we are primarily interested, since it gives us a more comprehensive understanding of how changes occur.

In considering the process of adaptation, we will be concerned with the continual and evolutionary interaction between a social group and its immediate social/physical environment. Since the focus here is on sociocultural change, these are the two levels which are directly involved in a particular case of adaptation. The population-environment interaction is an important part of ideas about biological evolution. It is also an extension of ideas of cultural ecology, where how the group maintains its relationship to its environment is considered (Barth 1956; M. Harris 1966; Lewontin 1978; Orlove 1980; Moran 1979; Murphy and Steward 1956; Rappaport 1968; Steward 1955; Sahlins and Service 1960; Stini 1975). Maintenance of a balance in this relationship is important, of course, but we will additionally be interested in how a group develops and changes its interaction with its environment in the process of adaptation.

The process of adaptation, then, involves two sets of forces. One set concerns the internal potentials a group brings to a particular setting, potentials that provide the possible alternatives with which to adapt. The other concerns the external challenges in the environmental setting that select from among the group's available alternatives those which are most appropriate for adaptation. The interaction of these two forces initiates and directs the course of change. We would like to examine each of these forces and then how they interact in the process of change.

(1) Internal potentials: As indicated, a group's internal potentials involve the alternatives it brings to a change situation. Its potentials consist of the needs and resources that it brings to the adaptive situation. A *need* includes whatever its members must have in order to survive and function in a particular setting. For example, all human groups have a physical need for food and a social need for internal cohesiveness. A *resource* includes whatever can be used to maximize the group's well-being in a particular setting. Subsistence technology and a social value on cooperation, for example, can contribute to a group's subsistence. Resources are not absolutely necessary for survival but can enhance the functioning of a group.

Adaptive potentials include both the group's members and their characteristics. In biological evolution, characteristics may be such morphological traits as physical endurance and the ability to produce antibodies to certain diseases. In cultural adaptation, they may be behavioral traits like social values and family structure. The characteristics of all individuals taken together constitute the group's total abilities for adaptation.

A group's internal characteristics can range from genetically fixed to highly plastic. A fixed trait is one that has few alternatives for expression. Fixed morphological traits, for example, include eye color and blood type. Fixed behavioral traits include certain facial expressions and a universal human norm against incest within the nuclear family. Fixed traits cannot be altered by environmental influences, and so they are *innate*. A genetically plastic trait is one that can have different expressions. Morphological examples include an individual's body shape and metabolism rate, both of which can be altered by exercise and diet. Plastic behavioral traits include cultural definitions of gender roles and social values. The specific shape of a plastic trait depends on how it is molded by particular circumstances. Values on interpersonal behavior, for example, can vary widely. An individual raised as a middle-class Anglo American might have a strong emphasis on individual identity, self-reliance, and personal "freedom." These traits were functional as immigrants left social ties in their homeland and had to make it on their own in an expanding frontier. The same person, on the other hand, might value cooperation and responsibility to the group if raised like Eskimos in the Arctic, where cooperative seal hunting assures subsistence in the long winters. Such specific traits are therefore more *developed* or learned. The more plastic a trait, the more it can be modified by environmental influences, and the more varied its expressions will be across populations.

All the characteristics of a group's members determine the group's total potentials for adaptation. In some cases, certain traits might provide only a limited resource. For example, some believe that all humans have limited physical ability to resist the human immunodeficiency virus (HIV, or the AIDS organism). But a great deal of effort at the cultural level has been devoted to developing medical vaccines and treatments, as happened with smallpox. In other cases, traits might provide a range of adaptive responses. Both a biological ability for verbal language and data processing technology, for instance, permit us to inform people all over the world about medical developments to meet the AIDS challenge.

Furthermore, a group's adaptive potentials should be considered in its collective functioning. If the group is to maximize its full range of adaptive abilities, all the characteristics of its members must function together in a compatible manner. For example, American culture consciously emphasizes "competition," as in sports and business. In reality, though, the society would be torn apart if everyone were completely competitive. If we examine actual behavior, the vast majority of the people are cooperative most of the time. People drive in the right lane of a road, use public rest rooms according to their gender, and exhibit a host of other cooperative behaviors in their daily lives. Though a value on "cooperation" may be more covert, it is actually a more prevalent norm.

As indicated, a group's potentials constitute its alternatives for adaptation. These provide the range of options a group has that help to meet specific environmental conditions. In order for any particular trait to be adaptive, it must contribute to the effective functioning of the group in two ways. First, it must enhance the internal functioning of the population. If its members were continually in conflict, a group would disintegrate. People's behavior must essentially be coordinated and complementary if a society is to function effectively. And second, a trait must enhance how a group interacts with its environment. The collective behavior of a group must maximize a productive balance with the specific conditions in which its members live. Both of these functions must be present for a particular trait to make an overall contribution to a group's survival and continuation.

(2) **External challenges:** A group's environmental challenges consist of the constraints and opportunities in its external setting. A *constraint* is a condition which must be overcome in order for the group to survive and continue. For example, an infectious disease can impose a limit on population density. If a group exceeds such limits, an epidemic may threaten its survival (Dunn 1968; Cockburn 1971; Dubos 1965). On the other hand, an environmental *opportunity* is something which can enhance a group's survival and continuation. An opportunity is not necessary for existence. But, depending on how much it is utilized, it can contribute to a group's adaptiveness. For example, the existence of certain strains of annual plants in the ancient Near East made possible the development of agriculture based on domesticated crops (Braidwood 1967).

It should be noted that when the focus is on sociocultural adaptation, a group's "environment" can include its larger demographic, socioeconomic, and political setting. This is particularly true for minorities and ethnic groups within a pluralistic national society (Barger 1977, 1982; Barth 1956).

Environmental challenges direct the course of adaptive changes by selecting among a group's alternatives. A group comes to any setting with a certain range of potentials. Of all its traits, the ones emphasized are those that help meet limitations and that help take advantage of opportunities. For example, a religious belief about spiritual purity may help contain an infectious disease and thus may gain a greater sacred meaning (Dunn 1968; Dubos 1965; Khare 1962). Environmental conditions can also de-emphasize traits which are susceptible to limitations. For example, a group may give an infectious epidemic a religious interpretation that calls for the group to disperse and thus minimize the spread of the disease (Dunn 1968; Dubos 1965). Those traits which contribute to a group's adaptation, then, may be emphasized more, and those which are more maladaptive may be de-emphasized.

*(3) **The process of change:*** As we indicated, one meaning of the term *"process"* is the sequence of events involved in change. In this sense, there are four stages of adaptation:

First, a group exists in relative balance with its environmental conditions. Taking infectious diseases as an example, a group's members may have developed biological resistance to microorganisms upon previous exposure to the agents. The diseases can also be controlled by medical technology like antibiotics and by sanitation practices that reduce exposure. The group is thus in a functional balance with existing disease agents.

In the second stage, the homeostasis between the group and its environment is upset. This can be caused by a group trait. In the disease example, industrial pollution stresses immunological functions, making many people susceptible to a particular viral infection. Or it can be caused by some change in the environmental conditions, such as the introduction of a new disease organism like the Asian flu or HIV. The new imbalance between the group's potentials and its environmental conditions threatens its optimal functioning and therefore poses an adaptive challenge.

At the third stage, the group changes its traits in order to adapt. Of all its alternatives, it emphasizes those which are most effective in restoring a balance with its environment. For example, medical research may produce a new vaccine against the new disease. An evolutionary example, of course, would be the death of those who had little resistance to the disease, leaving those with greater resistance to continue the group. It is at this stage that adaptation actually occurs, when the group's traits are reorganized to restore a balance with its environment (which includes the new disease organism).

In the fourth stage, a new balance between the group and its environmental conditions is initiated.

Any group is continually involved in all four stages at the same time. It will be in balance with some condition, facing an imbalance with others, and be in the process of adapting with still other conditions. In the long run, then, it is the overall balance with many simultaneous conditions which sets the group's relative adaptation.

The second meaning of *process* focuses on how forces interact and direct events toward a particular outcome. As indicated, this is the primary meaning with which we are concerned as we seek to comprehensively understand how social changes occur. In considering this process, there are three important points that need to be emphasized:

First, the basic process of adaptation is a *reorganization* of a group's interaction with its environment. The group can change its own traits or can change something in its environment. For example, in the civil rights movement, leaders like Martin Luther King had to develop internal organizations that were credible and effective in representing the cause of African Americans. But they also called upon the external support of other social groups to help make reforms. In balance, the larger society has been reorganized to provide African Americans with some important new educational, occupational, and other opportunities. In terms of its internal potentials, the group can develop new adaptive traits or eliminate old maladaptive ones. On the other hand, as is probably the usual case, an existing adaptive trait can be emphasized more or a trait that distracts from homeostasis can be de-emphasized. An example of emphasizing an existing trait would be the development of new strains of crops more resistant to plant diseases. An example of de-emphasizing a trait can be seen in the banning of DDT in the United States after its serious ecological impacts were determined. It should be noted that the synthesis of different parts of a system is at the heart of a number of concepts about social change. We can see this in ideas about innovation, syncretism, mazeway reformulation, and dialectics (Barnett 1953; Wallace 1956; Marx 1904; Dahrendorf 1964).

The second point is that in adaptation it is the *system* which changes, not just traits. Whatever specific changes occur, the ultimate adaptive impact on a group is set by the overall balance in how its total resources interact with its total environmental challenges. Neither the internal potentials of a group nor its environmental challenges is sufficient to explain change. We need to examine how these two sets of forces interact to direct the course of change. For example, in the civil rights movement, minority groups by themselves have not had the political power to make major social changes. But by mobilizing both their own people and external supporters, they have been able to amass sufficient strength to make important reforms. In a system, each part responds directly or indirectly to changes in other parts. Events at either the internal or external level can affect the other level. A group's optimal functioning at both levels is generally necessary for the group as a whole to maximize its chances for survival and continuation (Williams 1966; Stern 1970). In the process, the integrated balance of the whole can be modified.

The third point about process is that the *time* period for examining adaptation should also be specified. Since no system is in complete balance, a continual process of reorganization occurs as some changes are stimulated by other changes, which in turn stimulate yet other changes (Parsons 1964; Marx 1904; Dahrendorf 1964). The adaptive balance of changes can therefore vary or even reverse over a period of time. For example, industrialization may have had some adaptive advantages in a period when a rising standard of living had positive health impacts for many groups. In another period, however, the health hazards of pollution for certain groups has counterbalanced gains of industrialization. Also, rates and degrees of change, as well as the particular types of changes, should also be considered in terms of the relative equilibrium between a group's traits and its environmental challenges. The more a system is imbalanced, the more rapid and the greater the changes necessary to restore optimal functioning that best contributes to the group's survival and continuation. This is evident in the recent social changes in Eastern Europe.

It should be noted that the process of adaptation does not mandate that the same form be continued nor that traits be original to the group. For example, contemporary American culture is a product of the contributions of many other cultures. It includes everything from "french-fried" Andean potatoes to Japanese electronic products. But this does not mean that Americans today are any less "American" than in George Washington's time. Adaptation, in fact, involves a comprehensive and continual process of balancing many traits, in the context of many simultaneous challenges.

We should also note that chance can play a role in the process of change (Lewontin 1978:225–228). The existence of functional traits in a group does not necessarily mean that they will be present when and where needed to meet a particular environmental challenge. For example, the manufacture and distribution of a new immunization for an infectious disease may not have been developed before an epidemic occurs.

In summary, change should be seen as the *rule*, not the unusual. In a system, a change in one part automatically impacts directly or indirectly on other parts. A dynamic system is continually in a process of reorganizing itself to maintain the best balance possible. When we think of social changes, the "goal" of change should not be a particular trait or direction but rather *better adaptation*.

Adaptation of Midwestern Farmworkers

We believe a systems model of adaptation offers a useful framework for understanding specific cases of social change. As we have indicated, we are most interested in explaining *how* and *why* the FLOC movement has been able to achieve basic reforms for midwestern farmworkers. It is the systems adaptation model that we will use to examine the FLOC movement. In particular, we will focus on several key questions:

(1) Farmworkers' potentials: What *internal potentials* among midwestern farmworkers have been a force for social reform? What needs have they brought to the adaptive setting? What resources have they used to make meaningful changes in their living and working conditions? What have *their* views been on farm labor reform? Has FLOC reflected what farmworkers themselves want, and have FLOC's methods for achieving its goals been in accordance with its own constituency?

(2) Environmental challenges for farmworkers: What *external challenges* in the farmworkers' socioeconomic environment have been a force for farm labor reform? What constraints has FLOC had to overcome? In particular, what opposition have farmworkers had to overcome? Also, what have been the opportunities for reform? What support within the larger society has helped FLOC achieve its goals, and how have these been mobilized?

(3) Social adaptation of midwestern farmworkers: In terms of the process of adaptation, what internal changes has the FLOC movement actually made in the lives of farmworkers? What changes have been made in the larger agribusiness system in which farmworkers work? And what changes has FLOC made in the larger society in which farmworkers live? How have these changes affected the farmworkers' well-being? In other words, how adaptive has the FLOC movement been for midwestern farmworkers?

In summary, we will draw upon the ideas about social adaptation to examine the farm labor movement in the Midwest. We will first describe the context of farm labor reform in the next two chapters. This will involve reviewing farmworkers as a social group in the United States and then documenting the development of the FLOC movement. Following the adaptation model, we will examine in the next two chapters the internal and external factors that have influenced the course of the FLOC movement. We will then summarize the impacts of the FLOC movement. Finally, we will examine the adaptive forces involved in the FLOC movement. As we examine the FLOC movement, we will consider ideas about social change along with the events and forces involved in farm labor reform. Also, we will examine theory and fact from both directions and use ideas about change to understand the FLOC movement. Furthermore, we will use the FLOC movement to test and refine our understanding of social change.

CHAPTER 2

Midwestern Farmworkers

Every day Americans eat foods that are picked and processed by migrant and seasonal farmworkers. Yet farmworkers themselves often go hungry and are one of the most socioeconomically deprived groups in the country. Farmworkers' problems have been documented for much of this century (London and Anderson 1970; Daniel 1981; Goldfarb 1982; Majka and Majka 1982; Jenkins 1985). Over the decades, farmworkers have come from many ethnic backgrounds. Whether Chinese, Japanese, Filipino, Mexican, Black, Haitian, or Vietnamese, farmworkers have primarily been non-European immigrants. Besides being poor, they have usually been dispossessed by a number of factors. Warfare, famine, hyperinflation, extreme economic disasters, and other misfortunes in their home areas have left them with few subsistence choices. They have gone into farm labor looking for economic survival. Many have also followed the dream of self-sufficiency and even prosperity for their families. No matter what their reasons, very few have realized their hopes.

The estimated three million farmworkers in the United States generally fall into two categories. One type is the *migrant* worker, who travels with annual harvest seasons. This is the farmworker usually depicted in the popular image. Migrants are generally based in the southern border areas of the United States. They winter in the Imperial Valley of California, the lower Rio Grande Valley in Texas, and central and southern Florida. As indicated in Figure 2.1, there are three main migrant streams in the United States: the East Coast, the Midwest, and the West Coast. Some workers may leave their home base area as early as March and move north with the planting season. But most migrate between June and September to harvest crops. They are a hardworking people, but most migrants

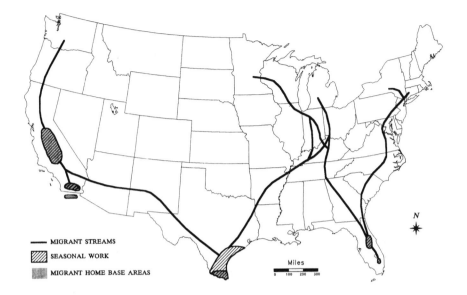

MIGRANT STREAMS
SEASONAL WORK
MIGRANT HOME BASE AREAS

Figure 2.1: Main Farmworker Base Areas and Migrant Streams

are employed only four or five months in a year. They have to rely on casual labor, welfare, and charity for their survival during the slow winter season.

The other type of farmworker is the *seasonal* worker. These people are generally employed much of the year in one location. They work mostly with one crop which requires continuous care, such as citrus and grapes. Besides harvesting the crop, they perform a variety of other tasks, such as pruning and irrigation. Compared to migrants, seasonal workers have more stable employment and may work up to ten months of the year.

Farmworkers are involved mostly with "table" crops, such as fruits and vegetables. Some are involved in other types of agriculture, such as chicken ranching or tree production in nurseries. Most Americans do not realize that farm labor involves specialized skills, though these may not be considered technical trades. For example, picking and packing table grapes requires care to ensure the product is visually appealing as well as undamaged.

Farmworkers belong to many different ethnic minorities. The largest ethnic group is Mexican Americans. There are also many Filipinos in the West Coast stream. The East Coast stream is composed mostly of African Americans and Puerto Ricans. In recent years, Haitians have also entered the East Coast stream, and

Vietnamese and Central American refugees have entered the West Coast stream. Mexican Americans make up most of the Midwest stream.

There is a common misconception that farmworkers are "illegal aliens." In some areas like southern California, the lower Rio Grande Valley in Texas, and southern Florida, there are a number of undocumented immigrants. Most undocumented workers, however, go to large urban areas, where they find employment in low-paid and low-profile jobs like restaurant kitchen work and building cleaning.

Most farmworkers are American-born individuals, naturalized citizens, or legal immigrants. Anglo Americans often do not realize that almost one-third of the United States used to be part of Mexico. Besides Texas and California, most of the American Southwest became U.S. territory after the Mexican-American War of 1846. The "Mexicans" in these areas thus became "Mexican Americans." Many other Mexicans came to the United States during the revolution of 1910–1920, seeking safety and a means to support their families. During and after World War II, the federal government operated the bracero program, where agricultural workers were recruited in Mexico and routed to growers who applied for labor to produce specialty crops. Many of these workers and their families remained and settled permanently in the United States. Now every year, a number of farmworkers do come north from Mexico. Some come only to earn money to help support their families and then return home. But for numerous reasons, many decide to remain in America.

European Americans also tend to forget that there are immigrants from many cultures in America. The ancestry of almost all Americans include people who left their homelands seeking better conditions. This history has contributed to core American values like "self-sufficiency," personal "freedom," and "industriousness." These values were formed as immigrants left kinship ties and social networks behind and sought to make it on their own in a new land. Many European Americans, however, arrived with far greater advantages and resources than those possessed by the people who are now farmworkers. European Americans arrived at times of economic expansion and could move into new jobs. Their language, educational background, value systems, and other traits were more similar to the "mainstream" American culture. It is still true that European immigrants today generally have advanced education and professional skills. Such newcomers can be seen among most university faculties and student bodies as well as in key positions in industry and business. It is also still true that immigrants who go into farm labor are socioeconomically dispossessed and come from ethnic minorities.

Agribusinesses and Farmworkers

The Structure of Farm Labor

The structure of the agricultural system is a primary force in the poor living and working conditions of farmworkers (Burnaway 1976; Galarza 1977; Majka and Majka 1982; Jenkins 1985; Hightower 1978). As indicated in Figure 2.2, large agribusinesses dominate this system. Many of these are public multinational corporations which focus on food processing and distribution, like Campbell Soup Company. In California, Texas, and other areas, there are also a number of private wealthy family corporations with large land holdings also involved in the production of specialty crops and products, like fresh grapes and wines. At the beginning of the season, these agribusinesses set annual marketing and profit goals. This, in turn, determines the price structures for different crops.

In regions like California, southern Texas, and central Florida, farmworkers may be hired directly by large agribusinesses and wealthy family growers (called *rancheros* in Spanish). They work on farms (*ranchos*) irrigating the crops, pruning, and taking part in ongoing operations. In these cases, company supervisors (*patrones* or "bosses") often act with great latitude in the hiring, overseeing, and firing of workers. Many supervisors have a bad reputation for harassing workers and for assigning women the more desirable jobs in exchange for sexual relations.

Migrant farmworkers are hired during labor-intensive periods like harvesting. These temporary work forces are recruited by labor contractors or "crew leaders" (also called *patrones*), who hire and supervise the workers in the fields. Many labor contractors provide housing, transportation, and other essential services when these are not furnished by the companies or growers. This system is particularly subject to abuses, and labor contractors are notorious for fraudulent and patronizing treatment of their workers. In a 1984 survey of California grape workers, for instance, we found that many names and Social Security numbers on employee lists were maintained by labor contractors (Barger and Reza 1985b). They filled the "slots" with different workers each year. We were told that the crew leaders

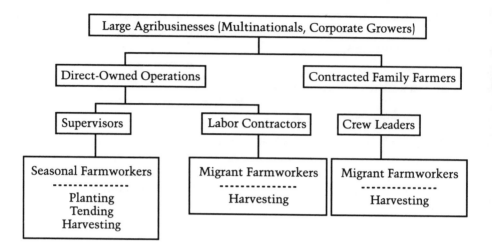

Figure 2.2: Farmworkers in the Structure of the Agricultural System

would then claim all the unemployment and Social Security benefits under these different names. Similar practices were observed among company supervisors on the large ranches.

In the Midwest and on much of the East Coast, family farmers (also called *rancheros*) are interjected as another level in the agricultural system. These small growers contract to raise tomatoes, cucumbers, and other specialty crops for the large food-processing corporations. A company negotiates with the individual farmer for the entire season's crop, but farmers have traditionally had little bargaining power in the prices paid. The corporations, however, have established long-term relations with their farmers, which ensures a continued supply of their basic crop needs. With many crops, the company provides its own seedlings to growers, to ensure consistency in its products. The farmer's crop is thus "dedicated," since only that company purchases the harvested crop.

These growers use farmworkers primarily to harvest their specialty crops. Most have built small labor camps in the fields near the crops. These camps usually consist of one-room family cabins, with central toilets and showers. In these regions, the growers are the focus of agricultural operations. The individual character of the grower can therefore make a big difference in the conditions farmworkers experience. Many farmers are well intentioned and try to provide their workers decent housing and wages. But some growers blatantly exploit farmworkers. For example, some may promise work for more migrants than they will actually need. Then they use the excess of workers as leverage to reduce wages, threatening to replace anyone who complains.

The farmer works with a crew leader (called *troquero*, from "trucker" in Spanish), who acts as a labor contractor. Many crew leaders have an infamous reputation for maltreating and cheating their own workers. For example, a crew leader may take soft drinks to their crew in the fields and then later deduct the costs from the workers' pay at inflated prices. Many have been known to hold back Social Security payments from wages, which they pocket instead of filing the funds with the Internal Revenue Service. They have also been known to overhire workers to reduce wages or to simply promise one wage rate and pay a lower one.

At the bottom of the agricultural system are the farmworkers. These are the people who contribute their physical labor to the production and processing of specialty crops which help feed others in America.

The Development of Farm Labor in America

There is a long history of immigrant ethnic minorities going into farm labor in America (Acuña 1988; Borjas and Tienda 1985; Cardenas 1976; Cockcroft 1986; Galarza 1964, 1970; Gomez-Quiñones 1982; London and Anderson 1970; Majka and Majka 1982; Meier and Rivera 1972; Reavis 1978; Sable 1987; Samora 1971, 1977; Scruggs 1988; West and Macklin 1979). In the late 1800's, Chinese who had been imported to build railroad lines turned to agricultural labor after the rail boom. In the early 1900's, Japanese workers were briefly recruited for farm work until some began organizing and staged strikes and others went into agricultural production themselves. Many Mexicans fleeing the 1910–1920 revolution also went into farm labor. To minimize labor costs, agribusiness lobbied for national policies promoting an influx of Mexican immigrants. During the Depression in the 1930's, poor Anglo "Okies" entered agricultural labor, and over 400,000 Mexicans and other minority workers were excluded from the market and deported. During and after World War II, Puerto Ricans and Filipinos were recruited, and in recent years, Haitians and other dispossessed groups have also gone into farm labor.

In the early 1900's, a number of factors generated a substantial expansion of agricultural labor (Scruggs 1988). Industrialization, urbanization, and immigration created large markets for food products. Railroads connected urban consumers with agricultural regions. Irrigation projects permitted the conversion of semiarid regions in central California and other regions in the Southwest into fertile agricultural lands. Canning and refrigeration technology permitted expansion of the market for perishable goods like fruits and vegetables. These developments shifted American agriculture from small family operations to accelerated intensive large-scale production. Mass production of foods in turn created a substantial need for seasonal farm labor.

Farmworkers, however, were subjected to severe conditions. High overhead costs in agricultural technology and transportation led agribusiness to minimize employee wage costs in order to maximize profits. The seasonal nature of agricultural employment, strenuous labor, long hours in the fields, and low wages created the cycle of exploitation, underemployment, poverty, and misery depicted in *The Grapes of Wrath* (Steinbeck 1988). Asians, Mexicans, and other deprived minorities were also victims of racial discrimination. The Depression was a period of significant labor organizing in America, but agribusiness interests were successful in excluding farmworkers from the 1932 National Labor Relations Act and other labor laws. Farmworkers were thus bound to a system that exploited their labor while denying them an active role in decisions that affected their well-being.

One significant example of the economic and political nature of the agricultural system which has exploited farmworkers is the bracero program (Cardenas 1976; Galarza 1964, 1970; London and Anderson 1970; Majka and Majka 1982; Reavis 1978; Samora 1971, 1977; Scruggs 1988; Valdés 1989, 1991). In World War II, the flow of Americans into the armed forces created a substantial demand for seasonal farmworkers. In 1942, pressure from agribusiness led the federal government to establish a system to recruit agricultural laborers from Mexico and place them with agribusiness operations. This system persisted long after World War II, into the 1960's. Even though the braceros, as the Mexican workers were known, were legally not supposed to be involved in labor disputes, growers regularly used them to replace workers on strikes. This ready pool of workers officially recruited by the federal government thus provided growers with a resource for undermining the organizing of farmworkers and for breaking strikes. The bracero program thus serves as a vivid example of how American agribusiness has exploited farmworkers. This type of exploitation has gone on for at least a century.

Farmworker Conditions

Farmworkers are among the most deprived groups in the United States. Their disadvantaged living and working conditions have been documented for generations (S. Allen 1966; Burnaway 1976; Columbia Broadcasting System 1960; Cockcroft 1986; Daniel 1981; Friedland 1969; Fuller and Mason 1977; Galarza 1964, 1970; Goldfarb 1982; Harper, Mills, and Farris 1974; McWilliams 1939, 1944; Moore 1965; National Broadcasting Company 1980; President's Commission on Migratory Labor 1951; Samora 1971, 1977; H. Schwartz 1945; Smith 1970; Solis 1971; Sosnick 1978; U.S. Senate Subcommittee on Migratory Labor 1970). Many studies and reports provide evidence of the disadvantages and hard life experienced by farmworkers like María Elena Ortega, who has spent most of her life in the fields (Buss 1985 : 245–281).

It should be noted that farmworkers see some advantages in their occupation. Some say that they like the family being able to work together. Many also report that they like working out in the open. Almost all with whom we have talked say that farm labor is work that people with few technical skills can get, and so it provides them with a chance to earn some income. Another advantage which some farmworkers report is that during the short harvest seasons they can afford to eat well. When they return to Texas or Florida for the winter, they say, they use their ready cash to stock their kitchen shelves with food. But after that they may have little. Some remember when they were children they would go through garbage cans to collect scraps of meat, fat for lard, and leftover fruits and vegetables. The kids would take these home, wash them, and eat them for dinner.

"We've always had so little"

Farmworkers experience among the most disadvantaged conditions in America. Their average annual earnings are far below official poverty levels, an estimated $6,000 to $8,000 for a family of five (Galasch 1975; Indiana Advisory Committee 1974; Sosnick 1978). As one worker puts it, "We've always had so little."

The poverty and deprivations experienced by farmworkers are certainly not due to being "lazy." Farmworkers perform labor that is physically strenuous and often deforming. Working in the fields is a labor that few other Americans can understand. From nearby roads, farmworkers can be seen bent over in the mud or working in 100-degree heat. One notorious practice is making workers use a short-handled hoe, which makes them stoop over for hours. Workers say

Migrants pick tomatoes in Ohio, September 1982, on a hot and humid day. Child labor is a common condition among farmworkers, setting a life-long pattern of physical strain, limited education, and poverty. In this case, 41 percent of the workers in this muddy field were children under fifteen years old.

supervisors require this so they can tell if someone is not working, because the person would be standing straight. Women report that the stoop labor is particularly painful when they are pregnant.

Farmworkers' low income is primarily due to low wages and structured seasonal underemployment. Farmworkers also face constant job insecurity. Even when they have found work, crew leaders and supervisors threaten to lay them off if they do not work harder. They may also be fired if they complain about being paid late or less than promised. Many are threatened with losing their jobs to mechanization, which has in fact left many without any means to support their families (Friedland and Nelkin 1972; Hightower 1978; Pratt 1973). Chronic unemployment and underemployment is thus a constant condition among farmworkers, leaving little hope of breaking free of poverty.

Though farmworkers never earn enough money to make it through the year, many do not apply for welfare. Most state with pride that they want to make it on their own, even if this is very hard. Some report that when they have asked for food stamps, people have called them "dumb" and "lazy."

Child labor is common among farmworkers (Coles 1970; Indiana Advisory Committee 1974; McGill 1929). Most farmworkers' children are born into poverty, and they have to work hard at odd jobs to help the family survive. They assume responsibilities at a very

A migrant labor camp in Indiana, 1982, illustrates the deprived conditions experienced by farmworkers in America for over a century. The main house, in which three families lived, had a leaking roof, rotten stairs, and holes in the walls. The other housing units were converted chicken coops infested with lice. The bathroom/shower building had toilets that overflowed. Also, dangerous farm equipment and pesticides were stored where children were playing. Though authorities determined that these conditions violated a number of laws and regulations, the grower was not subjected to any penalties.

young age, and in many fields we have observed that over forty percent of the workers are children. It is not unusual to see children struggling to carry heavy baskets in hot or muddy fields to the loading trucks. When work is available, children are needed to maximize family earnings. Unfortunately, many migrant children drop out of school early. Others may start school many weeks late, after getting back from the harvest seasons up north. They may also have to leave school early the next season. Parents express anguish about their children having to work so hard and miss so much school. But, they say, they have no choice if the family is to survive. Indeed, the average farmworker has only a sixth-grade education. This sets a lifelong pattern of deprivation for farmworker children. When born into this harsh system, such children find it hard to break out of the cycle.

Housing and sanitation facilities in migrant camps are clearly substandard (Indiana Advisory Committee 1974; Reno 1970). Families are usually provided a small, one-room shack in the migrant labor camps, but some workers recall being provided only an old chicken coop with three walls and an open front. Toilet facilities often consist of outhouses. Neither fresh water nor toilets have normally been available in the fields. While traveling, farmworkers may have only streams beside the road in which to wash.

Farmworkers' health and nutrition are among the poorest in the nation (Acosta et al. 1974; Barnett and Call 1979; Bleiweis et al. 1977; Chase et al. 1971; Coye 1985; Education Commission of the States 1979; Jacobson et al. 1987; Kaufman et al. 1975; Larson et al. 1974; National Rural Health Care Association 1985; West 1964; Wilk 1986). Not surprisingly, farmworkers have an average life expectancy of only forty-nine years. They also have high rates of infectious and chronic diseases, malnutrition, and infant and maternal mortality. Some women report that within three or four days of giving birth, they would be back in the fields, taking breaks to nurse the baby and then returning to work. Farmworkers also experience high rates of dental problems and industrial accidents. Despite such poor health conditions, health care and other services are frequently unavailable or inaccessible to farmworkers (Shenkin 1974).

"We knew . . . that pesticides were really bad"

Farmworkers are often subjected to hazardous working conditions. In particular, it is estimated that 300,000 farmworkers are exposed to pesticides each year (Davies 1977; Siewierski 1984; Ware 1978). There is no such thing as a safe pesticide. Many insecticides affect the nervous system, much like military nerve gas. Large doses can kill an adult in minutes, and low-dose exposure can severely damage the nervous system and brain. Many herbicides and some insecticides can cause cancers and birth defects, like Agent Orange used in the Vietnam War. And there are some pesticides that can only be categorized as *bio*cides. Several fumigants used in preparing fields and in storing grains, for example, are designed to kill everything from molds to insects and mice. Some of these fumigants also cause cancers and birth defects. All of us who eat these foods are at risk of consuming pesticide residues, but farmworkers are daily exposed to hazardous levels of these chemicals.

The experience of being sprayed can be frightening in itself. María Elena Ortega recalls being sprayed with Sonalin, an herbicide, in Texas in 1987. María Elena is usually a cheerful woman and has a bright smile, but a year after the incident tears ran down her cheeks as she told the story, pained at the memories that were still too fresh:

"It was when I was driving on a rural road around Los Fresnos,

María Elena Ortega participates in the 1988 FLOC convention in Toledo, Ohio, with FLOC President Baldemar Velásquez (left) and Vice President Fernando Cuevas (center). After María Elena was sprayed with the pesticide Sonalin in 1987, her digestive and nervous systems were seriously impaired. Usually a bright and cheerful woman, she told her story of pesticide poisoning and resulting disabilities with tears on her face. The emotional scars she suffered are as traumatic as the physical damage she has experienced.

Texas. Hector, my son, was with me. We were driving with the windows down, when suddenly Hector shouted, 'Watch out!' I looked out the window and heard a noise and saw a yellow swirl. Then all the sudden I gasped and felt like I was choking. I breathed it in, and it was all in my eyes and nose and hair, and I was coughing. It was even on my feet. I had stopped the car, and it was all over the windshield. I got out of the car. But then I got back in and parked the car on the side of the road. Hector and I hollered at the plane, then it turned back on the other side of the cucumber field, and my son yelled, 'Let's go, Mom!' So we left.

"I felt really terrible. It was really bad inside. I told Hector that we had to tell somebody. We knew from working with the UFW and FLOC that pesticides were really bad and that this was really wrong. Then I threw up and felt really nauseated. Hector, too. I knew about the UFW farmworker center in San Juan, Texas, so I called them. They gave me the number of the Department of Agriculture to report it, so I called them. I talked with an inspector, and he said to wait, that he was on the way. We waited forty-five minutes. I felt weak and was sweating and my vision was blurred. I had a pain breathing, and my stomach hurt. The inspector took a sample from the car, and we took him to where it happened. He told us to go to a doctor. Both he and the UFW center said we should go see Dr. Diaz.

"My son drove, and we picked up my brother. He said we should call an ambulance, but my son said it would be too late. By the time we got to a doctor, I was only half conscious. We washed several times. I threw up black slime, and my saliva was like a thick white foam. My heart was bad, they said 'forty.' I heard them say, 'Really bad.' Then I saw a light going at a high speed, and I saw the doctor like an angel, with people looking over his head. They gave me something with needles, and oxygen. And the next thing I knew I was in a hospital.

"Afterwards, I was so upset that I couldn't even think about the kids. My voice changed some, too. I couldn't remember things, and started doing things backwards. Like I'd try to write one word but it turned out to be another. My coordination was bad. I couldn't pronounce things or write. They told me not to eat many things, because they made me sick. Whenever I was exposed to chemicals, it would affect me for three or four days. I was disoriented, like not being able to find my way driving and I'd stop at yellow lights. I had a burning sensation in my stomach. I had a pain in my neck, like this," she said, grabbing the back of her hair and pulling it up. "I got stupid and absent-minded. Once I forgot three days. Once I had to stop when driving, and I didn't know where I was, and I cried. And once I was with my sister, Norma, and for one and a half hours I freaked her out.

"The union recommended a lawyer. The owner of the land wouldn't even answer, and the pilot wouldn't accept letters. They had to be delivered through the court. We have a big hospital bill. All we want is for them to be responsible."[1]

María Elena is still worried about the long-term effects of pesticides, and sometimes she cries when she thinks about being sprayed. She knows farmworkers who have been sprayed and couldn't work ever again because their nervous systems were so damaged. She also knows farmworkers who have been exposed to herbicides. Some of these people have developed cancer, or have had children born without arms and legs or with parts of their spines missing. Farmworkers are generally exposed to many different pesticides, not just one. They are, therefore, likely to cause many different health problems. The long-term dangers of even low-dose exposure are still being discovered.

"They do anything they want to us"

Farmworkers in America experience many forms of discrimination (Johnson 1976; McDonagh 1955; Perry and Snyder 1971; U.S. Senate Subcommittee on Migratory Labor 1970). One is a prejudice against minority ethnic groups. This is evident among some growers, one of whom referred to his workers as "rented slaves" (Moore 1965). Many workers remember the discrimination and injustices they experience. Children cannot understand why they are not allowed to use the rest rooms at gas stations and stores or why supervisors and sales clerks curse at them.

Among the most notorious exploiters of farmworkers are their crew leaders. One woman, for example, reports how a crew leader would loan her family small sums to buy groceries, then when payday came he would say that they didn't have any money left after repaying him. If they complain about work or living conditions, they are told to shut up or they will lose their jobs. There are many cases of farmworkers being cheated out of Social Security contributions and other wage withholdings. Another common practice is to withhold part of a worker's wages for a "bonus" payment at the end of the harvest. This practice is designed to ensure workers will remain to pick the last of the crop, which is thin and therefore uneconomical for migrants to work. Many crew leaders treat their workers harshly at this time, trying to make them quit. They then may split the forfeited "bonus" with the grower.

One woman recalls trying to talk about such abuses with her mother, but her mother told her not to talk about how bad things were. She now understands, she says, that her mother was simply too tired and couldn't take on any more worries.

Farmworkers themselves often focus on the growers when they express their frustration and anger at having little recourse for the conditions their families suffer. There are certainly many examples of growers who are racist and who exploit their workers. FLOC president Baldemar Velásquez once talked about a case when he was a child. His father had arranged work for the family, hoeing sugar beets in Ohio during a slow part of the summer work season. The grower had promised one pay rate, but when the job was finished paid much less. The father had to suffer humiliation in front of his family. One reason farmworkers focus their resentment on the growers is that this is the part of the system with which they are in direct contact.

Perhaps the greatest disadvantage experienced by farmworkers is being excluded from the decision-making processes that affect their well-being (Burnaway 1976; Craddock 1979; Daniel 1981; Galarza 1977; Galasch 1975; Goldfarb 1982; Majka and Majka 1982; U.S. Senate Subcommittee on Migratory Labor 1970). For example, farmworkers are specifically excluded from the National Labor Relations Act. In numerous states, they are also excluded from the scope of many labor laws, such as those providing workers' compensation and unemployment insurance. Even where they are covered by laws and regulations, standards are generally reduced or unenforced. This includes child labor laws, minimum wage rates, and occupational safety standards. Farmworkers also do not receive work benefits, like medical insurance and paid holidays, which are taken for granted by other American workers.

In summary, farmworkers experience conditions far below what are considered normal standards by most other American workers. In contrast, "migrant" petroleum workers on the Alaska north slope and on ocean derricks receive considerably higher wages and are provided abundant meals, cleaned sleeping quarters, movies and other off-duty entertainment, health insurance, and retirement pensions. Yet farmworkers are an essential link in the production of food for other Americans, a product as vital to the national well-being as petroleum. They also make significant contributions to the local and regional economies where they work. Not only do they help produce agricultural products, but they spend much of their income in the same area where it was earned (Barger and Reza 1984a, 1984b). Yet farmworkers do not receive the same protections and benefits as other American workers. Despite extensive documentation of their deprived conditions for over seventy-five years, their disadvantaged situation has persisted for generations.

Farmworkers in the Midwest

Each growing season, about sixty thousand farmworkers come into the central midwestern states of Indiana, Michigan, and Ohio (Barger and Reza 1984a, 1984b; Cardenas 1976; Carlson 1976; Good Neighbor Commission 1977; Indiana Advisory Committee 1974; Johnson 1976; Murrillo 1971; Rubel 1966; Valdés 1989, 1991). Most are Mexican Americans from the lower Rio Grande Valley in Texas. In recent years, many have moved their base to central Florida, where they can work citrus crops during the winter. Migrants come into the Midwest, following the midcontinent migrant stream, to work with a variety of crops. These include tomatoes, cucumbers, cherries, sugar beets, apples, peaches, strawberries, asparagus, and nursery plants.

The agricultural system in the Midwest has long been dominated by large food-processing corporations (Valdés 1991). In the early twentieth century, for example, the Great Lakes Sugar Company exercised considerable control over beet production. It set prices paid to growers, determined acreage allotments, and recruited workers from South Texas and Mexico. During the World War II era, the tomato industry began expanding its operations in the area, taking advantage of nearby urban markets and the availability of migrant workers. By the 1940's, Campbell Soup, Heinz, Libby, Stokely Van Camp, Hunt, and other food-processing corporations were firmly established in the region. The labor needed to harvest the crops and to work around-the-clock shifts at the plants brought in migrants during the summers.

The earliest farmworkers in the Midwest were Irish, Slav, and other impoverished or displaced European immigrants (Valdés 1984, 1991; Cardenas 1976). These immigrants left agricultural work as soon as industrial jobs became available in nearby cities. Mexican American farmworkers began migrating into the Midwest during and after World War I, after the major flow of European immigrants had subsided. Many came to work specialty crops like sugar beets. Others came originally to lay railroad tracks, then later turned to agricultural labor. During the Depression, many local farmers gave out-of-work Anglos preference when hiring workers, and many Mexicans and Mexican Americans were deported. But when some Anglo workers expressed ideas about labor organizing, the farmers quickly turned back to using Mexican Americans.

During World War II, more Mexican Americans were brought in to work in the fields, along with prisoners of war and Jamaican workers (Valdés 1984, 1991; Cardenas 1976; Scruggs 1988; Carlson 1976). The bracero program placed many Mexican workers into the Midwest. The availability of permanent jobs in the canneries provided many families with the opportunity to settle out of the migrant stream, in small towns in the region. Most of these new residents were American-born workers. After the war, the introduction of machine harvesters for sugar beets reduced the need for farmworkers. But many were still required to hoe sugar beets and to pick tomatoes and pickles, which were increasing in acreage. Growers preferred Mexican Americans, who had a reputation as hard workers. Their large families also provided a built-in work force. Both seasonal and in-stream migrants, however, experienced many forms of overt discrimination. They were refused service in restaurants and barber shops, and their children were teased and jeered in schools. As detailed earlier, many farmworkers were also cheated by growers and crew leaders.

The demographic background and farm work experience of midwestern farmworkers are indicated in Table 2.1, based on a field survey of tomato workers that we conducted in 1983 (Barger and Reza 1984a, 1984b). This survey indicates that male heads of household tend to be middle-aged and second-generation farmworkers, having worked in farm labor most of their lives. They have five to six people in their families, and most have only a primary school education. The vast majority are American citizens or legal immigrants, with most originating from Texas. Unlike the border states and other areas, very few were suspected of being undocumented aliens. About 53 percent of their annual income is earned in the Midwest. It is worth noting that tomato workers alone spend about $5 million a year, or about a quarter of their total income, in the local area where it is earned.

Midwestern farmworkers exhibit the same disadvantaged conditions that have been documented for other farmworkers, as seen in Table 2.2. Estimates of farmworkers' earnings are hard to make. Records are usually kept only for the head of household, even though all family members contribute their labor. Also, earnings vary by the crops worked, how the weather has affected crops, and how much of the year they have been able to find work. But *all* families in the survey reported a combined household income far below the official poverty level. They also reported chronic underemployment, particularly during the winter months. They endure substandard housing and sanitation facilities, high rates of child labor, and poor education.

Midwestern farmworkers also reflect the poor health profile of other farmworkers, as indicated in Table 2.3. Malnutrition, upper respiratory infections, chronic diseases like diabetes, back injuries, and dental problems are common ailments. These workers also report high rates of exposure to dangerous pesticides. We estimate that almost all are in need of some health care.

Midwestern farmworkers themselves feel that they experience much poorer conditions than the local population in the areas where they work. The vast majority state they have more child labor, worse housing, poorer health, and greater discrimination. Almost one-fourth reported being displaced by agricultural mechanization, and a majority feel their livelihood is threatened by such changes. A

Table 2.1: *General Characteristics of Midwestern Farmworkers*[a]

Some ability to speak English	71%
Church or religious affiliation:	
"Evangelical" Protestant	3%
"Mainstream" Protestant	0%
Roman Catholic	97%
Participation in religious activities:	
None	5%
Once a year or so	11%
Once every few months	26%
Once every few weeks	42%
At least once a week	16%
Place of birth:	
Mexico	19%
Florida	22%
Texas	59%
Citizenship:[b]	
Mexico	11%
United States	89%
Home base:	
Midwest	3%
Florida	34%
Texas	63%
How much like farmwork in general:	
Not at all or not much	19%
Some or very much	81%
Average age	36
Average family size	5.6
Average educational level completed	6.8
Average years worked in farm labor	18.9
Average generations worked in farm labor	2.1
Average annual months of employment in farmwork	7.3
Average annual months of employment in nonfarmwork	1.7
Average annual months of farmwork in the Midwest	3.4
Average number of times a year sprayed by pesticides	6.6
Average number of workers in family[c]	3.6
Average number of adult (18 +) workers in family[c]	2.6
Average total 1982 household income before taxes	$6,447.00
Average total household earnings while in the Midwest[d]	$3,395.00
Average total household spending while in the Midwest[e]	$1,650.00

[a]Based on a 1983 survey of midwestern tomato workers (Barger and Reza 1984a, 1984b). The research population consisted of Mexican American male heads of household (*n* = 38).

[b]Only one individual (2% of the sample) was suspected of being an undocumented noncitizen.

[c]No data exists for more than 10% of the sample.

[d]Annual income earned in the Midwest is 53%.

[e]The total estimated spending of tomato workers while in the central Midwest is about $5 million. Some 49% of their total annual income is earned in the region, and 25% of the annual income is spent in the same area.

Table 2.2: *Living and Working Conditions of Midwestern Farmworkers*[a]

Annual income less than $10,000	100%
Gainfully employed less than 8 months of the year	29%
Have been displaced by agricultural mechanization	24%
Feel threatened that mechanization will replace farmworkers	65%
Socially isolated while in the Midwest[b]	66%
Believe have more child labor[c]	76%
Believe have poor housing and sanitation facilities[d]	92%
Believe have greater exposure to hazardous pesticides[d]	79%
Believe have more diseases and health problems[d]	84%
Believe have poorer education[d]	74%
Believe experience greater discrimination and prejudice[d]	61%
FARMWORKERS EXPERIENCING SEVERELY DEPRIVED CONDITIONS[e]	95%

[a]Based on a 1983 survey of midwestern tomato workers (Barger and Reza 1984a, 1984b). The research population consisted of Mexican American male heads of household ($n = 38$).
[b]Social isolation was concluded if the individual has only one or no regular interactions with people outside the field/camp work setting.
[c]In comparison with other people who live in the Midwest. Based on the survey data, it is estimated that about 3,000 children are involved in harvesting tomato crops in the central Midwest.
[d]In comparison with other people who live in the Midwest.
[e]Represents those who exhibited negative conditions in at least 6 of the 11 items indicated.

majority also report being socially isolated while working in the Midwest, having very few meaningful social contacts outside their crews. Based on the survey data, we estimate that almost all midwestern farmworkers clearly experience deprived conditions.

As with other farmworkers, midwestern migrants experience discrimination in many ways. They are excluded from many labor laws, such as workers' compensation for job-related injuries. Even where they are covered, standards are often reduced, as with child labor laws, and even these are generally not enforced. Most midwestern states include farmworkers in minimum wage laws. But farmworkers actually earn far less, because they are normally paid piece rates over the whole harvest season. It is estimated that they earn about $2.50 an hour.

There have been no legal restrictions on an employer withholding part of a farmworker's pay for an end-of-the-season "bonus." Medical

Table 2.3: *Health Conditions of Midwestern Farmworkers* [a]

High blood pressure (DBP $\geq$ 90 and/or SBP $\geq$ 160)[b]	10.5%
Self-reported health condition:	
Poor or fair	48%
Good or excellent	52%
Have current health problems that would like to see a doctor about[c]	26%
Self-reported health symptoms in the past year or 12 months: [d]	
Have been in a hospital	56%
Had an accident or injury requiring medical treatment	16%
Deafness or ear trouble (other than temporary colds)	53%
Trouble seeing or eye problems (other than glasses)	13%
Ever lost any teeth	32%
Dental or gum problems	42%
Back injury	13%
Neck/back pain for at least a month	32%
Joints pain for at least a month	11%
Cold or flu	74%
Persistent cough attacks	13%
Increased cough and phlegm for at least 3 weeks	13%
Wheezing or whistling sounds in the chest	13%
Severe pain across the front of the chest for at least a half hour	5%
Heart failure or "weak heart" with any severity	0%
Infections of the kidneys or bladder	3%
Loss of vision or blindness from several minutes to several days	3%
Difficulty in speaking or slurred speech from several minutes to several days	3%
Prolonged weakness or paralysis lasting up to several months	0%
Numbness or tingling sensations from several minutes to several days	13%
Any reason to suspect may have diabetes	8%
Goiter or other thyroid trouble	31%
Illness which cut down the appetite	11%
Difficulty swallowing for at least 3 days	5%
Yellow jaundice, which made the skin or eyes turn yellow	0%
Abdominal operation	0%
PROPORTION EXPERIENCING ABOVE AVERAGE HEALTH PROBLEMS	42%
Told by a doctor in the past year that had serious health problems:	24%
Seriously incapacitating or life threatening	0%

Table 2.3: *(continued)*

Somewhat incapacitating	18%
A mild health problem	5%
Has been sprayed by pesticides more than ten times during past year[e]	21%
ESTIMATED TO BE IN NEED OF MEDICAL ATTENTION	97%

[a]Based on a 1983 survey of midwestern tomato workers (Barger and Reza 1984a, 1984b). The research population consisted of Mexican American male heads of household (n = 38).
[b]No data exists for more than 10% of the sample.
[c]Respondents reported an average of 26.3 months since they last saw a medical doctor. There was an average 5.4 presentations for medical care during the past year.
[d]Items taken from the nationally standardized Health and Nutrition Evaluation Survey (HANES), U.S. Center for Health Statistics.
[e]Respondents reported being sprayed with pesticides on an average of 6.6 times during the previous year, with a range of 0 to 40 times.

insurance and workers' compensation for farmworkers are voluntary on the part of the employer. While farmworkers are legally supposed to receive unemployment insurance, this is rarely enforced. It wasn't until a 1988 ruling by the federal Occupational Safety and Health Administration (OSHA) that sanitary facilities and clean drinking water began to be provided farmworkers while in the fields.

An example of how midwestern workers, like other American farmworkers, have been excluded from the decision-making process can be seen in the tomato industry. Traditionally, the large food-processing corporations have stipulated unilateral contracts with farmers before the spring planting season. These contracts specify price structures, strains of tomatoes, and pesticide use. Farmers receive comparatively high returns from tomatoes, even though the crop is subject to harsh weather conditions and other risks, such as drought. Farmers in turn arrange with crew leaders to recruit field workers. The crew leaders usually receive returns based on the earnings of their workers, who are at the bottom of the system. Farmworkers are the ones who perform the actual labor in planting, tending, and harvesting the crops. These farmworkers are subject to a host of decisions made at higher levels, decisions which affect their living and working conditions. Such decisions have, in the past, resulted in low wages, underemployment, poor housing and sanitation, and exposure to hazardous pesticides. Since farmworkers have had little input into these decisions, they can, at best, only react to the decisions, once they learn of impending or actual conditions.

Solutions to Farmworkers' Conditions

There is little agreement on how to improve farmworkers' living and working situations. It is clear, however, that there have historically been few improvements over the past century.

One alternative for improving farmworkers' conditions is for them to leave farm labor. We have heard people ask why, if conditions are so bad, farmworkers don't find other kinds of jobs. Indeed, this is the premise of some government service programs which provide farmworkers with job skills training. But this view presumes that a variety of desirable jobs are available in the national economy. And people often forget that even a "normal" unemployment rate is 5 percent of the work force. This view also ignores the fact that farm labor is essential in agricultural production of a great many foods. So when one person does leave farm work, the job itself remains. Another steps in to take his or her place. Thus deprived conditions persist, regardless of who performs the actual labor.

The main challenge, then, is *how to make farm work an acceptable occupation.* The goal should be to develop acceptable conditions for those people whose labor produces food for other Americans. We should not expect simply to cycle people through an occupation that inherently involves deprived conditions. Many farmworkers have told us that they prefer their occupation, citing a number of reasons. They have developed the necessary job and life skills for this kind of work. They also enjoy working outdoors, having their families together, and other aspects of farm work. In the history of American labor, textile workers, coal miners, and many other laborers, many of whom were recent immigrants, have experienced similarly poor conditions. They received low wages and were subjected to dangerous work settings and child labor. Such occupations, however, have become stable and economically productive. Farmworker leaders have asked why this cannot also be true with farm labor and thus they have rejected changing jobs as a false "solution."

A second possible solution is for those with the greatest resources in the agricultural system to pass on some of the benefits they receive to farmworkers. Historically, however, this has rarely occurred (Galarza 1977; London and Anderson 1970; Daniel 1981; Burnaway 1976; Majka and Majka 1982; Jenkins 1985; Hightower 1978). The large agribusinesses and wealthy growers have rarely taken the initiative to improve farmworkers' conditions. Instead, they have been the main ones to exploit farmworkers, using these people to increase their own economic position. While a possible solution might be for those at the top to pass out benefits to those at the bottom, this method has shown little probability of effectively improving farmworkers' conditions.

A third alternative for resolving farmworkers' poor conditions is to enact laws and regulations which extend to farmworkers the same rights enjoyed by other American workers. As we have seen, farmworkers are specifically excluded from many legal rights. Even where there are legal protections, standards are often reduced and provisions are unenforced (Craddock 1979; Goldfarb 1982; London and Anderson 1970; Sosnick 1978). Laws and regulations, then, have sometimes provided minimal working and living standards for farmworkers. But these have generally proven to be inadequate and ineffective in resolving many of the basic defects in the agricultural system which produce the problems in the first place.

A fourth possible solution is to provide public assistance programs for farmworkers. There are a number of health, nutrition, education, job training, and other social programs available for farmworkers. There are several problems with these, however. Many programs are not always accessible. For example, many migrant health clinics have a dedicated staff, but services are limited by restricted resources (Shenkin 1974). Also, a number of farmworkers have told us that they do not use some programs like welfare for the unemployed even when they are available. They say that they work hard to support their families and that their sense of dignity is more important than the services received.

Farmworker leaders have argued that such public assistance programs are in effect political subsidies for agribusinesses (Burnaway 1976; Goldfarb 1982; Galarza 1977; Majka and Majka 1982; Hightower 1978). They point out that agribusinesses do not have to provide their workers with the same wages and benefits as other industries. Instead, taxpayers bear the costs for such benefits, rather than the employers. Most important, many assistance programs tend to address only survival needs. They do not resolve the basic deprived conditions experienced by farmworkers. Farmworkers are hardworking people, their leaders argue, and deserve the same benefits as other American workers.

When the historical record is reviewed, only one alternative has made a significant impact in improving farmworkers' rights and conditions. As we will see in the following chapter, this has been the farm labor movement, led by the United Farm Workers (UFW) in California (Barger and Reza 1985b, 1989; Denny 1979; Friedland and Thomas 1974; Goldfarb 1982; Hoffman 1978; Jenkins 1985;

Meister and Loftis 1977; Rudd 1975; Sosnick 1978; Walsh 1978; Walsh and Craypo 1979). Farmworkers under UFW contracts no longer experience poverty and child labor. They now receive such benefits as medical insurance and retirement pensions.

A social reform movement, then, has proven to be the most viable solution for eliminating the deprived conditions of farmworkers in America. It is interesting to note that labor movements have also proven to be the main alternative for American workers in other industries who have experienced serious disadvantaged conditions. Once they gained upgraded conditions, these workers were able to make significant contributions to American society and to the national economy through their taxes and buying power. The lessons of history thus indicate that the farm labor movement has the greatest potential for improving the working conditions of farmworkers. In the next chapters, we will examine this alternative, particularly where midwestern farmworkers are concerned. We will review the history of the Farm Labor Organizing Committee and then explore the internal and external forces that have helped shape social reform for midwestern farmworkers.

CHAPTER 3

The FLOC Movement

A number of studies document the impacts of the United Farm Workers of America (UFW) on improving farmworkers' living and working conditions (Chávez 1976; Ross 1989; Barger 1987; Barger and Haas 1983; Barger and Reza 1984a, 1984b, 1985a, 1985b, 1987, 1989; Allen and Keaveny 1988; Day 1971; Denny 1979; Friedland and Thomas 1974; Goldfarb 1982; Gomez-Quiñones and Arroyo 1978; Hoffman 1978; Jenkins 1985; Jenkins and Perrow 1977; Kiser and Woody Kiser 1979; Kushner 1975; Levy 1975; London and Anderson 1970; Majka 1981; Majka and Majka 1982; Meister and Loftis 1977; Meier and Rivera 1972; Rudd 1975; Sosnick 1978; Walsh 1978; Walsh and Craypo 1979; Young 1974). The successes of the UFW came after a long series of farm labor reform movements in California (Acuña 1988; Galarza 1964, 1970; Jenkins 1985; London and Anderson 1970; Majka and Majka 1982; McWilliams 1939; Meier and Rivera 1972; Samora 1977). It is interesting that California agriculture has represented a blend of capitalist and feudal character in the production of specialty crops, dependent upon the preferential treatment of state and federal governments. Some precedence for organizations of workers were found in attempts to organize cooperatives, but the ready supply of displaced laborers and the power of agribusinesses successfully undermined most attempts at labor organizing. In the early 1900's, the Industrial Workers of the World (IWW) and the Packing House Workers both tried to organize field workers. In 1903, one of the earliest strikes in agricultural labor was staged by Mexican and Japanese sugar beet workers in Ventura, California. The strikers won the right to negotiate with the growers instead of the labor contracting company that had recruited them. In 1913, another strike by Mexican American farmworkers was harshly suppressed by local police and the National Guard. There were several attempts to form unions in the early 1900's, and though none were successful, farmworkers gained experienced leaders who pressed for better wages and conditions.

In 1928, the Mexican Mutual Aid Society (MMAS) was asked to represent a group of cantaloupe workers on strike in the Imperial Valley of California. Even though the strike was broken by "imported" workers and vigilante groups, the MMAS developed a harvest contract which subsequently served as the basis for the policy of the California Department of Industrial Relations. This includes elimination of the practice of withholding 25 percent of the workers' wages as a "bonus" until the end of the season.

The Great Depression brought an influx of displaced Anglos ("Okies") into farm labor, and also deportations of more than 400,000 Mexican and Mexican Americans. Farm labor organizing activities, however, actually increased during this time. In 1933, the Cannery and Agricultural Workers Industrial Union (CAWIU) led the largest agricultural strike up to that point in the San Gabriel Valley. Workers, mostly Mexican Americans, were incensed over wage reductions to as little as nine cents an hour. Despite violence, the workers eventually won wages of twenty-five cents an hour and ten-hour days. The workers also achieved a major step by winning union recognition, though the labor organization which eventually emerged did not last. In all, there were thirty-seven labor strikes in 1933, affecting most major crops. The growers responded by forming the Associated Farmers of California (AFC), to oppose "communist" unions and to establish a permanent lobby in Sacramento.

Farm labor organizing and strikes continued in California and Texas throughout the 1930's and 1940's but with few successes. Some labor unions emerged that were affiliated with the Congress of Industrial Organizations (CIO) and the American Federation of Labor (AFL). One organizer in the National Farm Workers Union (NFWU) strike in 1947 against Di Giorgio Farms in Kern County, California, was Ernesto Galarza, a former migrant farmworker and a respected scholar with a Ph.D. from Columbia University. An investigation by a California House subcommittee headed by Richard M. Nixon helped suppress this strike by bringing political pressure to undermine the labor organizers. Though legally restricted from being involved in labor disputes, braceros were frequently used to break strikes and union organizing.

In the early 1960's, events led to the beginnings of significant changes in farm labor affairs. In 1961, after several attempts in the 1950's to form a viable farmworker union, César Chávez and Dolores Huerta organized the National Farm Workers Association

(NFWA) in Delano, California. Another farmworker union, the Agricultural Workers Organizing Committee (AWOC), had been established in the area by the AFL-CIO. In 1965, a group of Filipino farmworkers arrived in the San Joaquin Valley to harvest grapes. When they learned their wage rate had been arbitrarily reduced, they went on strike. They asked AWOC for help, and the two groups formed a coalition.

The strikers faced unusual challenges in labor history, but these were met with creativity. For example, a strike line at a factory could be set up at bounded entrances to meet workers. But the grape fields were vast and had entrances at many points. It was impossible to surround the fields with picket lines. So the farmworkers set up a roving picket line, moving in caravans to the fields being worked. They used loudspeakers to urge pickers to join their cause. Other innovative tactics were also developed. The Teatro Campesino (Farmworker Theater), organized by Luís Valdez, put on skits for the strikers, emphasizing key issues in the struggle. They also presented skits in the picket lines for workers out in the fields, calling on them to join their companions for the benefit of all farmworkers. As a result of such creative efforts, more and more farmworkers joined the movement.

In August 1965, the NFWA and AWOC merged into the United Farm Workers Organizing Committee (UFWOC), AFL-CIO. César Chávez became director, and Larry Itliong, leader of the Filipino strikers, became assistant director. A few weeks later, the new organization won a government-supervised election among the grape workers on the giant Di Giorgio ranch. In the next months, the new union won more elections on grape ranches and wineries in central California. The growers' claims that farmworkers were not interested in unions and that outside agitators were causing all the problems had been proven wrong. But, though it had demonstrated support among farmworkers, the growers refused to negotiate with the UFWOC.

In their struggle with the large agribusiness interests, the UFWOC began to open up another front, external popular and political support. The farmworkers' leaders called for a boycott against Schenley, one of the largest of the Delano growers. They followed Schenley's grapes to shipping points and set up picket lines. Union, student, and urban sympathizers now had an active role they could play, and support for the boycott spread. Walter Reuther, head of the United Automobile Workers, came to Delano in December. He pledged $5,000 a month to support the movement. In 1966, Senator Harrison Williams held public hearings in California. Then Senator Robert

Kennedy publicly supported the farmworkers. All these events gave considerable publicity to the farmworkers' cause.

In the spring of 1966, UFWOC organized a 230-mile *peregrinación* (pilgrimage) to the state capitol in Sacramento. En route, thousands of farmworkers and supporters joined the cause. In Sacramento, the marchers and their supporters appealed to the state government to enact protections for farmworkers. During the march, Schenley announced it would recognize the UFWOC and negotiate a contract.

Later, in August 1967, the great grape boycott was born. The large Giumarra ranch had refused to meet with the UFWOC. Giumarra did not have an identifiable brand name, and the ranch shipped grapes with other growers' labels. The union responded with a new boycott, but this time they included *all* California table grapes. The rationale of the boycott was that the combined socioeconomic power of millions of Americans could counter the unilateral power of the large agribusiness interests.

Support for the boycott mushroomed. Organizers were sent to cities around the country. A majority of Americans approved of the boycott, and significant numbers refused to buy grapes in support of the farm labor cause. Mayors, city councils, labor unions, church organizations, political candidates, and many others endorsed the boycott. In an attempt to reduce the impact of the boycott, growers diverted table grapes to wineries. At the same time, the Department of Defense purchased huge quantities of grapes. Still, the boycott continued to grow and to make a significant economic impact on the grape industry.

In 1968, César Chávez and other UFWOC leaders became aware of the hazards of pesticides to both farmworkers and consumers. So they added pesticides to the strike-boycott issues. The boycott continued to expand, and support groups appeared all over the country to advocate the farmworkers' cause.

In 1969, several growers from the Coachella and San Joaquin valleys began negotiating with the UFWOC. Talks were bogged down by the pesticide issue, but eventually contracts were negotiated. These contracts contained key clauses regulating the use of pesticides. DDT and several other pesticides were thus contractually banned on UFWOC ranches, long before the federal government took similar actions. Over the next year, similar contracts were signed with other growers. The UFWOC consolidated its achievements in winning new rights and benefits for farmworkers.

In 1972, the UFWOC became the United Farm Workers (UFW), a fully chartered labor union of the AFL-CIO. In 1975, California passed the Agricultural Labor Relations Act (ALRA). This law legalized farm labor organizing and collective bargaining in the state. A government labor relations board was created to oversee farm labor elections and good-faith bargaining. The struggle had taken farmworkers from central California through a long strike and popular boycott. It had mobilized many segments of the American society in support of the farmworkers' cause. This was the beginning. There would be other struggles to win rights and benefits for farmworkers in other areas. For one thing, the UFW faced the intrusion of the Teamsters, whose "sweetheart" contracts with growers were made without the involvement of the farmworkers themselves. Later a long strike and boycott against the lettuce industry won new advancements for farmworkers. Another table grape boycott launched in 1984 continued the commitment of César Chávez and other UFW leaders into a new era. Recent research has indicated that the UFW still enjoys widespread support among California farmworkers and the public (Barger and Reza 1985b, 1989; Barger 1987).

The UFW represents a social reform movement. Its overall goal has been to include farmworkers in the opportunities and benefits enjoyed by other American workers. Its efforts have gone far beyond gaining wage increases. The ultimate issue has been control of farmworkers' working conditions. The UFW's ideology has defined both the problems and solutions for farmworkers in terms of labor rights and social justice. A predominant goal of the UFW has been to establish and maintain union recognition for farmworkers.

It should be noted that the UFW's ideology emphasizes nonviolence. César Chávez had a long commitment to this philosophy. He actively studied the ideals and the practices expressed by Mohandas Gandhi and Martin Luther King, Jr. The force of his moral leadership in the farm labor movement was in part based on this commitment to nonviolence.

A major factor in the UFW's success has been its strong internal support among farmworkers (Barger and Reza 1985b, 1989; Denny 1979; Hoffman 1978; Jenkins 1985; Jenkins and Perrow 1977; Levy 1975; Majka 1981). For a reform movement to be legitimate, it must have the endorsement of the group it claims to represent. The UFW was successful in organizing California farmworkers through grassroots house meetings, marches, rallies, and media campaigns. So the UFW has maintained a central place in farmworkers' minds. In a 1984 survey in California, for example, there was almost universal agreement that the UFW has been good for farmworkers (Barger and Reza 1985b, 1989). Also, 83 percent said that farmworker conditions had improved as a direct result of the UFW's efforts and activities. Most significant, 78 percent said they would vote for the UFW in a union election on the ranch where they worked. In general, farmworkers overwhelmingly support the UFW as the most viable alternative for improving their lives (Barger and Reza 1985b, 1989; also see Barger and Reza 1984a, 1984b). In contrast, the Teamsters' efforts to represent farmworkers have failed to generate any internal support, even where they enjoyed an alliance with agribusinesses in California (Friedland and Thomas 1974; Walsh and Craypo 1979).

Another major factor in the UFW's success has been its ability to mobilize considerable external support for its cause (Barger 1987; Jenkins 1985; Jenkins and Perrow 1977; Majka 1981; Majka and Majka 1982; Walsh 1978; Walsh and Craypo 1979). Any effort of social change automatically threatens existing vested interests. The social context of the UFW movement has included strong obstacles. Agribusiness has had a long tradition of socioeconomic power to maintain control over farm labor. Agribusiness' vested interests have historically been backed by the power of the state. This is evident, for example, in the exclusion of farmworkers from the National Labor Relations Act. It is also seen in the enactment of the bracero and other programs that ensure cheap agricultural labor. Being a disadvantaged minority, farmworkers themselves have inherently had very little economic or political power to make meaningful changes in their conditions. Because its goal is reform, rather than revolution, the UFW movement has respected general social norms and has utilized "legitimate" channels for making change.

External support from other segments of society has therefore been essential for farmworkers to overcome the considerable power of agribusiness. As stated earlier, the UFW has been successful in winning the backing of many church, labor, political, and civic groups. Such support has been successful in changing the structure of agribusiness to provide farmworkers with greater benefits for their contributions.

A major strategy along these lines has been widespread popular participation in UFW-sponsored boycotts (Barger 1987; Barger and Haas 1983; Field 1985; L. Harris 1975). In the original boycott of table grapes in the 1960's and of iceberg lettuce in the early 1970's, it is estimated that over 12 percent, or 20 million Americans, boycotted in support of the UFW. The rationale of these boycotts is that the combined power of millions of American consumers can counterbalance the powerlessness of farmworkers. In effect, if the corporate growers cannot sell their products, it does not matter how much economic and political power they have. And if the only way they can sell their products is to share power with farmworkers, then the whole system will be altered. Farmworkers can then have an active and effective role in determining their own conditions. Another key benefit of the boycott strategy is that it only needs about 10 percent participation of the public to be successful. At this level, the wholesalers and shippers reduce their prices. This, coupled with reduced sales, is enough to make the production of the boycotted goods a losing operation.

The boycott is a highly creative strategy. The traditional structure of agribusiness has been designed to keep the large growers and corporations in power. The UFW, however, simply invoked new "rules," ones that supported its goals. Once basic rights were guaranteed through binding labor contracts, farmworkers had their own voice. Then they were not dependent upon structures and practices put in place by other segments of society.

Research has documented that there is overwhelming popular support for the UFW, its goals, and its methods (Barger 1987; Barger and Haas 1983; Jenkins 1985; Jenkins and Perrow 1977; Majka and Majka 1982). For example, in a 1986 public survey in California, 74 percent of the respondents said they had a favorable opinion of the UFW (Barger 1987). Some 85 percent agreed with the UFW's goal of improving farmworkers' rights and conditions through collective bargaining with agribusinesses. Over 57 percent believed a boycott was a legitimate means for achieving farm labor representation; and 22 percent said they had participated in at least two UFW boycotts. These levels of participation are far greater than what is needed to make a boycott a success. Such external support has been effective in counterbalancing the relative powerlessness of farmworkers. It has posed a significant challenge to the political and economic strength of agribusinesses in California.

The fact that the UFW has been effective in mobilizing both internal and external support has been a critical factor in its achievement of considerable reforms in farm labor affairs. Furthermore, it has been effective in improving the living and working conditions of farmworkers in those areas where it has been active. Workers under UFW contracts no longer endure poverty and child labor. Instead, they now receive such benefits as medical insurance and retirement pensions, and they have experienced both social and economic stability.

Even farmworkers not working under a union contract have benefited. For example, all farmworkers in California are now covered by unemployment insurance and the state's Agricultural Labor Relations Act. Unionization has traditionally brought many positive carryover effects for nonunion workers as well (Roach and Roach 1981). There are also some intriguing indications that the success of the farmworker movement may have positive impacts on the agricultural system as a whole (Coffey 1969; Rochin 1977). A more stabilized work force reduces worker alienation, absenteeism, and turnover, and therefore, it normally brings an increase in overall production.

It should be noted that in recent years the UFW has faced new challenges. When Republican George Deukmejian ran for governor of California, he was heavily supported by agribusiness. When he took office, he undermined the Agricultural Labor Relations Board (ALRB) as an effective agency to regulate farmworker affairs (*Bakersfield Californian* 1984; Chávez 1985; *San Francisco Chronicle* 1984a, 1984c, 1985; *Los Angeles Times* 1984b; *Packer* 1984). He appointed an attorney who had represented growers to the board, staffed the agency with people who had close relations with agribusiness, and cut the ALRB budget. Such moves resulted in cases of unfair labor practices by growers not being investigated and the nonenforcement of existing ALRB rulings against growers. The UFW could win union elections on ranches, but these victories were never realized in labor contracts. To counter such political reversals in the hard-won rights of farmworkers, the UFW called a new citizens' boycott of nonunion California table grapes (*Fresno Bee* 1984; *Sacramento Bee* 1984; *Los Angeles Times* 1984a; *Catholic Universe Bulletin* 1984).

A major issue in these new events is whether the UFW indeed represents farmworkers. The UFW has recently been criticized as being behind the times, played out, and lacking followers (*Village Voice* 1984; *San Francisco Chronicle* 1984b; *San Jose Mercury News* 1984). If farmworkers themselves do not support the UFW, its goals, and its methods, then the union loses its social and moral legitimacy as a force in farm labor affairs. If, on the other hand, it does validly represent farmworkers, then it can be justified in seeking to achieve its goals. Surveys of Californian and midwestern farmworkers document that they are overwhelmingly in support of the UFW (Barger and Reza 1984a, 1984b, 1985b, 1989). This research indicates that the UFW's efforts in representing farmworkers are legitimate.

Another issue is whether the UFW has sustained its external support for the farm labor cause. In order to overcome political and economic opposition through "legitimate" channels of change, it must have the continued support of its allies and supporters in other segments of society. The new grape boycott, in particular, calls for mobilizing popular support for its goals. Research indicates that while the public is not very well informed about the issues, people strongly endorse farm labor reform, the UFW, and its methods, including the boycott (Barger 1987). Since the UFW has the support of both farmworkers and the public, its current challenges are largely political. To maximize its limited resources, the UFW has been focusing on mobilizing external support, particularly for the grape boycott.

The story of the United Farm Workers highlights several important points for understanding other cases of social reform. In particular, both the internal and external forces involved in social change must be examined. How these interact with each other to direct the course of change is crucial to understanding events and outcomes. The history of the UFW thus serves as a model for understanding the farm labor movement in the Midwest.

The Farm Labor Organizing Committee

While the UFW was heavily involved in seeking farm labor reforms in California, a similar group was becoming active in the Midwest. The Farm Labor Organizing Committee (FLOC) has led a reform movement to achieve improved rights and conditions for farmworkers in Ohio, Michigan, Indiana, and Illinois (Barger and Reza 1984a, 1984b, 1985a, 1987; Valdés 1984, 1991). As indicated in Table 3.1, the FLOC story covers several decades. The emergence of the FLOC movement was concurrent with the civil rights movements and the farm labor movement in California. FLOC is modeled along the same lines as the UFW, and its philosophy includes securing labor

Table 3.1: *History of the FLOC Movement*

1967	FLOC is founded by Baldemar Velásquez
	FLOC strikes farms in northwestern Ohio and wins 33 contracts
1968–1976	FLOC focuses on community organizing
1976	FLOC is called in to direct the Warren, Indiana, strike
1976–1977	FLOC organizes farmworkers in northwestern Ohio
1978	FLOC strikes Campbell Soup's tomato operations in Ohio
1979	Campbell mandates mechanization of tomato harvest
	FLOC formally organizes as a labor union
	FLOC calls for a boycott against Campbell Soup
1980	Many churches, unions, and others endorse FLOC and boycott
	Local FLOC support committees form around country
	Campbell offers funds to farmworker agencies in Ohio, refused

Table 3.1: *(continued)*

1981	FLOC organizes Campbell's workers in Texas/Florida base areas
	Ohio senate investigates farmworker conditions
1982	Catholic archdiocese of Boston sponsors FLOC-Campbell talks
1983	"Sharecropping" issue in cucumber operations arises
	FLOC marches 560 miles to Campbell's Camden headquarters
1984	FLOC organizes Ohio and Michigan Vlasic cucumber workers
	FLOC initiates corporate campaign
1985	Campbell agrees to talks with FLOC
	Statement of Understanding
	Establishment of Dunlop Commission
	Formation of Campbell growers' associations
	FLOC wins union elections on Campbell tomato farms
1986	FLOC signs a contract with Campbell and its Ohio tomato growers
	FLOC signs a contract with Vlasic and its Michigan pickle growers
1987	FLOC signs a contract with Vlasic and its Ohio pickle growers
	FLOC signs a contract with Heinz and its Ohio/Michigan pickle growers
1988	FLOC and Heinz develop drought relief program
1989	FLOC signs a second contract with Campbell and its Ohio tomato growers
	FLOC signs a second contract with Vlasic and its Michigan pickle growers
	Sharecropping phased out
1990	FLOC signs a second contract with Vlasic and its Ohio pickle growers
	Sharecropping phased out
	FLOC signs a second contract with Heinz and its Ohio/Michigan pickle growers
	Sharecropping phased out
	FLOC organizes Dean's pickle workers in Ohio/Michigan
1991	FLOC organizes Dean pickle workers in Texas/Florida base areas
	FLOC signs a contract with Dean Foods and its Ohio/Michigan pickle growers
	Sharecropping phased out

rights as the main solution to farmworkers' problems, with an emphasis on nonviolence. The two organizations have worked together in seeking to achieve common goals. Cooperative efforts have included formally endorsing the other's boycotts and joint organizing efforts in Texas and Florida.

Prior to FLOC, there had been several unsuccessful attempts to organize farmworkers in the Midwest. During the 1930's, agricultural employment in the Midwest increased sharply due to expanded production of labor-intensive fruits and vegetables. With migrant workers only in an area for a short time, however, organizing efforts were limited. Many Mexican American and Mexican farmworkers were deported, and the U.S. Department of Labor Placement Service helped growers hire field workers. Both of these actions were used to eliminate organizers and sympathetic workers. It was not until the middle 1960's that any enduring effects came from efforts to organize midwestern farmworkers, when Baldemar Velásquez began organizing FLOC.

Baldemar Velásquez

FLOC's founder, Baldemar Velásquez, was born in 1947 in Pharr, Texas, a small town in the lower Rio Grande Valley. He was the third of nine brothers and sisters in the family of Cresencio Velásquez and Vicenta Castillo. His father was born in Driscoll, Texas, and when Cresencio was orphaned at eleven, he entered migrant farm work, as a means of survival. Baldemar's mother, Vicenta, was born in Pharr, where her parents had fled in 1910 to avoid the Mexican Revolution. Baldemar says that his parents have had two main impacts in his life, "One, they taught me to work hard, with intensity. And two, Mom's Christian conviction has taught me to have strong faith."

Baldemar recalls his early years in the migrant stream: "We traveled in a canvas-covered truck. I remember people huddling all around the sides of the truck, trying to keep warm with blankets and a can of hot ashes." He remembers working in the fields at about four years of age. Also, he has memories of his family living in crowded conditions, sometimes having only one little room to themselves.

In 1953, when Baldemar was six, the family settled out of the migrant stream in Gilboa, Ohio. The family continued working in the fields and canneries during the summer season, but the children were able to go to school. In the first and second grades, Baldemar did not know English well and did not always understand what the teachers were saying. "I had to work three or four times longer to do what other students were doing." He remembers other kids making fun of him for being Mexican, and he remembers feeling isolated. He was good at sports, but in the seventh grade Baldemar remembers being told by an Anglo student, "You're a good athlete, but look at your grades. You're still a dumb Mexican."

Rising to the challenge, Baldemar made the honor roll in the following year. In high school, he gained recognition for his athletic abilities in baseball, football, basketball, and track. When he had first entered high school, his counselor tried to track him in vocational skills, but Baldemar insisted on enrolling in college-preparatory courses. Baldemar adds, "I did not really decide on college till my senior year. An English teacher convinced me to go since I had all the college-prep classes."

In 1965, Baldemar enrolled in the engineering program at Pan American University in southern Texas. While there, he explains, "I began seeing my roots in the Texas Valley, where all the injustices and oppressions are magnified. I took a class in Texas history and it opened my eyes to the exploitation of Mexican people and how farmworkers fit into it." He became interested in social sciences. A priest, Father Sweytzer, helped Baldemar get financial aid, and the following year he transferred to Ohio Northern College. A year after that, he transferred to Bluffton College, a Mennonite institution, where he finished college. In 1969, Baldemar married Sara Templin. Her father, on the faculty at Bluffton College, had lived in India for several years and knew Mohandas Gandhi personally. He shared Mennonite and Gandhian philosophies with Baldemar, which influenced Baldemar's convictions about farmworker justice.

While at Bluffton, Baldemar volunteered to work for the Congress of Racial Equality in Cleveland and lived with an African American family for a few weeks. "That experience made me realize that I should work to change conditions for farmworker families." The next summer, he says, he thought a lot about organizing farmworkers. He worked cherries in Michigan to pay off college loans. Then he went to Wisconsin and met with Jesse Salaz, who was starting *Obreros Unidos* (united workers) for farmworkers in that area. When he got back to Ohio, Baldemar talked to his father about organizing the farmworkers.

Baldemar says he knew that the older men thought he was too young. So he asked his father to help. "He would get his friends together. They would listen to me, mostly for amusement as well as not to disappoint my dad, but enough of the idea caught on with them. I started convincing the older people that this was an interesting thing and a good thing."

One event in the early years of organizing stands out in Baldemar's mind. He was invited to a local meeting of the National Farmer's Organization. "A lot of the farmworkers came, and half the room were farmers, half were Mexican farmworkers. For the first time, they heard me mention the farmworker cause to the farmers directly. One man said that I told those farmers in their own language exactly what he and others felt. That incident made me realize that I was not speaking for myself but for the sentiments that were being felt by other farmworkers."

Another incident that Baldemar considers formative was challenging a trespassing law at the Libby cannery camp in Leipsic, Ohio. "I went to pass out FLOC literature, and the security cop told me he would arrest me if I went in. I started a commotion at the fence so workers inside would get interested. I then went into the camp and started giving them flyers. I told the guard in both Spanish and English that the workers were not slaves. To have me challenge authority by stepping over the fence, it made them think. The word spread like wildfire and by the end of the week, all the workers were on our side. One lesson that I learned there is not to be afraid of the powers that be, especially in front of other workers."

Baldemar's personal philosophy has been influenced by the ideas of Martin Luther King, Jr., Mohandas Gandhi, and César Chávez. In particular, he has strong convictions about social justice and nonviolent resistance to oppression. Baldemar also comments, "As far as personal philosophy is concerned, I think we are waging two battles all of the time. One is in the natural realm and the other is in the spiritual realm. There is a passage in the Scriptures that says, 'We battle not against flesh and blood but against powers and principles.' I think we have to be constantly discerning the spirit of the situation."

Baldemar's religious beliefs are an important part of his social convictions. "This is what it is all about," he says. "As long as you have faith, you have hope. You've got to admit that with the farmworkers there is so much hopelessness and perhaps the situation that farmworkers face in many cases are hopeless. But in the Scriptures it also says, 'In Jesus all things are possible.' It is that faith that helps us overcome those things that we cannot overcome on our own, in many cases, in spite of ourselves. At times I would ask my parents how were we going to make do, how are we going to pay bills or debts. They would say, *'Nomas Dios sabe'* (Only God knows). And somehow it was always there."

Baldemar states that sometimes he has made mistakes. "One of the biggest things I had to learn was some traditional managerial skills. I had no training in these things and didn't know anything about this when we started organizing. It is something I am still learning about. I am trying to understand more about personnel relationships and know that a lot of communication is necessary."

Baldemar says that FLOC has had a big impact on his family. "Generally, I think the experiences that the kids have had on the picket lines, on marches and demonstrations, are invaluable educational events that few kids have the opportunities for. It is important that they understand what happens to people who are victims of oppression in this world, and that such things do occur."

Though he had achieved many advantages not available to most farmworkers, Baldemar never forgot the conditions in which he was raised. He remembers the poverty his family endured, especially the time he and his brothers huddled in a bed while snow drifted in through the walls of their home. He remembers the maltreatment by growers, like the one who cheated his father and paid only half of what they were promised for the work they had done. Baldemar also remembers the insults and racial slurs of local Anglos.

These experiences in the long term served to shape his convictions and his commitment to making meaningful changes for other farmworkers who have suffered similar injustices. "We call on the agricultural industry to recognize that farmworkers have legitimate concerns for their families," he says. "We do hope for a healthy industry, in which all workers, from top managers to farmworkers, can earn a living that is conducive to a healthy family. That is the new notion they have to accept, and that is what we call upon them to do."

The Early Years

In 1967, when Baldemar Velásquez was twenty years old, he began forming FLOC with his father and a small group of farmworkers. They were initially concerned with the immediate problems of farmworkers. They sought to address their poor living and working conditions and the discriminations they endured. They primarily focused their attention on the growers, who, in their view, provided meager conditions in the labor camps and paid them poverty wages.

In the summer of 1968, FLOC called for meetings with tomato growers in Lucas County, in northwestern Ohio. Few growers responded, and negotiations were not even able to start. FLOC then called for a strike. The quick response by farmworkers soon shut down tomato operations in the area. Some growers reacted violently, displaying guns and threatening the workers. Local law enforcement officers also harassed the strikers' picket lines.

Despite the threats, FLOC won a surprisingly quick victory (Valdés 1984). The fear that their crops would rot in fields compelled thirty-three growers to sign contracts with FLOC. These contracts gave FLOC the right to organize farmworkers, provided a wage increase, and guaranteed that FLOC members not be fired or harassed for their union convictions.

The victory, however, was short-lived. In the next three years, the growers developed tactics to circumvent FLOC. Some, for example, temporarily switched crops. Then, when the local press and Anglo communities took the growers' side, the Mexican Americans who had made their homes in these communities, and who spent their earnings locally, were ignored.

One objection of the farmers, however, had an element of truth to it. They claimed that their own ability to provide wages, housing, and other benefits were governed by the prices paid by the large food-processing corporations.

For specialty crops like tomatoes and pickles, this has certainly been true. Each winter, a company determines its produce requirements for the coming year. The company then signs a contract with each individual farmer for his or her entire season's production; and prices, pesticide use, and other conditions are set before planting. In order to ensure consistency in its products, the company sells its own seedlings to its growers. That company, and only that company, then buys back all the harvested produce.

In this situation, the farmers themselves have little bargaining power because their market is limited to a few large corporations. Since a company wants to ensure a consistent supply of produce, there is some inducement to pay its growers a reasonable price. Rates, however, may vary some from farmer to farmer. Specialty crops like tomatoes and cucumbers generally provide farmers with higher profits than staples like corn or soybeans. But from these earnings, the grower must pay farmworkers and provide them with housing. He or she also takes a higher risk, depending on weather and other factors that affect yields.

Farmworkers are in direct contact with these growers. It is therefore natural to see them as the most obvious factor in their deprived conditions. There are certainly some growers who are racist and who cheat their workers. There are also growers who show human respect for farmworkers and provide them with the best facilities and conditions possible. The negative cases, unfortunately, are all too common, and most farmworkers have experienced maltreatment. So it was natural that FLOC initially focused its efforts on the growers.

FLOC leaders, however, soon realized that the large corporations would have to be involved in any long-term reforms. "It was a big mistake to go after individual farmers," says Baldemar, "instead of focusing on the large corporations. We spent a lot of years doing that, and it was a mistake."

The companies, however, denied any direct responsibility for the well-being of workers. They argued they could not interfere in the affairs of their growers. In response, FLOC pointed out how preseason price structures and other conditions of the corporations clearly did affect the growers' affairs.

Assessing the situation, FLOC leaders decided that they needed to be better prepared for dealing with these companies. They turned their attention to building a strong support base. From 1970 to 1976, FLOC focused on a broad community organizing effort. They raised basic civil rights issues like the discrimination experienced by farmworkers. They created food and gas cooperatives and developed legal aid programs for farmworkers. During this time, FLOC's membership grew to about seven hundred people. Most of these were seasonal workers who lived in the general area.

In 1976, a spontaneous strike of farmworkers in Warren, Indiana, involved FLOC in its primary mission as a labor union (Valdés 1984). The strike involved overrecruitment at a Morgan cannery. Following a common practice among growers and canneries, more people had been brought in to work than there were actual jobs. This was done to ensure low wages. If any workers complained they were getting less than they were promised, they would simply be replaced by unemployed workers. When the farmworkers arrived and discovered there were far fewer jobs than promised, they struck the Morgan cannery. The workers constructed a barricade to keep tomatoes from being delivered for processing. They called on FLOC to represent them.

A federal district judge was asked to issue an injunction against the strikers. After reviewing the situation, the judge publicly condemned the owner, John Morgan. He cited discriminatory hiring, inadequate and unsanitary housing, the lack of unpolluted drinking water, and filthy latrines. Yet, to the shock of the strikers, the restraining order was issued. Morgan was given ten days to resolve the problems, sufficient time for the cannery to process the waiting tomatoes.

The strikers refused to take down the barricades and were arrested. Fortunately, press coverage of the strike increased public awareness of farmworkers' conditions. It also brought to light the use of the Immigration and Naturalization Service (INS) to deport workers, to avoid paying them for work done and to intimidate strikers. Too, the press noted how the state government failed to investigate or monitor farmworker conditions.

The Warren strike was eventually settled. Both cannery workers and field pickers received higher wages. It was also agreed that the camps were to be repaired and maintained by a janitorial staff.

The Warren case was an important learning experience for FLOC. Baldemar notes that "it was a major event in that it tested our negotiating and mobilizing ability. It also gave us a taste of the forthcoming fight with the Campbell Soup Company." Following the Warren strike, FLOC leaders renewed their efforts to build the union. Moral and financial support came from the Catholic church and from local labor unions. The Communication Workers of America (CWA) and the American Federation of State, County, and Municipal Employees (AFSCME) were particularly supportive.

The Campbell Strike

By 1978, the FLOC movement had developed a meaningful reform ideology, based on social justice and labor rights for farmworkers. This philosophy emphasized that farmworkers had been denied basic working rights and benefits, particularly those enjoyed by most other American workers. Farmworkers' disadvantages were seen as a result of their economic and political powerlessness. The ultimate concern was that they had no direct role in determining those conditions which affected their lives.

FLOC's solution to these problems was labor organizing and collective bargaining. FLOC's initial goal, then, was union recognition, where workers exchanged their labor for fair wages and benefits. This would make farmworkers an equal party with those who used their labor. This was a reform ideology, since it called for farmworkers to be included in the basic norms and structures of American society.

FLOC's ideology included several creative components. Perhaps the most innovative was the call for three-way contracts between farmworkers, growers, and the canning corporations. From the farmworkers' point of view, this meant that they should be able to participate in the system as equals. It also meant that they should be able to share in the opportunities enjoyed by other American workers. The three-way contracts, however, represented a whole new approach in labor history. Since production of specialty crops involved multiple levels, FLOC maintained that the three main parties concerned must all be participants. In particular, this included the large food-processing corporations. It was they who ultimately determined the structure of the industry, which affected both the farmworkers' and the farmers' well-being.

In the spring of 1978, FLOC called for meetings with growers and the food-processing corporations to discuss farmworkers' conditions. In letters to growers, FLOC asked them to work together with farmworkers, but only 21 of 550 agreed to meet with FLOC. No representatives of the companies responded.

When it appeared that the growers and corporations would not voluntarily show any regard for their concerns, 2,300 farmworkers in northwest Ohio voted to strike Campbell Soup and Libby tomato operations. Baldemar Velásquez explains it was "basic discontent" that motivated the strikers to take such actions. The workers had been distressed with their conditions for years. Now the proposed meetings had raised their hopes for meaningful changes. When they were disappointed, the strike allowed them the chance to express their frustration. Baldemar also feels that this continuing discontent helped maintain the workers' strike.

The strike focused on Campbell Soup and Libby for several reasons. Most of the workers active in FLOC had worked for these operations, and so the strike targets reflected their personal discontent. Another consideration was that limited resources could be most effectively used when focused on specific goals. In terms of practical strategy, if a settlement with one of the top companies could be achieved, this would open the door for the whole industry.

The strikers picketed the tomato fields in northwest Ohio which supplied Campbell and Libby. They also picketed the canneries, and FLOC held rallies and organized marches. Then Baldemar Velásquez went on a hunger strike in support of the farmworkers' cause. It should be noted that before the strikers conducted any activities, they were well trained. They learned about nonviolent techniques, the legal limits of different actions, and their rights. Furthermore, the presence of nuns, clergy, and lawyers on the picket lines did much to restrain violence against the strikers. The picket lines were successful in pulling out many workers from the fields. When the summer season was over, it was estimated that about 25 percent of the local tomato crop was not harvested that year (Valdés 1984).

During the summer, however, the companies had thrown their weight into the confrontation. Campbell offered higher prices to its growers. It apparently assumed that the growers would pass on

FLOC farmworkers vote to strike Campbell Soup and Libby tomato operations in Ohio in 1978. Midwestern farmworkers have demonstrated continuous support for the FLOC movement, even when this jeopardized their meager earnings. As Baldemar Velásquez has said on many occasions, "What have we got to lose? Only the deprived conditions we have experienced all our lives."

some of the extra earnings to their workers to diffuse the strike. This was not the case, however, and the workers were further offended. For its part, Libby filed a lawsuit against FLOC for losses from the strike. These actions, however, gave the farmworkers' cause more visibility.

Several growers were particularly hostile. Some faced the picket lines with guns pointed at the workers. One ran his pickup truck into the strikers' lines. Another grower sprayed a picket line with pesticides. Even farmworkers sympathetic to the FLOC cause who were working on farms not being struck were sometimes fired and blacklisted.

The growers tried to pressure the crew leaders to keep their workers from supporting the strike, Baldemar recalls. "Once we were in Leipsic, picketing the Libby plant. One crew leader kept riding around the plant in a Cadillac full of goons. That night the farmers also came in with their own goons. The crew leader in the Cadillac saw the dogs and the squad cars that were being used to harass us. He saw me stand up to the police and the farmers. Afterwards he came up to me and said, 'Baldemar I've been against you all this time. But now I see what's happening, and now I'm on your side.'"

Baldemar also cites another incident. "Out of all the crew leaders, we had about nine or ten who were very helpful. The growers tried to pressure some of the most influential crew leaders, like Fernando Cuevas, FLOC vice president. Fernando was known as an early FLOC sympathizer. On one occasion during the pickle season, the farmers cornered him and started yelling at him. When other crew leaders saw Fernando being cornered, something clicked in them. They realized what the growers really thought of *them*. They went and helped Fernando. Something made them realize what side they were really on."

There was also a strong reaction from the local Anglos. On several occasions, farmworkers were beaten. One night, a cross was burned at the strike headquarters. Even public organizations stepped over their legal limits. Public schools let classes out early so the children could pick tomatoes. The main impact was that the children learned that stoop labor in the fields is very hard work. Few lasted in the fields after a couple of days. Another case involved the director of the Findlay office of the Ohio Bureau of Employment Services, who was also the owner of a migrant camp. He referred workers to struck farms. This was an illegal action, since an employment bureau cannot refer workers when a labor dispute is in progress. The INS was called several times to check FLOC picket lines for undocumented aliens. Several U.S. citizens who looked "Mexican" were subsequently arrested without due process.

Local sheriff's deputies and police in particular harassed the strikers. Sometimes they showed up at picket lines with riot gear and attack dogs. They arrested strikers on a number of occasions for minor violations. In other circumstances, such charges would result in a ticket rather than being jailed.

That summer, FLOC farmworkers learned how formidable their task was. They were facing the deep-rooted structure of the midwestern agricultural system. This was the system that had deprived farmworkers in the first place. The main barrier was not necessarily an intention to mistreat farmworkers on the part of either the growers or the corporations. Rather, it was an "inertia factor." The system had so settled into a style of operation that it would take considerable energy to overcome its inertia.

The food-processing corporations, which benefited most from the system, had considerably more resources to resist changes than FLOC had to make changes. The hostility of many growers was in many ways understandable. In recent years, family farmers had been in an increasingly tenuous economic situation. Many incurred

Campbell Soup responded to the FLOC strike by stating it did not have any relationship with midwestern farmworkers. In 1979, however, the company mandated that its Ohio growers mechanize their tomato harvests, in order to circumvent the farm labor issue. FLOC cited this action as evidence that the corporation *did* have a direct role in setting conditions for farmworkers. The mechanical harvesters, however, did not work well in the mud, and many growers had to rely on field workers to harvest their crops.

large debts at the beginning of the season to buy seeds, fertilizer, and pesticides and to purchase or maintain costly machinery. Often they operated on thin profit margins. When the economic survival of growers in the strike area was threatened, some reacted bitterly.

The Campbell Boycott

As the strike continued into the 1979 season, Campbell Soup made a fateful decision. The company mandated that the ninety farms that supplied its tomatoes mechanize their harvests. This move greatly reduced the number of farmworkers required and was therefore designed to reduce the impact of the strike.

It should be noted that machines were not the preferred means of harvesting tomatoes in the region. Only a few acres were machine harvested in the late 1960's (Carlson 1976). Growers preferred hand pickers because they yielded greater quantity and quality per acre. Workers could go through the fields several times as the tomatoes ripened. Mechanical harvesters, however, uproot the whole crop in one pass and are therefore less efficient. They also are easily bogged down in the muddy fields of the region. In addition, shifting to mechanical harvesters involved raising whole new strains of "rock tomatoes." These strains require different techniques and equipment to be processed at the canneries. Following Campbell's action, other canneries and growers implemented machine harvesting of tomatoes. By 1982, about 85 percent of the tomatoes in northwestern Ohio were machine harvested (Valdés 1984).

Campbell's move to mechanize the harvest raised new issues in the farmworkers' struggle. The company had claimed that it had no direct relations with farmworkers in its operations. It had also said that it could not intervene in the internal operations of its growers. Yet, the mandate to mechanize clearly contradicted both of these claims. It made clear that the large food-processing corporations *were* directly involved in determining farmworkers' conditions and could mandate how the growers ran their operations.

Displacement by mechanization thus became another issue in FLOC's campaign. FLOC stated that its position was not to stop mechanization. Baldemar Velásquez noted that stoop labor in the mud was an undesirable condition. FLOC did demand, however, that the farmworkers displaced by mechanization be given first choice at the new jobs operating the harvesters. It also called for retraining the rest of the displaced workers for other viable occupations.

In protest to Campbell's move, FLOC staged a sit-down in front of a harvester on one farm. The sheriff's forces arrested about twenty of the workers. When several parents rushed to get their children on the sidelines, some were clubbed and also arrested. When FLOC lawyer Jack Kilroy went to arrange bail for those arrested, the sheriff informed him that he was under arrest. Kilroy asked what the charges were and was told his car was blocking a driveway. When Kilroy expressed disbelief, five deputies jumped him and knocked him to the ground. One deputy grabbed his hair and pounded his head on the pavement. Kilroy lay unconscious in a pool of blood, with a fractured skull, permanently disabled.

This event was perhaps the lowest point of the farmworkers' struggle. It was particularly traumatic for the children. Fernando Cuevas, FLOC vice president, reports that his seven-year-old son was with Kilroy at the time. He said his son suffered nightmares about what he had seen for six months afterwards. FLOC filed a lawsuit against the sheriff. He and his officers were subsequently restrained by a court order from approaching any FLOC members or strikers.

Many growers continued to react with hostility toward FLOC.

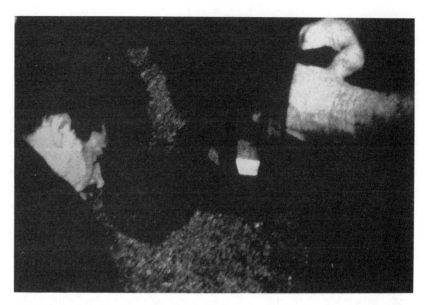

One of the lowest points in the FLOC movement was when its attorney Jack Kilroy was beaten unconscious by sheriff's deputies. He is shown here lying in a pool of blood with a fractured skull. Other violence against FLOC workers included cross burnings, arson, and gunshots fired at strike leaders.

Not only were they financially jeopardized by the strike, they now had to make new heavy investments in tomato harvesters. Some cursed and shouted at FLOC workers on picket lines along their fields. They also tried such practices as planting corn around their tomato fields, to hide their operations from FLOC picketers.

In the summer of 1979, FLOC held its first constitutional convention, in Holgate, Ohio. César Chávez, head of the United Farm Workers, was the keynote speaker, and he took a solid stand in support of the FLOC cause. His presence and actions initiated close relations between the UFW and FLOC.

At this time, FLOC was officially constituted as a labor union. The convention itself was a well-organized event. Logistical arrangements were anticipated and coordinated. Activities were thoroughly prepared, and deliberations followed standard procedures. The farmworker members were actively involved in the proceedings. This convention marked a new level of organization for FLOC as a cohesive and effective social unit.

The convention was important because it demonstrated the substantial internal support for FLOC among farmworkers themselves.

Farmworkers actively participated in the selection of representatives, the election of FLOC officials, and the formulation of resolutions. Many strikers were present as observers. Many other farmworkers who were working on farms not being struck also came to the convention.

Just as important, the convention served as an occasion to mobilize external support. FLOC's legitimacy was recognized by the support of César Chávez. The breadth of support, though, was demonstrated by the representatives of labor, church, political, and civic organizations around the country who attended.

During the convention, FLOC called for a consumer boycott of all Campbell Soup products. Included were Campbell subsidiary products like Vlasic pickles, Swanson's frozen dinners, and Pepperidge Farms foods. The rationale for the boycott was that the collective socioeconomic power of millions of supporters could counterbalance the dominance of the large agribusiness. This, in turn, could overcome the farmworkers' powerlessness to participate actively in determining their own conditions.

In calling for the boycott, FLOC in essence changed the rules of the conflict. It was no longer a private affair between two parties, but the dispute had become a public concern involving larger issues of social justice. Focusing its limited resources on a high-profile company like Campbell Soup proved to be an asset to the FLOC boycott strategy. If success could be achieved here, then the whole system could be changed. Other large companies could then be approached, to broaden these changes.

Over the seven years of the boycott, FLOC found a broad response among allies and supporters from many walks of life. Labor unions donated funds to FLOC and urged their members to honor the boycott. Many Catholic, mainstream Protestant, Jewish, and interfaith religious organizations also backed FLOC. A number of civic and political groups also joined the cause. More than a million Americans boycotted Campbell products in support of the FLOC farmworkers. The FLOC cause clearly appealed to basic American values such as social justice and human dignity. Over the years, FLOC was able to draw upon these broad social forces in support of its cause.

Campbell's initial reaction to the boycott was to maintain its position that it did not employ farmworkers and could not intervene in the internal operations of its growers. But FLOC pointed out how the mechanization mandate indicated Campbell *did* directly affect farmworkers. Then Campbell claimed that FLOC did not have the support of the farmworkers. Here, it was referring to FLOC's small numbers of dues-paying members. FLOC countered that without contracts farmworkers were not able to pay dues. Still, two thousand workers had gone on strike and had signed authorization cards, legally designating FLOC as their representative in labor negotiations.

It should be noted that Libby was initially included in this boycott effort. Libby, however, chose to get out of production, sold its Leipsic plant, and concentrated its business in marketing. At the time, Libby was involved in an international boycott against Nestlé, its parent company. Nestlé was being boycotted because of its marketing practices with baby formula in underdeveloped countries; such practices had increased infant diseases and the parents' economic deprivations. With Libby withdrawn from the conflict, FLOC was then able to turn its full efforts to dealing with Campbell Soup.

The Struggle Continues

In 1980, R. Gordon McGovern became president and chief executive officer of Campbell Soup. McGovern devoted considerable energy to reorganizing the company. The company introduced new products, such as Prego spaghetti sauce and Le Menu frozen dinners, to appeal to a changing American life-style. Such new products, of course, were immediately added to the FLOC boycott list, in an effort to maximize the pressure on Campbell Soup.

Under new leadership, Campbell Soup shifted its manner of dealing with the FLOC movement. It did not accept any direct responsibility for farmworkers, but it did express concern about their conditions. For example, the company offered funds to the Ohio Council of Churches to operate a retraining program for tomato workers displaced by mechanization. This action was presumably in response to the displacement issue raised by FLOC. After FLOC objected that the offer circumvented the real issue of self-determination for farmworkers, the council debated the matter and decided to refuse Campbell's offer. This action increased the pressure on Campbell to deal directly with FLOC.

By 1980, a number of local FLOC support committees were being organized in major cities in the Midwest and East, including Ann Arbor, Indianapolis, Chicago, Detroit, and Philadelphia. The primary role of these volunteer groups was to advocate the boycott in their home areas. The groups were coordinated by FLOC through boycott retreats, rallies, and newsletters. The support committees were instrumental in grass-roots organizing in their local communities to advocate FLOC's cause and the boycott. They proved to be a very effective auxiliary to FLOC's efforts. They drew upon personal and professional networks of their members to represent the FLOC cause in many different segments of the local scene (Barger and Reza 1985a, 1987).

FLOC and the boycott increasingly won endorsement from many groups throughout American society. Religious bodies, such as the Council of Churches in Indiana and Ohio, endorsed the boycott. Labor unions, like the Indiana and Ohio AFL-CIOs and the United Auto Workers, also publicly backed FLOC. FLOC organized special campaigns to further the boycott. For example, one effort focused on the Campbell labels program, which provides schools with educational and sports equipment in exchange for labels from corporate products. It is estimated that eventually over 1,200 parochial and public schools dropped the Campbell label program (Barger and Reza 1985a, 1987). In general, widespread support for the boycott grew through a snowball effect, as boycotters informed and enlisted new boycotters. Each year, Campbell Soup found the pressure continually increasing, despite its every effort to counter the boycott.

The impact of the boycott was clearly being felt by the company. For example, one student at Indiana University at Indianapolis told a professor that he had just been hired as sales representative for Campbell Soup. When she reacted with "Campbell Soup!," he said, "I know. They exploit farmworkers." He did not seem to believe this charge, but he did appear concerned about the reputation of the company for which he was going to work. He also said that in the hiring process, company officials had told him sales of Campbell's products were down in central Indiana and that they attributed this to the boycott.

Campbell Soup felt a social as well as an economic pressure from the boycott. For example, when the Church Federation of Greater Indianapolis considered a resolution to endorse the boycott, the company sent its representative, Rodger Dean Duncan, to present its case. Baldemar Velásquez came to present FLOC's case. After a public debate and with both representatives present, the federation voted to endorse the boycott. The company was given six months, however, to resolve the dispute with FLOC before it would take effect. Following this event, the first real (though unofficial) dialogue between FLOC and the company took place, as Baldemar and Duncan privately discussed the issues.

It should be noted that FLOC had relatively few opponents. Campbell Soup was an obvious adversary, of course. But even other major food-processing corporations preferred to remain quiet and see what would happen. A number of local growers and Anglos opposed

FLOC, but not all. Many churches, labor unions, and political groups openly endorsed FLOC. Some groups chose not to take a stand, but few took a stance *against* FLOC.

In the winter of 1981, FLOC began organizing in the Texas and Florida base areas of most midwestern farmworkers. About 3,400 workers signed authorization cards naming FLOC as their bargaining representative.

That year, an Ohio Senate committee headed by Neal Zimmers began an investigation of farmworker conditions. This committee found that the food-processing corporations were very much involved in farmworker conditions. It concluded that since they held the economic power, they should be included in farm labor actions. The Senate report further supported the legitimacy of FLOC's primary goals.

In 1982, the Ohio Council of Churches endorsed the boycott, urging Campbell Soup to enter into a dialogue with the farmworkers and farmers. At the same time, the Justice and Peace Commission of the Catholic Archdiocese of Boston, headed by John Moynihan, called for talks between Campbell and FLOC. Under this sponsorship, Ray Page, vice president of corporate relations for Campbell Soup, and Baldemar Velásquez met three times. Campbell offered to fund several farmworker welfare projects through FLOC, but FLOC refused. FLOC felt this addressed only short-term issues and kept Campbell in the position of making unilateral decisions. The company would be free to take away provisions as it pleased. FLOC asserted that the only meaningful solution involved changes in the structure of agribusiness, specifically union recognition for farmworkers. This would guarantee farmworkers a representative voice in determining their own conditions.

In 1982, FLOC held its second constitutional convention in Defiance, Ohio. This event was located near the Campbell tomato and V-8 processing plant in Napoleon. César Chávez was again the keynote speaker. The convention gave further evidence that FLOC workers were well organized and that FLOC was operating as an effective social unit. The workers took an active role in electing FLOC officers and in discussing resolutions. The democratic process in these deliberations illustrated how effective farmworkers could be in deciding their own affairs.

That fall, Baldemar Velásquez went on a twenty-four-day fast, consuming only water. He says this was a period of meditation on his life and on FLOC's direction. Though the fast was initiated privately and for personal reasons, it inevitably focused public atten-

The 1982 FLOC constitution convention was held in Defiance, Ohio. Over two hundred delegates represented about two thousand workers who had signed cards authorizing FLOC to collectively bargain on their behalf. This convention illustrated the democratic participation of farmworkers in the movement, as they nominated and elected FLOC officers and passed resolutions. Baldemar Velásquez, FLOC president, sits to the left of the podium, and Fernando Cuevas, vice president, to the right. The presence of United Farm Workers (UFW) President César Chávez (seated left of Velásquez) was an important factor in FLOC's gaining legitimacy in its struggle for midwestern farmworkers.

tion on FLOC and the Campbell boycott. In the long run, Baldemar says, it renewed his faith and his resolve for FLOC's cause.

Over the years of the strike and boycott, FLOC had to face a continual organizational problem. Its leaders and staff were essentially volunteers, people willing to work for the cause for only their basic subsistence. A core group persisted, but there was always a turnover of staff essential for basic operations. This often resulted in a loss of continuity in several ways. When some staff members left the organization, they took with them practical experience and valuable contacts. The replacement staff were not always familiar with previous efforts and had to relearn basic lessons. The most serious problem, though, was that the limited staff resources had to be concentrated on one particular activity; in the midst of this activity, though, the staff might then have to turn their concentration on the next issue. Sometimes, everyone would be pulled out of what they were doing and thrown into dealing with a crisis situation or new

Baldemar Velásquez leads a strategy meeting in 1982 with other FLOC organizers during the Campbell strike and boycott. FLOC leaders and staff sacrificed much to win justice for midwestern farmworkers. With no regular income, they worked part-time and relied on donations of supporters to maintain their organizing efforts.

opportunity with minimal discussion or planning. These occurrences often undermined continuity in day-to-day operations. This style of operating proved to be frustrating to some staff members. Many had joined FLOC to work on a particular effort but then felt they could not see these interests through to completion. This frustration led a number to eventually leave FLOC, and the discontinuity was thus perpetuated.

Given these problems and having to face new challenges on short notice, FLOC developed a flexible organizational style. Its staff was still composed largely of the union's main officers and volunteers. Limited material resources and personnel remained focused on the primary event at that time, such as organizing strike lines or a rally. However, before each event, planning sessions were held. Specific activities were identified, logistics planned, and workers and supporters assigned individual responsibilities. If the event was a long one, daily staff meetings evaluated activities, made plans, and assigned tasks as needed. After each event, an evaluation session was held to identify lessons learned and to discuss how these would be incorporated in FLOC's operations. This organizational style maximized effective management of limited resources.

New Issues and Strategies

In 1983, several important events in the development of the FLOC movement occurred. One involved the "sharecropper" issue in the pickle industry (called *medios*, or "halves," in Spanish). This practice had been the norm in Ohio and Michigan, key states in the production of cucumbers (commonly called "pickles"). Under this arrangement, farmworkers are hired as "independent contractors." The workers receive half of the proceeds for the cucumbers they pick. The pickle harvest was a part of the farmworkers' annual cycle, coming before the tomato harvest. But the sharecropper practice removed farmworkers from their status as "employees." Therefore, labor laws and regulations that applied to the farmworkers' other jobs were bypassed. For example, there were no minimum wage guarantees and no possibility for workers compensation or unemployment insurance coverages. Even more significant, child labor restrictions would not apply because the growers were not seen as employers of the children working in the fields. Since children were working for their families, they would not be covered.

Baldemar Velásquez recalls his experience with this system. "When I was a child, I remember my family worked as sharecroppers. We all had to work, and work hard, because our pay was fixed according to what the whole family could pick. I wanted to run and play, to be a child, but we had to think of the whole family. I knew my mother was sad that I had to work, so I tried to be brave and not complain."

Perhaps the most devastating aspect of the sharecropping practice involved taxes. Since the workers were not employees, Social Security and other taxes were not withheld or filed. Instead, farmworkers had to file these themselves. Furthermore, self-employed business income taxes were higher than the rate for wages. Farmworkers were generally unaware of these implications, and many experienced serious consequences. A number were audited by the Internal Revenue Service and found to owe thousands of dollars in back taxes. For a family well below the poverty level, paying just the base back taxes was impossible, without adding in the penalties and interest accrued. Many pickle workers thus found themselves in perpetual debt with no hope of relief. Growers were reluctant to alter the sharecropper system, though, because the practice relieved them of many bookkeeping responsibilities. They also expressed concerns that any changes could subject them to a "grandfather" condition, where they could be found responsible for the farmworkers' back taxes.

In 1983, the sharecropper issue intruded into the FLOC movement. A federal district judge in Michigan ruled that a pickle grower did not violate child labor laws on his farm. It was clear that children had worked in his fields. But it was decided that their parents were independent, self-employed contractors, so the grower had no direct responsibility in the matter. Many FLOC farmworkers were affected by this case, and the issue of child labor gained new visibility. At this time, FLOC developed a nationwide "Hear the Children" publicity campaign, highlighting the child labor issue in the Campbell boycott.

The most important impact of the case was that the FLOC movement broadened to include workers who harvested cucumber crops. Campbell's subsidiary, Vlasic, was the processor for about sixty pickle growers in Ohio and Michigan, the primary area in the country for pickle production. Cucumbers proved to be a ripe area for FLOC to focus its efforts. For one thing, in order to ensure quality, the crop must be hand picked and harvested while still small and fresh. Since pickle workers usually went on to harvest tomatoes, many were already involved with FLOC. Furthermore, the same workers were involved with a number of other crops. For these reasons, FLOC easily gained a hold in other areas. Following the Michigan case, FLOC began actively organizing workers involved in Vlasic pickle production.

Another major event in 1983 was a 560-mile march of about one hundred FLOC workers from Toledo to Campbell headquarters in Camden, New Jersey. The purposes were to dramatize the farmworkers' cause and to make a mass appeal to Campbell to negotiate. In August, the marchers were joined outside Philadelphia by César Chávez and other supporters. After a rally in Philadelphia, some four hundred people marched across the bridge to the Camden cathedral and participated in a mass for the marchers.

Perhaps one of the most moving events in FLOC history occurred when fifteen priests washed the feet of the farmworkers. The next day, the marchers arrived at Campbell Soup headquarters and asked to speak with the company's president, Gordon McGovern. McGovern was out of town, however (though the marchers' itinerary had been known for over a month). The company did consent to a meeting, however. In October, Baldemar Velásquez met with Ray Page, but no progress was made.

Also in 1983, the Ohio legislature passed a bill which upgraded minimum standards for migrant housing. Campbell Soup initiated a housing program with nineteen of its Ohio tomato growers who boarded migrants. Only seven growers participated, however, and migrant housing on pickle farms was not included in this program. Campbell also established a company ombudsman for migrant affairs and hired a Hispanic for this position. His primary responsibility was to inspect farms under contract to Campbell to ensure they met legal requirements for living and working conditions. While FLOC condoned efforts to improve farmworker conditions, it argued that Campbell was still putting itself in the position of making all decisions unilaterally. The company could therefore withdraw its efforts at its convenience. The basic problems would always exist, Baldemar said, as long as the farmworkers had no voice in determining their own situation.

In 1984, FLOC began active organizing among Vlasic pickle workers in Ohio and Michigan. About 1,800 new members were enlisted in the movement, all of whom signed authorization cards designating FLOC to negotiate in their behalf.

Also in 1984, another major strategy was added to the FLOC movement, a corporate campaign. Ray Rogers and Ed Allen had developed this strategy to help the Amalgamated Clothing and Textile Workers Union achieve its victory in winning collective bargaining with the J. P. Stevens company. The strategy was to use interlocking

In the summer of 1983, FLOC workers marched 560 miles from Toledo, Ohio, to Campbell Soup's headquarters in Camden, New Jersey, to petition the company to recognize farmworkers' right to collective bargaining. Such events strengthened the resolve of midwestern farmworkers and generated considerable support from churches, labor unions, and other segments of American society.

corporate structures and investors to pressure a company. For example, supporters who had stocks in Campbell Soup were asked to attend shareholders meetings where they raised the farmworker issues and made motions that the company negotiate with FLOC.

As a part of the campaign, FLOC discovered that the Philadelphia National Bank (PNB) had close ties with Campbell Soup. The PNB chairman was G. M. Dorrance, whose family controlled the majority of Campbell stock. The PNB also held many Campbell shares in trust for the Dorrance family. Another link was that Gordon McGovern, president of Campbell Soup, sat on the board of the PNB's parent corporation, CoreStates Financial. FLOC called for the help of its union, church, and other supporters who had accounts and investments with the PNB. These supporters raised the FLOC issues to the bank's officers and board and asked that they urge Campbell to negotiate with FLOC. Similar steps were taken with the Prudential Life Insurance company, whose chairman served on the board of directors of Campbell Soup; Prudential had substantial investments in Campbell Soup as well. Thousands of FLOC supporters wrote the chairman, asking his position on the FLOC issues and urging him to bring these issues to Campbell board meetings. Support for the FLOC cause thus reached to the top levels of Campbell Soup through the corporate campaign.

By 1984, considerable social forces had been mobilized in support of the FLOC cause. Hundreds of organizations had formally endorsed FLOC and the boycott. In addition to the Indiana and Ohio AFL-CIOs, FLOC received new labor support from the International Executive Board of the United Auto Workers and a number of state-level American Federation of State, County, and Municipal Employees unions. Many religious organizations also supported FLOC. Besides the Indiana and Ohio councils of churches, the archdioceses of Columbus, Cincinnati, and Detroit endorsed the boycott. Several conferences and commissions of the Christian Church (Disciples of Christ), the United Methodist church, the United Church of Christ, and the American Friends Service Committee took stands in support of FLOC. A number of political and civic organizations also endorsed FLOC, including the Democratic party of Oregon, the Consumers League of Ohio, the Indiana State Council of NOW, and the National Association of Farm Worker Associations. Local FLOC support groups across the country were networked by FLOC through boycott retreats and newsletters. Supporters also made donations and raised funds to support FLOC's efforts.

The boycott effort reached a new peak in 1984, when the National Council of Churches deliberated an endorsement of the boycott against Campbell Soup. The NCC appointed a mediation commit-tee, which recommended endorsement of the boycott if Campbell had not resolved its dispute with FLOC by the following May.

At times, Campbell Soup responded to the FLOC issue in ways that appeared surprisingly devious. For example, once a company spokesman wrote a letter to the editor in the *Cleveland Plain Dealer*. This statement was later reproduced without credits and titles, so that it appeared to be the newspaper's editorial. It was then sent out to schools and others who had inquired about the FLOC issues. This action seemed a poor business practice, which could seriously damage the company's public image. Indeed, schools and churches that were shown the original and revised versions of this article readily quit participation in the Campbell labels program. It seems unusual that a company so concerned with its positive public image would take such an action.

For FLOC's part, it had clearly made a long-term commitment and was not going to give up. As Baldemar Velásquez stated many times during the struggle, "What have we got to lose? If we quit now, we will just go back to the same poor conditions we had before and will have gained nothing." FLOC was clearly in the struggle to stay.

FLOC Wins Farmworker Rights

By 1985, Campbell's net earnings over the previous five years had dropped to less than 6 percent. How much of this loss was due to the boycott is hard to estimate. Whatever the boycott's effect, it was clear that the company could not afford further economic problems. Certainly, the boycott exerted both economic and social pressures on Campbell.

In January 1985, Campbell agreed to meet with FLOC. Baldemar Velásquez and Ray Page began a series of meetings to resolve the issues. Despite critical differences, the talks involved serious nego-tiations. On May 13, FLOC and Campbell signed a formal statement of understanding, which included two important provisions:

The formation of a private labor relations commission: It was agreed that a commission would be formed whose general func-tion would be to mediate between the parties concerned to find workable solutions. In particular, the commission would arbitrate matters by holding hearings on the issues and by setting rules and regulations for representation proceedings. These proceedings were to include farmworkers in Ohio and Michigan working on farms selling tomatoes and cucumbers to Campbell. The commission would also set rules and regulations for subsequent collective bargaining and would establish a procedure for hearing and deciding grievances by the parties covered. The commission included four representatives of the parties involved. Monsignor George Higgins of the Catholic University of America and Douglas Fraser of the United Auto Workers were asked to represent FLOC. Tom Anderson, a local agricultural businessman, and Don Paarlberg, on the faculty of Purdue University, were asked to represent the growers. John T. Dunlop, a Harvard professor and former U.S. Secretary of Labor, was asked to head the board, which became known as "the Dunlop Commission."

The formation of associations of growers: Campbell agreed to cooperate in the formation of associations of its tomato and cucumber growers in Ohio and Michigan. These groups would specifically participate in representation proceedings and collective bargaining. Campbell committed itself to consider the effect of collective bargaining agreements on growers' costs in its own relations with its suppliers.

In addition, both parties agreed to suspend all boycott and anti-boycott activities when representation proceedings began, provided procedures were free of unfair labor practices. The parties also agreed to investigate farm labor issues and to search for cooperative solutions to improve farmworkers' living and working conditions.

This understanding included several creative points. It provided a means for all three of the parties (the farmworkers, growers, and company) to be involved in solutions. It also provided the means for transcending state laws and conditions by providing an authority to which all parties were subject. The understanding did not resolve the major issues. But it did provide an effective means for resolving them.

In the meantime, the Ohio Catholic Conference of Bishops had endorsed the boycott. The National Council of Churches set a new deadline of September 1 for a collective bargaining agreement as a condition for postponing its action on the boycott. The pressure on Campbell was still a present force.

In the summer of 1985, the Dunlop Commission began work to implement the understanding. Campbell held a series of meetings with its tomato and pickle growers to establish the growers associations. Many growers were reluctant to deal with FLOC and resisted joining an association. After a series of discussions, procedures for a secret ballot election on a farm-by-farm basis were developed.

When union elections were held on farms producing Campbell tomatoes, FLOC won by a substantial margin among the 3,100 farmworkers voting. The elections, however, were marred by several incidents. A few growers were accused of intimidating their workers, of bringing in local workers to work only on the day of election (to vote against FLOC), and of only permitting machine operators (not hand workers) to vote. Still, FLOC had won, and when the elections were completed, the commission called for the growers and FLOC to formalize representation procedures for the 1986 season. Because Vlasic pickle growers had not yet agreed to form an association, no elections were conducted among pickle workers that year.

In August 1985, FLOC held its third constitutional convention in Toledo. Once again, César Chávez was the keynote speaker, and the farm labor solidarity now presented a formidable social force. As on previous occasions, the convention reflected a well-organized social unit of farmworkers who were actively involved in farm labor issues.

In February 1986, history was made when FLOC signed three-year labor contracts with Campbell Soup and its Ohio tomato growers and its Michigan Vlasic pickle growers (*Cleveland Plain Dealer* 1986; *New York Times* 1986; *Toledo Blade* 1986). Two sets of contracts were involved in this settlement. One was a contract between FLOC, Campbell Soup, and the Ohio Campbell Tomato Growers Association. The other involved individual contracts between FLOC, Campbell, and the Michigan Vlasic pickle growers.

These contracts covered eight hundred farmworkers in Ohio and Michigan. The contracts set hourly wage rates for workers on harvesters and for truck drivers. Piece rates were also set for hand pickers, plus incentive payments for higher yields. In addition, the contracts established a paid holiday (Labor Day) and set up an experimental health insurance program. Full prior disclosure of conditions of employment (the time period, place, pay rates, and activities) was established. And at the end of the season, each worker was to be provided a full itemized written report of all earnings and expenses. This statement was to include wage basis, units or hours worked, total earnings, sums withheld, and net pay. Another important provision provided $2,000 in compensation for each family who went on strike against Campbell's operations in 1978. Also, union dues of 2.5 percent were to be paid to FLOC.

The contracts provided FLOC farmworkers with a whole set of new rights and benefits. Finally, they had won clear union recognition. Most important, though, farmworker participation in determining wages and benefits had been established.

One important provision of the contracts was the establishment of a grievance procedure. When a problem was noted, attempts would be made to resolve it informally in the camps between the workers, the FLOC representative, and the grower. If the problems persisted, the grievance was to be presented in writing to a FLOC-grower panel within forty-eight hours. If it was still not resolved, the Dunlop Commission would arbitrate and make a ruling. All these provisions were binding by a legal contract.

Our subsequent field work indicates that this has had a large and positive impact on FLOC farmworkers' sense of security. A number of FLOC workers have stated that they no longer feel subjected to the threats or whims of others. To these farmworkers, the new rights and benefits were "like a law."

In addition, the three parties agreed to set up special joint committees to investigate and resolve a number of problems experienced by farmworkers. These include substandard housing and sanitary facilities and inadequate day care. Health care and safety hazards, particularly exposure to dangerous pesticides, would also be examined. In addition, the sharecropping system was scheduled to be investigated.

In June 1987, FLOC signed a similar three-year contract with the H. J. Heinz company and its pickle growers in both Ohio and Michigan, which were served by a single grading station. Soon after the Campbell contracts were signed, Heinz had expressed a willingness to talk with FLOC about union representation for farmworkers involved in its operations. The Heinz contract also provided for union recognition, piece rates and incentives set in advance, conditions of employment, a grievance procedure, and study committees. Furthermore, it was also agreed that Heinz, its growers, and FLOC would use the Dunlop Commission as a private labor relations board.

In August, FLOC also signed three-year contracts with Campbell Soup's Vlasic pickle growers in Ohio. These Ohio growers, some of whom were closely involved in the original strikes against Campbell tomato operations, had originally resisted a formal agreement. Pressure from Campbell Soup and FLOC's church and other supporters, however, eventually persuaded them to sign contracts.

During the 1987 summer season, some 3,300 tomato and pickle workers were under FLOC contracts in Ohio and Michigan. By this time, FLOC was organizing workers with a card check system. Migrants involved with Campbell tomatoes and cucumbers and with Heinz cucumbers would sign cards authorizing FLOC to represent them. Then the signatures would be matched against a farm's list of workers. When a majority was reached, the workers on that farm would be brought under a FLOC contract.

While workers gained key benefits for the first time, it should be noted that the contracts also provided some important benefits for the growers involved. These farmers were allotted a larger acreage by the companies, which meant they would be able to realize greater earnings. Additionally, the three-year terms in the agreements improved the farmers' credit ratings for seeds, equipment, and other debts incurred in their annual operations.

In August 1988, FLOC held its fourth constitutional convention in Toledo. Volker Grotefeld, a German volunteer with an international church reconciliation program, was instrumental in organizing this event. The three hundred delegates at this event reflected important developments in the FLOC story. For the first time, proceedings were managed by farmworkers under union contract. These workers had a whole new perspective on farm labor affairs, since they were now personally involved in deciding their own working conditions. César Chávez was not able to attend. He was on a thirty-six-day fast to protest political undermining of California's farm labor laws and the hazardous use of pesticides, which endangered both farmworkers and consumers. Arturo Mendoza, a UFW board member, represented César to affirm the UFW's solidarity with FLOC.

Also attending the convention were representatives of organized labor in Mexico. Their presence reflected the collaboration of FLOC, the UFW, and Mexican labor unions in representing the interests of farmworkers on both sides of the border. This alliance was developed in response to an earlier threat that Campbell Soup would export its tomato and pickle operations. The coordination of the American and Mexican labor organizations was an effort to ensure that neither side would be played against the other. It also combined their total bargaining strength.

Farmers, too, have been concerned that they would lose their livelihood by the export of crops. This anxiety was voiced on one occasion when a grower lightly accused a Vlasic representative that "half of your winter relish already comes out of Mexico." The farmer's worry was validated by the Vlasic agent's response, "The labor's cheaper there." This concern has led some farmers to actively cooperate with FLOC on this issue, and several have even accompanied FLOC on visits to Mexico to meet with growers and farm labor unions there.

By 1988, FLOC had become a major force in farm labor affairs and

Ray Santiago, FLOC secretary-treasurer, calls for votes on a resolution during the 1988 FLOC convention in Toledo, Ohio. Over 3,200 farmworkers under FLOC contracts were represented at this convention. By this time, FLOC had won significant labor rights for midwestern farmworkers, including wage increases, clearly stated conditions of work, and clear grievance procedures. More important, however, FLOC workers had gained a direct voice in determining their working conditions. Furthermore, workers who have become involved in this process of self-determination have experienced personal growth, a greater sense of security, and greater integration into the American socioeconomic system.

a major resource for midwestern farmworkers. On an individual level, FLOC was able to help workers experiencing personal problems. For example, when one family was notified about the death of a close relative back in Texas, FLOC provided them with the means to go back home. In another case, when one worker had to leave an Ohio farm before the harvest was complete, FLOC explained the circumstances to the grower, so the worker would not lose either his incentive pay or his seniority for employment the next year. FLOC has also actively addressed common problems experienced by farmworkers. During the severe drought in 1988, for instance, many farmworkers were left stranded in the Midwest without jobs or money. FLOC worked with Heinz to raise funds to help these workers return to their base areas. FLOC also worked with a Michigan pickle grower, Scott Osier, and Campbell Soup in developing a model housing program for farmworkers on Osier's farm.

In 1989, in a notable step toward abolishing the sharecropping practice, Scott Osier, the Michigan Vlasic grower, agreed to hire workers on his farm as employees, rather than as independent contractors. Workers were guaranteed a set wage plus incentives, and they had Social Security and income taxes withheld for them. For its part, Campbell Soup agreed to underwrite any excessive costs to Osier. This historic agreement opened the door to resolving a major farm labor issue. It has also raised the hope of future cooperation in improving farmworkers' conditions and benefits.

In November of 1989, FLOC signed another three-year contract with Campbell Soup and the Campbell Tomato Growers Association in Ohio. This contract extended the three-party arrangements of the previous agreements and also continued the Dunlop Commission. It provided increased wages for farmworkers, particularly for planting and hoeing as well as new standards for field sanitation.

Within the following year, FLOC renewed three-year contracts with Vlasic and Heinz and their pickle growers in Ohio and Michigan. Perhaps the most important feature of these contracts was that they formally eliminated sharecropping arrangements by the 1993 season. All workers would be clearly classified as employees, paid an hourly wage rate with a minimum earnings guarantee. They would also receive incentives for quantity and quality of the cucumbers picked. In addition, they would receive workers compensation, unemployment insurance, and Social Security benefits. Clauses were also included that provided for field sanitation and protections against pesticides. Furthermore, only workers fifteen and older could be employed, thus contractually eliminating child labor.

It is important to note that over two thousand workers on fifty-two farms discussed the provisions. Many workers expressed a new sense of job security in reaction to the contracts. They also expressed satisfaction that their children did not have to work in fields any longer. They voted almost unanimously (97 percent in favor) to accept the new contracts. Fernando Cuevas, vice president of FLOC said, "We worked very hard together with the growers and corporations to agree to a contract that would give every farmworker the right to be a regular employee. But we felt that these important changes must be approved by the FLOC members themselves. There was a lot at stake, but we want the members to be actively involved in all stages of the union." From the vote, it was clear that midwestern farmworkers were solidly behind FLOC's leadership.

FLOC leaders have expressed a great sense of achievement at these developments. "Elimination of the sharecropping system was won by farmworkers," Baldemar Velásquez says, "not by lawyers or politicians." As Alinsky (1969:175) notes, success is much more meaningful to people who have achieved objectives through their own efforts.

With these new achievements, however, came a new challenge. Both Vlasic and Heinz expressed concern that they could not continually face competition from other pickle companies with lower operating costs. This primarily involved Dean Foods, the parent company of Aunt Jane's and Green Bay pickles, the last major cucumber producers in the Midwest. Dean's operations did not include the costs of providing better conditions for farmworkers. FLOC was thus even more obligated to pursue organizing Dean farms, both for the farmworkers' sake and for that of its current contractual partners.

During the 1990 season, FLOC opened talks with Dean Foods. FLOC leaders heard the same story they had heard years before from Campbell Soup. Dean said that it did not employ farmworkers, that it did not want to interfere in the business of its growers, and that farmworkers did not want a union. The threat of a boycott exerted some pressure to maintain the talks, and FLOC worked to involve the Dunlop Commission.

That summer, FLOC began organizing workers on Dean Foods farms. They devoted special effort to locate and document twenty-six camps involved with Dean's pickle operations. FLOC organizers began an outreach and education program with workers in these camps. They talked with the workers and distributed literature on the conditions won in the Campbell and Heinz contracts. They even got involved in settling five disputes between the workers and growers, using the established grievance procedure (even though this was done without contract provisions).

During the winter of early 1991, FLOC conducted a follow-up organizing campaign with Dean pickle workers in their base areas in Texas and Florida. Meetings with about a thousand workers were held by FLOC organizers and camp representatives of workers under Vlasic and Heinz contracts. In a card-check vote, 72 percent of the Dean workers authorized FLOC to represent them. FLOC and Dean Foods subsequently opened formal negotiations. The Dunlop Commission also became involved in its role of private labor relations board.

In August 1991, FLOC held its fifth organizing convention in Perrysburg, Ohio. The delegates represented over five thousand pickle and tomato workers under contract. Raúl Yzaguirre, president of the National Council of La Raza, one of the main Hispanic advocacy organizations in the country, told the farmworkers, "You have won dignity for our people. People throughout this nation believe in what you are doing. You are the vision of what is ahead." Diego Aguilar, president of the fifty-thousand-member Mexican agricultural workers union SNTOAC (Sindicato Nacional de Trabajadores y Obreros Asalariados del Campo), told the delegates, "We are together in the same cause, one family. Our road is long, but we will go united." Thomas Anderson represented the Dunlop Commission and spoke of the progress made for both farmers and farmworkers.

To many of the FLOC members and supporters present, one of the most exciting events was an address by guest speaker Wally Wagner, president of the Campbell Tomato Growers Association in Ohio. During the days of the strike, he had been a strong opponent of FLOC. Now he addressed the farmworker delegates, saying, "As you know, Baldemar and I have covered a lot of roads, and we went down a lot of them in different directions. We still don't agree on some things, but a lot of the mountains that stood between us have been removed. Now we understand the issues and each other. We have made much progress, and we will cooperate in the future." The farmers representing the Vlasic and Heinz pickle growers associations also gave speeches of reconciliation and cooperation. These appearances symbolized the tremendous reforms that had been achieved in farm labor affairs.

The 1991 convention was a landmark in the FLOC story. It represented new levels of organization and achievements in farm labor affairs. It symbolized a more complex, stronger, and democratic organization of midwestern farmworkers. Most important, the active involvement of the delegates in FLOC's decisions and resolutions illustrated their greater empowerment in the system that determines their conditions and livelihood.

In November 1991, a contract was signed which covered 1,200 farmworkers involved in Dean's pickle operations. This contract followed the three-way agreements structure already implemented with Campbell and Heinz. It also provided for a grievance procedure and phased out the last of the sharecropping system. With the Dean Foods contract, FLOC had successfully organized all the major pickle operations, involving over 5,000 farmworkers in the Midwest.

FLOC Reorganizes

After the first contracts were signed, FLOC encountered several new challenges. It still faced the effort of organizing pickle workers not yet under contract. It also had to maintain its ties with the many groups that had supported its struggle. Added to that, it had heavy new responsibilities in administering the contracts and in operating an organization that had grown from a small core group to thousands of members spread across several states.

Since 1986 FLOC has continued evolving its organizational structure to address farm labor affairs at a number of levels. This structure consists of the general membership, camp representatives, field organizers, operational staff, and the organization's officers and board.

(1) Membership: FLOC's ultimate purpose as a reform movement is to democratically represent its constituent group, farmworkers who labor in the agricultural system in the Midwest. (See Alinsky 1969.) The general members of FLOC include all dues-paying workers under contract. These members are the ultimate authority in setting organizational policies and operations and are formally represented by their chosen delegates at constitutional conventions. FLOC has made a concentrated effort to fully inform the members on issues, union organization, contracts, and their working rights. This is done in camp meetings at the beginning of the season and is followed up by house meetings with individual families during the season. These occasions are also used to elicit the members' views and input into current issues and events like contract negotiations. Sometimes special meetings are held in the Texas and Florida base areas to inform members about critical issues and to get their views. Meetings in preparation for constitutional conventions are also used to discuss issues as well as to elect the workers' delegates.

In addition, FLOC has sponsored festive events, such as Mexican dances and special celebrations, to further involve members with the organization. Other occasions also serve to build ties with members, such as when FLOC provides emergency services or when members use the grievance procedure. FLOC maintains communication with its members during the off season by distributing newsletters and disbursing end-of-the-season incentive payments to members. FLOC also issues a union card with the member's picture, which provides a useful means of identification for cashing checks and other purposes.

(2) Camp representatives: An important new addition to FLOC's structure is the camp representative. This is the person who represents the crew on a daily basis during the migrant season. The "camp reps" are responsible for monitoring the implementation of the contracts with their crews. They also initiate any grievance procedure and act as a liaison with union organizers and officers. At the beginning of the season, FLOC has a full discussion in the camps of

what responsibilities the camp rep will have and which traits might make someone a good representative of fellow workers. Then the reps (and their alternates) are selected by the crew members and FLOC field staff.

FLOC has special training sessions for the camp reps during the summer season. These meetings inform the workers about their rights under the contracts, provisions such as the incentives and the grievance procedure, and FLOC's structure and operations. The reps are especially trained in the grievance process and conflict resolution. These involve learning how to listen, identify the core issues, use the specific steps of filing the grievance, and negotiate solutions.

The camp rep meetings serve as an opportunity for involving the workers in current issues, like the future of the sharecropping system and even the acquisition of washing machines for labor camps. When the contracts came up for renewal in 1989, the camp reps were also involved in developing the negotiating platform. The meetings and discussions with FLOC leaders have fostered a broader awareness of labor issues and procedures among the workers. This is particularly true when camp reps compare the conditions and union activities in their own crews with the conditions and activities in other crews.

The camp reps play an important part in implementing the contracts at the place of work. They are there to make sure provisions are met, problems addressed, and questions answered. They also provide an important link for worker input into the organization. FLOC leaders see the camp reps as the critical level in building a strong and democratic union. When the contracts were renewed in 1989, provisions were included to pay the camp reps for expenses involved in performing their responsibilities.

Several problems have been encountered in the camp rep system, however. One is that some reps, who may be respected by other crew members, are not well informed about the structure of the agricultural system or the union organization. Though they are almost all willing and some have admirable interpersonal skills, at times they may not be very capable in fulfilling their responsibility. The training sessions are designed to develop their knowledge and skills, and FLOC has tried to work with those with limited backgrounds in particular. Another problem has been a turnover in camp reps from one season to the next. After investing training efforts into camp reps, each year some do not come back. This means the process has to start over. This will probably always occur with a migrant population. FLOC takes this into consideration and uses the training sessions to develop the skills of new reps as well as to further the development of reps with more experience. The organizers and older reps also assist the new reps in learning the ropes.

In the long run, the camp representatives have proven to be one of the most effective institutions in the FLOC structure. They are the direct daily link with the workers, both representing their crews with FLOC and implementing FLOC's achievements in the fields and camps. The camp reps have also been a source of new leadership for FLOC, and several have gone on to become organizers and to serve on the board of directors. Baldemar Velásquez says, "The camp rep system is giving farmworkers a new voice and authority. It is also creating a process that provides excellent leadership training. Farmworkers and growers are telling us the system is working and they strongly support it. The corporations back it too."

(3) Organizers: During the summer season, FLOC has a field staff of organizers to work with farmworkers in the camps. The organizers have perhaps the most demanding and critical job in the whole organization. Their primary responsibility is to be the direct representative of the union to the workers, and they generally act as a liaison between the workers and the companies. Each organizer is responsible for about twenty to twenty-five camps, and their activities are divided between contract administration and labor organizing.

Early in the summer, the organizers and FLOC leaders develop the primary goals for the season. At this time, the organizers are trained in the general issues, strategies, and contract provisions of the union. They are also trained in the skills needed to be effective in working with the workers, growers, and companies.

The organizers put in long hours traveling around Ohio and Michigan and on occasion, Illinois and Indiana. They try to regularly visit each camp under contract (currently over 120) or being organized. They try to meet with each family to discuss the union's role and contract terms, particularly the grievance procedure. They also meet with the camp as a whole to decide on the camp reps and discuss other important issues, such as negotiation efforts, contract ratification, convention plans and delegates, and coming fiestas and dances. On other occasions, they hold joint camp meetings with the growers and companies to discuss wage rates, incentive pay, and other terms of the contracts. In addition, they work with the crews in selecting a camp rep and then organize the reps' training.

Another important responsibility is organizing workers not under contract. For example, in the 1990 season, the organizers worked hard to inform Dean pickle workers about FLOC's purpose and operations, along with contract benefits enjoyed by Campbell and

Fernando Cuevas, Jr., a FLOC organizer (*on the right*), goes over contract provisions and grievance procedures with a camp representative at a Heinz pickle farm in 1989. FLOC has developed a flexible organizational structure to involve midwestern farmworkers in the organization and to develop their leadership skills. Fernando, Jr., has grown up with FLOC since his father became involved in the movement when Junior was six years old.

Heinz workers; they also worked hard to win them over to joining FLOC. During the following winter, most of the organizers worked in the Florida and Texas base areas to maintain contact with the Dean workers and urge them to join FLOC. As already noted, the organizers' efforts paid off in the spring of 1991, when Dean pickle workers voted to have FLOC represent them in negotiating a labor contract.

On a typical day, the organizers start each morning with a joint meeting. They go over the previous day's activities and events and discuss any issues, strategies, and skills that need to be considered or developed. Next, they set that day's goals and activities before they head for the camps. Then they may hold house meetings, investigate grievances, meet with growers and company officials, or become involved in other needed activities.

The organizers must have a variety of important skills. They have to be able to listen to and communicate well with the workers, growers, and company representatives. They also have to be fully knowledgeable of the contract provisions and laws regarding farm labor affairs. There is some turnover in organizers, and some may "burn out." Fernando Cuevas, FLOC vice president, has directed the field organizing since the first contracts were signed. He and the other core organizers have formed a consistent presence over the years since the first contracts were won. They demonstrate an exceptional level of commitment and self-sacrifice in their work. They have deep convictions about justice and self-determination for farmworkers. It is their commitment, in our assessment, that most inspires the workers themselves to support and participate in FLOC.

(4) Staff: FLOC has a central staff that maintains its daily operations. The office staff provides continuity in the running of the organization, keeping the extensive membership records, business files, and organizational accounts. They also produce newsletters and campaign materials and maintain equipment used by the leaders and field staff. The office staff also provides an essential service in relaying messages and following up on inquiries and actions. At times, there are an attorney and legal staff, who provide legal input into decisions, investigate legal issues, and represent workers and the union in any litigation.

(5) Board: At the heart of FLOC's organization are the officers and board members, composed of the president, vice president, secretary-treasurer, and three at-large officers. At the 1991 convention, Baldemar Velásquez was elected as president, Fernando Cuevas as vice president, and Ricardo Velásquez as secretary-treasurer. The FLOC officers are responsible for the overall operations of the union.

They develop policies and campaign strategies, and they conduct the negotiations with the food-processing corporations and the growers. They also act as FLOC's representatives to other organizations and to the press. Individual officers, like Cuevas, may coordinate specific campaigns, like organizing Dean workers in the Texas and Florida base areas. Most of the officers are in the migrant stream but come into the central office for board meetings and special sessions as needed.

In considering FLOC's structure, another element should be examined: its supporters. Throughout its history, FLOC has relied upon individuals and other organizations to help it achieve its goals. These allies include church, union, and civic organizations, and individual public figures like the Reverend Jesse Jackson. FLOC still asks their help on specific projects. For example, church, labor, and other organizations were asked to write Dean Foods urging it to negotiate with FLOC. "Besides the very important and tangible success of the letter-writing campaign, the project was morally uplifting for us," says Baldemar Velásquez. "It reminds us that we are blessed with good and caring friends." FLOC, in turn, lends its support to helping its allies achieve their goals. For example, FLOC has participated in an alliance of Hispanics in the Midwest and has taken a public stand with civil rights organizations. These alliances are a critical part of FLOC's existence, which both further establishes its own operations and ties it into larger networks and settings. FLOC also receives regular contributions from supporters; these donations are crucial in continuing its organizing efforts and in expanding its achievements. FLOC makes a continued effort to maintain its relations with supporters. It sends out regular newsletters and special mailings to keep its friends informed of current issues and FLOC's activities.

There is another structural level at which FLOC has been involved: a national network of farm labor organizations. FLOC and the United Farm Workers have cooperated closely in a number of areas. They have endorsed each other's boycotts and have extended practical help in the other's campaigns. They have also jointly organized workers in the Texas and Florida base areas. Their alliance in many ways provides a national framework for the organization of farmworkers. Both have been involved in an even larger level of organization, an international one. They have jointly established ties with farmworker and labor organizations in Mexico. They have hosted representatives from the other's organizations at their own conventions and have held joint meetings to discuss common interests. There is currently an interest and even a basis for an extensive alliance of farm labor organizations.

In summary, FLOC's organizational structure has seen a steady evolution over the years since the original strike against Campbell Soup. In much of its history, FLOC was clearly a movement organization. It coordinated mass actions both among its constituency of farmworkers and among its external supporters. When it began winning labor contracts, FLOC expanded its structure to include contract administration. FLOC leaders, however, have been able to look beyond the immediate tasks and issues. Their vision includes a broad goal of organizing farmworkers in other specialty crops, expanding alliances with other organizations and addressing other social issues like minority rights.

Over the years, FLOC has developed a cohesive, flexible, and effective organizational structure. It has achieved a remarkable feat, organizing a group that initially appeared to be unorganizable. Farmworkers' migratory life-style and work cycles provide little opportunity for unity. They work in any particular area only a few weeks in the year and in fact, have little permanence in any area. They are also a minority that has few consistent ties with other segments of society, including the industries that use their labor. Yet, FLOC has built an effective organization with this membership and has become a major force in farm labor affairs. One recognition of this effectiveness came in 1987 when FLOC was cited by *Washington Monthly* as among the best of American labor unions. In 1989, FLOC was also recognized when Baldemar Velásquez was awarded the prestigious MacArthur Foundation fellowship. FLOC has achieved the "unachievable" in bringing together midwestern farmworkers in an organization dedicated to their empowerment and well-being.

FLOC Looks Ahead

Although FLOC has achieved a major role in farm labor affairs in the Midwest, its leaders have visions of continued achievements. They have set goals in several areas to further the development of the organization and its members.

One FLOC effort is leadership development among its members. The primary goal is to build farmworkers' abilities to enforce their own rights. This is a continuation of its camp reps training efforts. In the 1990 summer season, for example, FLOC trained 160 of its workers in Ohio and Michigan in several areas. One emphasis was expanding their knowledge of their labor rights under state and national laws and under the contract agreements. They also learned about the grievance procedure. In addition, they were trained in conflict resolution skills. These included listening and identifying legitimate problems, as separate from their feelings. They learned, too, how to present a problem for formal consideration, how to think through an acceptable resolution, and how to negotiate to achieve desired goals. As a final step, the workers learned how to implement agreements.

FLOC has followed the rule that experience is the best teacher, so it has sought to involve its camp reps and members in leadership actions. In the 1990 summer season, for example, camp reps dealt with 242 grievance problems. All were resolved at the local level, and it was not necessary to utilize any formal processes. At training sessions, camp reps pool experiences and learn indirectly from each other's experiences. The direct role these farmworkers have played has built their own awareness, commitment, and confidence.

During the winter season, FLOC has conducted leadership training in the workers' Florida and Texas base areas. FLOC leaders, for example, have called meetings to distribute company checks for incentive payments, and at these meetings they have raised issues and suggested actions relevant to the members. A FLOC office was opened in Plant City, Florida, while the UFW office in San Juan, Texas, was used as a base in that area. Also, seven leadership development committees were organized during the early winter of 1991. These committees, composed of five to twenty-five families each, discussed the issues of pesticides and government immigration policies. One winter, FLOC members were involved in organizing Dean pickle workers. They also participated in conferences and workshops on farmworker and minority issues sponsored by church groups and civil rights groups.

Another FLOC effort is to continue the elimination of the sharecropping and tenant farming systems in pickle operations in other regions. FLOC leaders have been working with organizations in the South to address these issues there, and they have recruited two African Americans to conduct outreach and education among sharecroppers in Mississippi. FLOC has discussed similar arrangements with Mexican unions to organize workers involved in pickle operations in Mexico. FLOC estimates that as many as seventy thousand can be affected by these operations.

A third effort of both FLOC and the UFW is building relations with Mexican farmworker organizations. Delegations of Mexican unions, as already indicated, were invited to the 1988 and 1991

FLOC conventions. Additionally, FLOC leaders have conducted trips to Mexico to meet with these groups there. One purpose of developing this alliance is to ensure that the multinational corporations face the same labor conditions wherever they operate, rather than just exporting production to exploit cheap labor, as one Campbell field agent acknowledged was being done. It has also been noted that Campbell and Heinz farmers have been involved in this effort and have even accompanied FLOC leaders on trips to Mexico.

FLOC has not stopped its efforts with the resolution of the Campbell boycott or with its successes in organizing the pickle industry in the Midwest. FLOC has continued to develop its relations with church, labor, civic, and ethnic groups in its efforts to improve the lives of farmworkers and other disadvantaged groups. Baldemar Velásquez, for example, sits on the board of the Highlander Center, which is dedicated to the grass-roots organizing of deprived groups. FLOC leaders have also taken the initiative in working with companies and growers to acquire over $1 million in federal and state grants to improve farmworkers' housing and other conditions. Even though it has made substantial achievements, FLOC has maintained its original vision to gain basic rights and benefits for all farmworkers and has continued its efforts to accomplish this beyond immediate gains.

FLOC Achieves Social Reform

When FLOC was founded in 1967, midwestern farmworkers were experiencing among the most deprived socioeconomic conditions of any group in America. By the 1991 season, there were over six thousand people working under FLOC contracts. As we look over FLOC's record, there are a number of specific achievements that should be noted.

Perhaps the greatest of FLOC's accomplishments was that for the first time midwestern farmworkers gained a formal voice in their own conditions. The collective bargaining agreements have provided a new structure where farmworkers are now an equal partner in deciding what benefits they will accept for their labor. This does not mean that they have total control, of course. It does mean, though, that they can decide what they will give up and what they will not give up. And *they* make these decisions rather than someone else deciding unilaterally what will happen to them.

FLOC workers now enjoy considerably improved working conditions. They had won an increase of up to 25 percent in wages and incentive payments. Housing and sanitary facilities have been improved. In particular, labor contracts eliminated sharecropping in the area, along with the child labor that accompanied it.

One important change we have noted in many FLOC workers is a new sense of security. They know that they cannot be harassed or fired for protesting against unacceptable conditions or unfair treatment. They are aware that their jobs will be waiting for them next year. They can rely on earning a basic income with which to support their families. This sense of psychological security, we have observed, is a pervasive impact of the FLOC movement.

We have also observed a remarkable degree of personal growth in those farmworkers who have become involved in the FLOC movement. They have grown more interested in national and international affairs, developed leadership and organizing skills, and built broader social relations with others.

The new developments being experienced by FLOC farmworkers have many important long-term implications. FLOC workers can now expect to lead healthier, more stable lives. They can look forward to a higher and more beneficial standard of living. And they can expect to achieve a more productive existence, with a greater sense of achievement in their individual and family life.

FLOC farmworkers are also more integrated into a new social structure of farmworkers. Through FLOC, they have more contact with other farmworkers and can compare conditions, benefits, and ideas. A broader identity as *FLOC* workers is also taking form.

Since 1986, there has been a significant change in the agricultural system of which farmworkers are a part. FLOC's relations with the food-processing corporations and growers have been dramatically altered. Much of the hostility they displayed during the strike years has dissipated. Some farmers have willingly worked with FLOC in improving housing, field sanitation, and other conditions for their workers. Also, growers have realized benefits from the three-party contracts. They are guaranteed, for example, a more stable and experienced work force. This has resulted in an increase in pickle productivity by over 40 percent, according to Heinz figures. The three-year term of the contracts has improved the growers' credit ratings for farm loans. It is significant that the heads of the grower associations under contract were guest speakers at the 1991 FLOC convention. We have also noted an important change in how FLOC farmworkers view the companies and growers. They no longer see them as "the enemy." In essence, this reflects a new perception of *themselves* as equals.

Another major change in the agricultural system is that there are now new processes for addressing problems among the three major parties involved. A process for dealing with day-to-day problems is the grievance procedure included in the contracts. The Dunlop Commission provides a means for dealing with collective problems and conflicts. Because the commission functions as a private labor relations board, whose authority is guaranteed in legal contracts, it sidesteps lack of legislation and regulation as well as legal differences across state boundaries. Baldemar Velásquez notes that this new system "is based on mutual dialogue and respect. It enforces the same rules for all parties." The grievance procedure and the Dunlop Commission provide a *structure* for constructively resolving differences as they arise and before they get serious.

On a larger scale, FLOC farmworkers are now more integrated into the American socioeconomic system. They are more active participants, right along with the agribusinesses and growers. In many ways, the American socioeconomic system itself has also been changed. FLOC workers are now more integrated into the national structure through links with labor, religious, and other organizations. Their active involvement and their new networks bring FLOC farmworkers more into the national structure from their former isolation on the fringes of society.

Now FLOC workers have the opportunity to make more contributions to the American society. They can become productive taxpayers, instead of having to rely on tax-supported social services. Their children can receive more comprehensive education. Their greater purchasing power can help support the American economy. Most important, they can contribute their own potentials as more effective and responsible citizens. As the FLOC workers become more integrated into the American system, we can *all* benefit.

In noting these social reforms, Baldemar Velásquez says, "These changes should have been made a long time ago."

CHAPTER 4

The Internal Potentials
of the FLOC Movement

We have reviewed the story of FLOC and the important reforms it has been able to achieve for midwestern farmworkers. We have seen *what* has happened. Now we will turn to *how* FLOC has been able to achieve important changes in the agricultural system in which farmworkers are a part. The concept of adaptation calls for examination of two sets of forces that direct the course of social change. One set involves a group's internal potentials, and the other involves the challenges in its external environment. We will now examine the internal forces that have influenced the course of the FLOC movement, and in the next chapter we will look at the external forces involved.

The internal potentials that a group brings to a change situation involve two kinds of forces, needs and resources. Needs include whatever a group must have in order to function in a particular setting. Resources include whatever the group can use to maximize its well-being in that setting. Needs and resources together set the adaptive potentials of the group, and both are evident in the FLOC story.

In examining the internal potentials that have influenced the FLOC movement, we will first review the experiences of midwestern farmworkers. Some of farmworkers' existence we have already reviewed in Chapter 2. We know, for example, that midwestern migrants have suffered poverty, child labor, deforming work, exposure to pesticides, and many kinds of illnesses. Here, we will continue to examine farmworkers' lives but with a focus on their experiences regarding the FLOC movement. We will begin by looking at the life stories of midwestern farmworkers that tell how the FLOC movement has impacted on their lives. We will also review the results of a field survey of midwestern farmworkers. This survey indicates the degree of their involvement in the farm labor movement and explores those factors which have influenced their involvement. We will then summarize the different internal forces operating in the FLOC movement.

Midwestern Farmworkers Tell Their Stories

We have seen in the history of FLOC that the farm labor movement in the Midwest has achieved remarkable gains for farmworkers. Listing new benefits like workers compensation, the grievance procedure, and personal security can help us organize our knowledge of events. But in so doing, we can miss the *meanings* of these changes in their lives. To better understand the motivations and reactions involved in the FLOC movement, we asked several midwestern farmworkers to tell us their life stories. Their tales illustrate the variety of backgrounds and experiences evident in FLOC workers, including working for different corporations' operations, working tomato and pickle crops, and working as migrant and seasonal farmworkers. They also include workers who have been heavily involved in FLOC and those who became affiliated when their crew came under a FLOC contract. In particular, these stories compare their experiences before and after FLOC won labor reforms.

Fernando Cuevas

Fernando Cuevas is the vice president of FLOC. He has been an officer, an organizer, and a contract negotiator with FLOC since 1978. His commitment and endurance in pursuing FLOC's goals is illustrated by his activities on one hot July day in 1989, while we interviewed him and observed his work. Fernando drove to Bay City in northeastern Michigan for a series of meetings with farmworkers. On the way, he talked with crew leaders, growers, and company representatives in three migrant camps. That evening, he attended a general membership meeting with about twenty-five farmworkers at FLOC's regional office. Fernando then worked on an urgent grievance case, where a crew leader had been abusive toward a family. Fernando met with the parties involved until well past eleven at night, gathering information and discussing options under the grievance procedures in the labor contract. Fernando arrived back at FLOC headquarters at two in the morning. After a short night's sleep, he was back at work by nine the next morning, meeting with FLOC field organizers.

Fernando was born in Brownsville, in southern Texas. "I remem-

Fernando Cuevas, Sr., FLOC vice president, with his young daughter, directs a strike line on the edge of an Ohio tomato field in 1981. Watchful sheriff's deputies are in the background. Fernando, a former crew leader, has devoted considerable energy to the FLOC movement and has become one of its core leaders. He has shown creative initiative in organizing efforts. On this occasion, he had a portable toilet for the strikers mounted on the back of a pickup truck, in view of the field workers who had no such facilities. This visibly emphasized to the workers how they were denied even simple improvements.

ber being out in the fields with my parents and grandparents since I was five," he says. In May, the extended family would migrate to work in Arkansas, Michigan, and Ohio. In October, they would return to southern Texas. "My grandpa would tell me these captivating stories while we worked in the fields," he recalls. Fernando later realized that those stories were used to hold the young listener's attention. "I didn't want to miss anything," he says, so he had to maintain the work pace of his grandfather, a seasoned picker. He jokes, however, "When I was eight, my grandpa couldn't keep up with me."

Initially, Fernando's family had traveled with a *troquero* (crew leader) named Timoteo. He remembers Timoteo as an abusive boss, who often cheated the Cuevas family of some of their hard-earned pay. When Fernando learned of such incidents, he would complain to the adults in the family. However, his complaints were often stifled by his grandpa's response, "¡*No seas tan hocicón!*" (Don't be such a big mouth!). The family could not afford to lose their jobs by challenging the crew leader. Over the years, Fernando says, "I was so angry and frustrated. We were so helpless when we were treated so bad. We couldn't do anything about it."

When he was eleven, Fernando's family moved their base to Florida after the harvest season in Ohio. That winter, he used his grandfather's Social Security number to get work. He lived in a labor camp with more than two thousand workers. He recalls how this camp provided extra "services" to the workers. "They would take deductions from our pay to cover what we owed the camp's grocery store and bar!" When his grandparents decided to settle in Ohio, Fernando stayed with them for five years. At seventeen, he returned to Florida for the winters. Two years later, Fernando married Irene, whom he had met while working in Ohio. He and Irene now have ten children.

Like many migrant children, Fernando was not always able to attend school regularly. In elementary school, however, he was able to skip a whole grade. "Not many teachers showed much faith in me," he says. He finally dropped out of school when he was in the ninth grade.

When he was twelve, Fernando realized that crew leaders made more money than workers, and he decided he would become one. However, remembering the abuse his family received, he also decided he would not cheat or mistreat his crew. His bilingual skills and hard work gained the notice of growers and crew leaders. By age thirteen, he was given supervisory responsibilities. At eighteen, Fernando obtained a crew leader's license and began to achieve some economic independence. When he became a crew leader, his grandpa gave him some new advice: "*Un troquero no es troquero sin su gente"* (A crew leader is not a crew leader without his people). Fernando remembered this rule, he says, and always tried to treat well those who worked for him.

Being a labor contractor provided many benefits and a higher income. Fernando and his brother, Pino, would arrange for all the labor and transportation needed by different growers. They would also organize the tending, harvesting, and shipping of crops. By the time Fernando was thirty, he and his brother owned a small fleet of trucks to haul crops picked by the crews to the processing plants. Fernando had also bought some land in central Florida, which still serves as his home base.

Fernando first learned about FLOC in 1968. A family friend in Leipsic, Ohio, persuaded Fernando to join FLOC. "I paid a one-dollar annual fee and signed an authorization card," he says. His membership entitled him to a discount at FLOC's gas co-op. At the time, Fernando found this a useful benefit, since his trucks used a lot of fuel. Fernando soon forgot about FLOC, however, and focused on his contracting business.

In the summer of 1978, Fernando had arranged to harvest the pickle crop for a grower in northern Ohio. Due to bad weather, the pickle harvest was running almost a month behind schedule. Fernando had fifty-eight workers with him, all needing work. After an intense search, he found temporary work for his crew with a grower in Michigan. He soon found himself very busy. "Every day," he says," I had to drive my crew seventy-five miles each way. And we still had ten hours to pick and load the crop." Late one night after a long day, Irene told Fernando that a young man named Baldemar Velásquez was looking for him.

Initially, Fernando paid very little attention to Baldemar's efforts to contact him. Several times while waiting for Fernando, Baldemar would talk with people in the camp about FLOC's goal to unionize midwestern farmworkers. Fernando's brother, Pino, was particularly impressed by Baldemar's ideas and enthusiasm. Fernando finally met Baldemar and generally agreed with his vision for reform. He says, however, he did not really want to get involved at that point. He tried to distance himself from FLOC, by arranging for Pino to work with Baldemar while still receiving his share from their contracting business.

Several days later, Fernando learned that Baldemar and Pino had been assaulted by growers in Marion, Indiana, while trying to enter a labor camp. Fernando showed up at a subsequent court hearing with fifty-two workers. "We were ready to back up Pino and Baldemar." During the hearing, however, Baldemar's eloquence and legal reasoning made a powerful impression on Fernando. After the hearing was adjourned, Baldemar talked about FLOC's goals with a group of people in Fernando's home until late in the night. Fernando became convinced that conditions had to be improved for all farmworkers, not just those who happened to be part of his crew. "Baldemar and FLOC opened my heart and made me want to change the injustices," he says. "So that became my vocation, helping farmworkers to a new day of self-determination by our own participation."

That day began a special relationship between Fernando Cuevas and Baldemar Velásquez. Fernando soon became a tough negotiator. "I'd argue for better wages and benefits for my crews," he says. Some growers who had previously been very friendly with Fernando turned hostile. Fernando helped to arrange a meeting between Baldemar and twenty-eight other crew leaders. After gaining their trust, Baldemar was able to obtain valuable information about the price differences received by crews. "Some crew leaders realized others were being paid more," he says. They also realized they could benefit from joint negotiations with growers. FLOC was subsequently able to develop uniform wage standards for proposed labor contracts.

As Fernando became more involved with FLOC, his interest in the contracting and trucking business waned. He began to devote more and more time to FLOC's organizing activities. After long discussions with his family, Fernando made the decision to became a full-time organizer for FLOC. At FLOC's first constitutional convention in 1979 and at all the following conventions, Fernando has been elected to serve on FLOC's executive board.

Fernando has proven to be a tireless worker for the farm labor cause. During the strike against Campbell Soup, he was a key figure in organizing farmworkers and also in training other organizers. He gave speeches to church, labor, university, and other groups, and with effective persuasion, he won their support for the boycott. After the first contracts were signed in 1986, Fernando spent many long days organizing the workers in Campbell's tomato and pickle operations. These workers subsequently voted overwhelmingly in union elections to be represented by FLOC.

Fernando has also been a creative leader. For example, when FLOC decided to organize pickle operations, Fernando came up with new ways to involve Vlasic workers in northeastern Michigan. In 1984, he organized the first *pachanga* (celebration) in the area, to build social unity as well as labor solidarity among the workers. The festival has since become an annual tradition. On his way to the *pachanga* in 1989, Fernando stopped by a farm where a card count was due to be conducted. He found a representative from Vlasic and the grower also there. He reacted spontaneously and got a majority of the workers to sign authorization cards. Then he validated them with the grower's list, with the company representative as the witness.

Fernando believes his commitment to the farm labor cause comes from values formed early in his life as a farmworker. He remembers the anger and frustration with the way his family was mistreated. His own experiences have developed in him a concern for fairness, justice, and human dignity. "I thought I could solve the problems by being a good crew leader [who treats his own workers right]," Fernando says. As he became involved with FLOC, however, he realized that the issue was much broader. He saw that all farmworkers suffered injustices and that solutions had to work for farmworkers in general.

"FLOC changed my life completely," Fernando says. His children have also learned by seeing him and other FLOC activists at work. Most of his children have been involved with FLOC for most of their lives. They have put on "FLOC Kids" skits at rallies and fundraisers, worked in the FLOC office, and helped in field campaigns. Fernando "Junior," his oldest son, has also been an organizer and plans eventually to go into law and work on farm labor legal issues. Fernando also recalls how his family has developed over the years. "I used to be a typical Mexican father," he says. He considered himself the ultimate authority in the family. His children, however, used the democratic principles they had learned with FLOC, arguing that all the family should be involved in decisions. Now all the children expect to be a part of family affairs. Fernando says that these changes have been very positive for the whole family.

Looking back at all the years he has worked for the FLOC cause, he says, "It's a lifetime vocation for me. One of the highest points was actually signing that first history-making agreement between the growers and Campbell and FLOC. It proved for the first time that it can be done. We can win the right to negotiate our status with the growers who directly employ us and the food corporations who control them and the whole industry." Fernando emphasizes one point: "It came from those of us on the bottom. I'm very proud of that. Not just for me, but for all of us who migrate and work in the fields with skilled hands." The quality of Fernando's self-sacrifice and commitment to farmworker self-determination and justice was recognized in 1990 with his being awarded a Charles Bannerman Memorial Fellowship. (This fellowship is awarded by a Baltimore-based program which recognizes community activists who have made significant contributions to democracy.) When asked about what advice he has for other farmworkers, Fernando says, "Do not underestimate what farmworkers can do. Even if we're not educated, we can do a lot if we work together."

David Bermúdez

In July 1989, David Bermúdez sat in his home in Leipsic, Ohio, while we interviewed him about his long involvement with FLOC. David and his wife, Mariana, have lived with their ten children in Leipsic since 1956. The small town includes several hundred residents of Mexican heritage. It is located in the rich agricultural regions of northern Ohio, where many migrant farmworkers come every summer. Baldemar Velásquez also lived in this area for many years, and FLOC's early efforts were concentrated in this region. David is currently a seasonal farmworker, involved mostly with cucumber and tomato crops. Over the past twenty years, David has witnessed and participated in FLOC's evolution. He has worked with FLOC as a supporter, member, organizer, and as an elected board member.

David and Mariana were both born in Poteet, Texas. David only completed three years of elementary school. He recalls how he started into farm work when he was thirteen, after his grandmother died. "I lived with my grandmother when I was little and had everything I needed. When she died, all doors closed on me. I first started working in Texas, harvesting peanuts. I used to work barefoot because I didn't have shoes. I would get $3.00 a day for working eight hours, for five days a week. Since then, I've worked with cotton, asparagus, beets, cucumbers, and tomatoes. I still work planting tomatoes and on the harvesting machines."

David remembers first coming to Michigan when he was sixteen, after picking cotton in Arizona and in northwest Texas. He continued to migrate until 1953, when he joined the army for three years. In 1956, he and Mariana were married and together joined the migrant stream. When their first child was born a couple of years later, they decided to stay in Leipsic so that the children could have a better education. David comments, "I've worked on different agricultural and construction jobs in the thirty-five years or so we've lived here." During this time, David suffered several work-related injuries, including a major back injury and a broken knee. Still, he says, "We have to like every type of work we can do, if it helps us earn a living. When we have great needs, we cannot afford to avoid the difficult jobs." He adds that even when wages did increase, the

David Bermúdez *(on the right)* is shown with Alfonso Salinas, during a strike strategy meeting in 1981. David is one of the core FLOC farmworkers who, with great personal sacrifice and stamina, sustained the movement's efforts in its early years. Whenever a strike line, rally, demonstration, or volunteers were needed, David was always there to help.

family could not even stay ahead of inflation. "Before, things used to be less expensive. Even though we may be earning more money, it does not buy what we used to buy."

David talks about problems of people who have settled out of the migrant stream. He remembers one occasion when the family had used all of their money. He tried to get assistance through a government-funded service agency and applied for emergency aid for families with dependent children. After many delays in a lengthy application process, he was told that they could not be helped because the agency could only assist migrant workers and not seasonal farmworkers.

When FLOC was founded in 1968, David was one of the first members. "I went to a few meetings and signed a membership card," he says, "but I wasn't very active. Baldemar's father was a good friend of mine, and he would tell me what was going on." He says he was interested in the idea of a farmworkers' union. "Because of my background in farm work, I had learned how to pull for others who needed help at one time or another. I still do."

David says he became more active in FLOC around 1974, attending some home meetings. "I wanted to learn more about FLOC. I wanted to help improve our situation so farmworkers could have what we never had. I would find places here in Leipsic where FLOC could have general meetings.

He remembers, "In 1978, when we voted to strike the Campbell's and Libby's fields, we wanted more money for the workers, and we wanted the companies and the growers to recognize the union. If Libby and Campbell had cooperated from the start, everyone would have benefited, especially the local communities. Even when we had terrible wages like ninety-eight cents an hour, this was an important source of income for the local businesses. Mariana and I became very involved. We would take food to people who were on strike and were living in tents that FLOC had set up in the town of Belmore. In 1980, I remember having twenty FLOC members staying in our home. Every morning, Mariana would get up to make breakfast and lunch to take for the people out on the fields who were striking."

David now works under a FLOC contract on a farm that produces pickles for Vlasic and tomatoes for Campbell Soup. "FLOC has had a big impact on farmworkers' wages and conditions," he says. In 1956, when he first moved to the area, workers were paid nine cents for one hamper of tomatoes of about thirty-three pounds. By 1967, they were getting seventeen cents a hamper. These rates did not improve much, and by 1976 they were being paid only thirty-two cents a hamper. But in 1978, growers offered as much as fifty cents a hamper in order to break the strike. Before the FLOC contracts, David says, his family was earning about $2,000 during the summer season. If it was a good season, they could make $4,000.

"Now, with everything FLOC has done, farmworkers do not have it as difficult as we once did. In the beginning, the growers were very contrary. But things are better now that there are growers who have signed contracts." Then he adds, "Now the work is much better, even though the season is shorter because machines are being used for the tomato harvest. Already there is a difference; with the contract it is much better." David mentions FLOC workers can now be sure that their wages will be more than minimum wage standards. He adds that they also have greater job security and seniority rights. Where health conditions are concerned, David says, "We now know how to protect ourselves better from pesticides. We are more careful."

Fernando Cuevas, FLOC vice president, says David convinced the grower where he works to sign a collective bargaining agreement with FLOC. David says, "The grower I work for and I have developed a good deal of trust. We communicate honestly with each other. He told me that all of Campbell's growers in the area want to sign contracts. They like the benefits other growers with contracts have, like the larger acreage and the three-year agreements which improve the growers' credit rating."

Several months before, David and other FLOC members met with a group of growers in Detroit. The meeting was to initiate a more direct dialogue between the two groups. In the meeting, the growers and FLOC agreed to exchange written statements about their goals and the ways they could work together. He notes the significance of such a meeting: "The situation was not like that before. The growers would treat us as if we were crazy."

On a more personal level, David says, "FLOC has helped my family when we needed legal assistance and other things. Because of my experiences with FLOC, I have learned much about legal rights and politics. When the FLOC board members received training by the UFW, we learned that there will always be highs and lows. I've also learned that when you interact with many different people you have to be a good psychologist. Most people want to have whatever benefits are available. At the same time, they want others to be fair with them. I think I have helped Baldemar understand this idea a little better. On a few occasions, I felt abandoned by others. I thought that my personal needs or my family's needs were not being met. Or I thought that my opinions were not given enough attention. But I do not quit trying because of that. It has cost me a lot of work to get this far. If I were to quit trying, I would be abandoning not only the union but also other farmworkers who may need some help." David quoted a Mexican proverb, "¡*Ay qué sufrir para merecer!*" (In order to merit something, one has to work and even suffer for it!).

David says his message to other farmworkers is, "Never belittle unions. If it were not for the FLOC, we would have the same low wages and no benefits, like we used to have."

José Hinojosa

On a pleasant August evening in 1989, we interviewed José Hinojosa while he sat outside his cabin in a small labor camp near Fremont, Ohio. Inside were his wife, seven children, and his mother. José and several other men were barbecuing goat and chicken. Most of the migrants in this camp had come every year to pick cucumbers for a grower who had a contract with Heinz.

Standing by a van, José recalled his migration to the United States.

José Hinojosa is shown with his mother and family at an Ohio Heinz pickle farm camp in 1989. José has served as a camp representative and was elected by his crew to be a delegate to the 1988 and 1991 FLOC conventions. He is encouraged by improvements since the FLOC contracts were implemented and serves as an example of how workers' new status with growers has fostered a sense of security and confidence.

He was raised in Matamoros, Mexico, across the Rio Grande from Brownsville, Texas. He came to the United States when he was fourteen. His father and eight of the children came in search of the means to provide for their family. Conditions in Mexico had been very severe. "When we came," José says, "there was no work with the companies, so we had to go to the fields." They worked different crops in the Rio Grande Valley. Then they started migrating every spring from their home near Brownsville to Missouri, Ohio, and Michigan.

José continued this cycle when he got married and started his own family. Every June, they leave their home in San Benito, Texas, and go to Ohio. "We pick cucumbers until late August, when the tomatoes start ripening. We work on the mechanical harvester machines. We sort ripe tomatoes from the bad fruit, plant parts, and other matter." José says they used to harvest the tomatoes by hand. "Then, we used to work three or four weeks longer. But the growers started using the machines to be against FLOC. Now there is only work for about twelve people, instead of the many who used to work picking tomatoes."

In September, the family goes to Missouri, where they pick apples until mid-October. The family goes back to their home in Texas, where they work locally harvesting broccoli during December and January, onions during March and April; they plant tomatoes at the end of April. This annual cycle may at times leave them without available work for up to two or three months.

José talks about how the system has made it hard for farmworkers to support themselves. He says he has not liked the independent contractor (sharecropper) system. "Instead of paying about seven percent in taxes, we have had to pay maybe eighteen or twenty percent."

José says he first learned about FLOC in 1986. He had known about the United Farm Workers in California. He had not known much about FLOC, however, until the initial union elections were held as a part of the agreement with Heinz. When FLOC organizers informed the workers about the issues and elections, José says, "We were thinking they are starting something good for farmworkers." He and others thought this would lead to getting more benefits. "We decided to sign with the union. We will stick with the union and see how things work out."

José talks about one case where FLOC had a direct impact on behalf of his crew. One worker, Roberto, drove a tractor with the bin for loading pickles. Members of the crew began complaining that Roberto would load his own family's pickles first, making others wait in the hot fields. They also complained that Roberto did not give people their daily tallies, the record on which a family's earnings are based. Some workers felt that this was being done to make people mad so they would leave early. (This practice has been used by growers and crew leaders to keep workers' "bonus" pay for themselves.) Roberto eventually quit, but he went to FLOC saying he was fired and wanted to sue the grower. Following the grievance procedures, Fernando Cuevas investigated the matter and determined there was no fault on the part of the grower. In this case, the other crew members were relieved that tensions with the grower had been eased and everyone could concentrate on their work.

José was chosen by his crew to be a delegate to the FLOC conventions in 1988 and 1991. In 1989, he was chosen to be a camp representative for the union. He attended several meetings of the camp reps and was able to compare experiences with other reps and to see what new ideas people had. They also discussed the renewal of the contracts, and he was talking ideas over with other members of his crew.

José compares the workers' situation before and after the FLOC contracts. He says they would like even more earnings than under the current contract; they would like the incentive rates increased, too. He also says that he appreciates the people from FLOC because the workers are in better shape now. "The union has started something good," he says.

José also says that the workers feel more secure in their work now. "With FLOC, the growers cannot put the people down." Additionally, under the contract, those currently working for a grower have first chance for jobs next year. "Before, we couldn't be sure we would have a job the next time," he says. Also, when they have a problem, they know they now have the grievance procedures to help them do something about it.

José also talks about people who have gotten involved with the union. "They have changed," he says. "They can now tell the grower when they feel something is wrong. They can work together to make things better rather than just making complaints. The people are learning," he says.

José also points out that the workers are deciding more things for themselves. With insight, he notes that "the first major decision we made was whether we wanted the union." Since then, they have been involved in deciding the conditions for the new contracts. "Now we have a way to get more benefits. We don't have to depend on what others decide to give us."

"I believe in Cuevas and FLOC," José says. "The union can help us." He looks forward to the new contracts, a more secure job, more pay, better benefits, and a better life for himself and his family.

Isaías Alfaro

In the summer of 1989, Isaías Alfaro, his wife, and their four children sat in their small apartment in Leipsic, Ohio. The grower for whom they were working supplies Vlasic's pickles and Campbell's tomatoes. Isaías and his family became FLOC members in 1988, when their crew voted for the union. At the time of the interview, they were in their second year of working under a FLOC contract.

Isaías and his family live in Pharr, Texas. He notes that they are renting government housing there until they can save enough to buy their own place. "Before we came to Texas," he says, "we used to live in Río Bravo, Tamaulipas, in Mexico. I am a U.S. citizen, because I was born in San Benito, Texas. My wife and children were all born in Mexico. You see, I became an orphan when I was five, so I went to live with an aunt in Río Bravo."

Isaías has had little formal education. "I studied in Mexico until the second grade, in a school set up for peasants. In order to go to school in Mexico, I had to use my aunt's last name. I left school in the third year, though, because I had to work helping my aunt." When he was twelve, he started shining shoes to help his adopted family.

When he was eighteen, Isaías obtained the necessary evidence to prove that he had been born in the United States. He then started migrating on a regular basis. "I first worked in Texas, harvesting cabbages, onions, oranges, and green peppers. I also worked in a corn canning factory," he says. "When I was nineteen, I went on to Oklahoma. The next year, I went on to Oxnard, California, to harvest tomatoes."

In 1974, Isaías decided to stay in Texas and work cotton and other seasonal cash crops. In 1977 and 1978, he went to Illinois, where he worked on a poultry farm collecting turkey eggs. He remembers getting $3.50 an hour, but the job required that he work ten-hour shifts on a regular basis. On top of that, the job stipulated that unless he stayed there two complete months, he would lose a travel subsidy and a "bonus" of twenty-five cents an hour, which had been held from all his payments. Isaías comments, "I went for two years only because I needed the money." In 1978 and 1979, Isaías returned to California and worked in Can City and Salinas. "I worked for a grower who had hundreds of workers. We all lived together isolated out in a migrant camp, and a bus would take us from the camp to the fields." He says that he applied for regular jobs in many places, "But if you're not fluent in English they won't hire you. In order not to struggle aimlessly, we migrate and work in the fields."

In 1981, Isaías' family was able to join him in the United States. "As soon as they came, we started to migrate to the Midwest, working as a family. Last year, we worked here in Ohio on the harvest of small cucumbers. This year, we came to plant tomatoes, harvest cucumbers, and work on the tomato-harvesting machines."

Isaías says his sons were already young adults when they came from Mexico, and they did not want to start their schooling over again in the United States. "My girls are doing well," he says, "and they want to return to Texas sooner in order to start school on time. They may be able to register for school here and receive credit in Texas when we go back. But my sons want to stay to earn more money and want to keep coming back in the future. I don't know whether to stay or whether [to] go back with the girls only."

Isaías says farm labor has been hard. "When I first started coming to this area, they were paying me about $4.00 per hour. Now they are paying $4.45, and in the tomato harvester we are supposed to receive $4.75. Last year, we earned $5,700 during the entire year. In Texas, when we can find work, we receive $3.35 an hour."

He is grateful, he says, that they have not had any health problems while in Ohio, though they are eligible for Medicaid while in the area. In Texas, they do not have any medical coverage. "In Texas, I still owe a hospital for an X-ray test and some medication I received last year. Last November, I felt a very strong stomach pain and had to go to a hospital emergency room. I would have gone to a public clinic, but they couldn't make an appointment until about a month after I called."

Isaías recalls union organizing for farmworkers in Texas in the 1970's. "A man I knew even died from a shooting that took place in the fields. Some of the growers attacked the workers who were on strike and started shooting at them. The unionizing effort was not well organized, though. That was the first time I thought of joining a union. But I did not like the way it was organized. When I went to California in 1978, I remember hearing of César Chávez. They wouldn't let the union people into the camp to talk to us, though. Eventually that changed, and the union won. But I left California."

Isaías first heard about FLOC when he came to Ohio in 1981. "The first year we were approached about joining FLOC, but we did not want to get involved. At that time, I did not think that the benefits were something that the grower had to provide for us. I did not know that these were rights and that we were entitled to them. We had not experienced any troubles with our grower, and we knew that some other growers paid less. So we waited," he says. "I first became a member of FLOC in 1986, at the ranch where I'm working now. Some FLOC organizers brought us some information and talked to us. We then signed a form to become members. They even took our picture and gave us a membership card with our picture on it. We also had elections where I and others voted."

Isaías says FLOC has helped farmworkers. "Because of the union, we have been getting raises in the tomato and cucumber prices. But the union has not affected some things. Our grower knows that we are FLOC members and has not treated us bad because of that. The only complaint against him was last year, when he tried to pay us $4.10 an hour. We let him know that FLOC had told us we should be receiving $4.45. Even though he continued paying us at $4.10, he finally paid us at the higher rate. We got the thirty-five-cent difference about two weeks after we returned to Texas. A FLOC organizer went to San Juan and gave us the check with the money that was owed to us."

Isaías talks about how things are better off since they have had the FLOC contracts. "With the union, it is easier to get better wages from the growers. In Texas, workers get as little as $3.35 an hour. Here, we have gone from $4.10 to $4.45 an hour. And we are supposed to get $4.75 working on the tomato harvester. It is a good thing to be a FLOC member. In the cucumber harvest, we are getting $16.00 for every hundred pounds for the 'Number 1' pickles. Last year we were getting less. Also, it used to be that we had to go to migrant clinics where we had to pay for the medical services. But now we have Medicaid, and we get better treatment. All of these improvements FLOC has been able to get for us. For me, it is better this way."

Isaías says he fully supports FLOC. "Anyway you look at it, there is nothing like being united. In farm work, unions hardly exist. The way I see it, the union has helped us because at least they fight for the rights of farmworkers. If the union was to disappear, there would not be anyone who could put pressure on the growers. I do not think that the growers would pay us the same amount if we did not have the union."

Guadalupe Franco

In August 1988, we interviewed Guadalupe Franco as he stood outside a small trailer in a labor camp south of Fremont, Ohio. This summer had been the worst drought in the Midwest in recorded history. Temperatures had been over 100 degrees for weeks, as farmworkers worked in the fields, picking cucumbers going to Heinz. Lupe, his wife Francisca, and their six children had all been working in the fields to support the family during the severe weather.

Lupe was born in Matamoros, Mexico, across the river from Brownsville, Texas. He says economic conditions in Mexico were particularly depressed, and his family could not support everyone. So when he was nineteen, he came to the United States to find work. Presently, he is married and is raising his own family under tough economic conditions. He tells his children that it is hard work in the fields. So if they want an easier life, they should study hard and get an education.

Lupe talks about the problems farmworkers have with crew leaders. "Instead of demanding more for the workers from the grower, they try to pull more out of the people." He says, "A lot of crew leaders are crooked. They don't pay workers what they've really earned. And the crew leaders keep the people's taxes, instead of filing them with the government."

He also talks about growers. "A lot of growers are also crooked. They ask workers if they have their immigration papers. If they don't, they give them a job. They pay people without papers less because they can get away with it. They don't have to pay taxes either."

Lupe talks about one grower who was always putting up notices and rules. Lupe asks, "Why don't farmworkers have any rules of our own? For example, the cabins should have smoke alarms in case of fire. And the cabins should be inspected for safety." He also says the furnishings should be in good working order. Once, they had to buy a stove out of their small earnings because the one furnished by the grower didn't work. "This grower," he says, "is quick to say if he finds something in the cabin broken, and [he will] make the people pay for it." He suggested that the grower build canvas covers over the trailers and provide fans. These would help the workers rest better, with the temperature over ninety degrees even at night. This would even help the grower, he says, because the workers could do their jobs better.

The previous winter, Lupe and his family had gone to Florida to pick strawberries. In May, they had come north to Ohio from their home in Brownsville, Texas, to plant tomatoes, hoe sugar beets, and pick cabbage. At the time, they were picking pickles and planned to harvest tomatoes after that. They were thinking of going back to Texas for Christmas and then returning to Florida to work oranges. "This year has been really bad with the drought," Lupe says. "Normally, we could earn about $6,000, $3,000 over expenses. This would be enough to add a room to our house. We also try to put a little aside for our children's school. But this year, we might earn only $2,500 because things are bad all over for migrants."

This is the first year that Lupe and his family have worked under a union contract. "This has made a big difference," Lupe says. "We know for sure what we can earn. We didn't have any security before the FLOC contract."

Lupe says FLOC was a big help during the drought when many migrants didn't have the money to get back to their home areas. "If it weren't for FLOC," he says, "we would have had to get a loan at high rates." He states FLOC informed the workers about different resources available and set up a telephone hotline to refer migrants for public assistance. He also notes that in a cooperative effort with FLOC, Heinz had donated $25,000 to a matching emergency fund to help farmworkers return to their homes. In addition, FLOC had helped the workers get food stamps. When Lupe and his family dis-covered they had not received the full amount of assistance, they told the clerk they were with FLOC and were then treated fairly.

Lupe says unions are good in general, and particularly unions like FLOC that have good leaders. He believes Baldemar Velásquez is sin-cere, enthusiastic, and cares about the workers. Lupe was chosen to be a delegate at the 1988 FLOC convention. "My only disappoint-ment," he says, "was that there were not enough farmworkers rep-resented. More farmworkers need to know about FLOC and to tell others."

Higinio Pecina

In August 1989, we interviewed Higinio Pecina while he and his family were attending a FLOC *pachanga* (celebration) in Standish, in northeastern Michigan. He, his wife, and their ten children had been working on a nonunion pickle farm in the area. Though they were not working under a contract, they have been strong FLOC supporters for years.

Higinio was born in Matamoros, Mexico, across the border from Brownsville, Texas. Like many others, Higinio had come to the United States seeking better opportunities. Increasing inflation and unemployment in Mexico had made it impossible for him to support his family. He immigrated when he was twenty-six and went right into farm work. He worked first in Texas and then migrated to Ohio. About twenty years ago, he and his family had moved their base to central Florida. "We thought there was a better chance for work there during the winter months."

Higinio and his family usually leave for Michigan in June. "We hoe sugar beets and then pick cucumbers and peppers through Sep-tember. In October, we go back to central Florida. We pick oranges, cherry and regular tomatoes, strawberries, peppers, and cucumbers until May." The family has few complaints about farmwork itself. They are very dissatisfied, however, with the way they are treated by their bosses. Higinio talks about the grower they worked for in Ohio, for example. In 1982, they felt so offended by the way he treated them that they quit going there in the summer. Now they migrate instead to northeastern Michigan for work.

"I first heard about FLOC in 1978 when we were picking tomatoes in Pandora, Ohio," Higinio says. "This was when FLOC had gone on strike against Campbell Soup." He had talked with FLOC organiz-ers, and he liked what he heard. The following year, the family worked in Fremont, Ohio. There, they saw some of the FLOC organizers they had known in the Leipsic area. "We talked more about the union then," he says. In 1984, when they were working in Michigan, "they found me here." At that point, Higinio became more involved with FLOC, attending organizing meetings and rallies.

"FLOC is good for us," Higinio says. "They fight for better housing, better wages. We come a thousand miles and waste our money. Growers don't give us anything. We come here, and all they say is, 'Here are the rows. Start working.' They don't care anything for us."

Many farmworkers see FLOC as a labor union that can help them win better wages and benefits. But Higinio has a wider vision of FLOC as *un movimiento* (a movement) where many people combine their efforts to change their conditions. "Together we can fight the growers, but by ourselves we don't have any power," he says. He expresses willingness to struggle for farmworkers and has helped FLOC in organizing the workers in his crew and on other unorganized farms.

A Survey of Midwestern Farmworkers

The stories of midwestern workers help in understanding the feelings of farmworkers themselves about their work and about FLOC. However, we also need to know how their experiences are representative of midwestern farmworkers in general. If only a few people have such views, then FLOC's legitimacy and effectiveness would be in doubt. On the other hand, if there is wide support among midwestern farmworkers, then we can be assured that FLOC indeed represents its constituent group.

In order to establish the range of views about FLOC among midwestern farmworkers, a field survey was conducted in 1983 (Barger and Reza 1984a, 1984b). This survey took place before the FLOC contracts were instituted, and so it gives an indication of farmworkers' involvement in the movement at the height of the strike and boycott. The research population was defined as the estimated 25,000 farmworkers involved in the tomato harvest in the central Midwest. This was the group with which FLOC was most concerned at the time. The study group was further defined as the estimated 4,500 Mexican-American migrant tomato workers who are adult male heads of household. A total of 42 workers from 36 migrant camps were selected by a stratified random sampling design and were interviewed, with a response rate of 87.5 percent. The social and economic backgrounds and general conditions of these workers were discussed in Chapter 2. (See Table 2.1, Table 2.2, and Table 2.3.)[1]

In the analysis of the survey data, three sets of factors concerning tomato workers' views about the FLOC movement were examined. The first was the *knowledge* workers have about the farm labor movement, about FLOC, its goals, and its methods. Another factor was the workers' attitudes about the farm labor movement, particularly the degree of *endorsement* of FLOC, its goals, and its methods. The third factor concerned their active *participation* in the farm labor movement. A number of other factors were also analyzed to determine how they collectively influence views about the farm labor movement.

Knowledge of the Farm Labor Movement

The survey indicates that midwestern farmworkers have been fairly well informed about the farm labor movement. This is especially significant because this awareness was present during the height of the strike and boycott against Campbell Soup. As seen in Table 4.1, a majority had some awareness of the United Farm Workers and of its purposes and activities. Several factors may have contributed to this knowledge. At the time of the survey, the UFW had led the farm labor movement for almost three decades, and as such, it was well known. Also, the UFW had actively organized farmworkers in the home-base areas of Texas and Florida.

Almost half knew about FLOC. Over 40 percent understood FLOC's purpose was to improve farmworkers' conditions through labor organizing and collective bargaining. Even more were aware of the conflict with the Campbell Soup Company, though only a third were aware of the FLOC boycott. In all, about 45 percent had clear knowledge of the farm labor movement. This is a substantial proportion of a movement's constituent group. At the height of the FLOC boycott, then, midwestern farmworkers were relatively informed about farm labor issues.

Related field research suggests that in 1983 farmworkers' channels of information were somewhat restricted while in the Midwest. Most were in the region for only a few months of the year. Even then, they were usually isolated in rural labor camps. However, FLOC actively tried to inform farmworkers through camp and field visits. Also, both the UFW and FLOC had conducted mutual information campaigns in the Texas and Florida base areas. These efforts undoubtedly contributed to the awareness of many midwestern workers.

Table 4.1: *Farmworker Knowledge about the Farm Labor Movement* [a]

Have heard of the United Farm Workers (UFW)	61%
Understand the main purposes of the UFW [b]	58%
Aware of the UFW grape and lettuce boycotts a few years ago	58%
Have heard of the Farm Labor Organizing Committee (FLOC)	47%
Understand the main purposes of FLOC	42%
Aware of the FLOC strike against Campbell's Soup in Ohio	45%
Aware of the FLOC boycott of Campbell's Soup products	32%
KNOWLEDGEABLE ABOUT THE FARM LABOR MOVEMENT [c]	45%

[a] Figures represent awareness of the farm labor movement on the items indicated (n = 38).
[b] Responses to open-ended questions were evaluated for a perspective that the UFW and FLOC work for better rights and conditions for farmworkers, primarily through labor organizing and collective bargaining. About 96% of those who had heard of the UFW indicated such views, and 89% of those who had heard of FLOC.
[c] Represents an awareness of at least 4 of the 7 items indicated.

Endorsement of the Farm Labor Movement

The survey also indicates that midwestern farmworkers have overwhelmingly endorsed the farm labor movement as a viable alternative for improving their lives. As indicated in Table 4.2, there has been almost universal approval of those basic labor rights which constitute FLOC's goals for farmworkers. It should be noted that most of these are enjoyed by most other American workers.

The vast majority of midwestern tomato workers have strongly approved of the main farm labor movement organizations, as indicated in Table 4.3. There has also been widespread support for the labor goals of FLOC and the UFW, including collective bargaining. Furthermore, a substantial majority has endorsed the primary nonviolent methods of these organizations, including strikes and public boycotts. While the workers may not have had full knowledge of the FLOC movement, it does appear that they have had an understanding of the farm labor movement in general and of its goals. This awareness has provided a ready background for understanding the specific issues when workers were informed about the particulars of the FLOC movement itself.

When all factors are considered together, an overwhelming 84 per-

Table 4.2: *Farmworker Endorsement of Farm Labor Rights* [a]

THINK FARMWORKERS SHOULD HAVE BASIC RIGHTS TO:	
Earnings that average at least the minimum wage rates	100%
Payment of full wages each payday (instead of an end-of-the-season "bonus")	97%
Coverage by workers' compensation for work-related injuries	97%
Medical insurance benefits	100%
Unemployment benefits	100%
Access to fresh drinking water while working in the fields	100%
Access to restroom and hand-washing facilities while in the fields [b]	100%
Reimbursement for travel expenses in coming to work in the region [b]	100%
First choice of new jobs created when mechanization displaces old jobs [b]	100%
Retraining programs when displaced by mechanization [c]	100%

[a] Figures represent awareness of farm labor rights on the items indicated ($n = 38$).
[b] Midwestern farmworkers have generally not been covered for these items under either national or state labor laws. About 95% of the respondents endorsed all 10 of these labor rights for farmworkers.
[c] No data exists for more than 10% of the sample.

cent of the midwestern farmworkers endorsed the farm labor movement. In comparison, when a political figure receives such public approval, he is perceived to have a mandate from the people. Such rates reflect a high level of popular endorsement for any efforts of organized social change. The survey documents that FLOC has had a solid base because of farmworkers' attitudes about the farm labor movement. FLOC can be assured that its goals and methods for achieving basic rights and conditions for farmworkers reflect the basic views of its constituent group.

Participation in the Farm Labor Movement

A substantial proportion of midwestern farmworkers have been actively involved in the farm labor movement, as seen in Table 4.4. An individual may have positive attitudes, but this does not necessarily mean he or she will act according to such values. This is particularly true when socioeconomically marginal people like farmworkers may be threatened with losing what little they already have. This

Table 4.3: *Farmworker Endorsement of the Farm Labor Movement*[a]

Approval of organizations like the UFW and FLOC as good for farmworkers[b]	79%
Farmworkers should have the legal right to labor organizing and collective bargaining	92%
Growers/agribusinesses whose products involve farmworkers' labor should negotiate with FLOC/UFW[b]	82%
Would prefer working under a FLOC/UFW contract than under the personal arrangements of a crew leader	87%
If necessary, farmworkers should go on strike to achieve better working rights and conditions	82%
Approve of boycotts to help achieve better working rights and conditions for farmworkers	76%
Believe that public boycotts help achieve better working rights and conditions for farmworkers[b]	66%
Interviewer rating on positive attitude toward the farm labor movement	68%
ENDORSEMENT OF THE FARM LABOR MOVEMENT[c]	84%

[a] Figures represent approval of the farm labor movement on the items indicated (*n* = 38).
[b] No data exists for more than 10% of the sample.
[c] Represents a positive attitude toward at least 5 of the 8 items indicated. Missing data were conservatively included as a lack of a positive view.

is not the case for midwestern workers, however. They have acted upon their views about the farm labor movement. During the Campbell strike and boycott, over one-fifth indicated they were members of the UFW or FLOC. Half of these said they belonged to both farm labor unions. Also, almost a third had participated in the boycotts of these organizations.

The survey indicates that almost a third of midwestern farmworkers had been actively involved in the farm labor movement at the height of FLOC's struggle with Campbell Soup. Compared to other recent social movements, this is a fairly high proportion of participation (Howard 1974:1, 147–153; Freeman 1979). The active support of farmworkers, for example, is about three times the 12 percent level of the American public who participated in the UFW's grape and lettuce boycotts (L. Harris 1975). Given that migrants have been a fairly isolated group, this is a notable proportion of involvement.

Table 4.4: *Farmworker Support for the Farm Labor Movement*[a]

Member of a farm labor organization[b]	21%
Participated in the UFW boycotts[c]	29%
Participated in the FLOC boycott[d]	29%
Interviewer rating on active, involved in the movement	24%
ACTIVE SUPPORT FOR THE FARM LABOR MOVEMENT[e]	32%

[a] Figures represent active support for the farm labor movement on the items indicated ($n = 38$).
[b] Of those that stated they do belong to a farm labor organization, 50% claimed UFW and the other 50% claimed both UFW and FLOC. Of those who are not members, 55% (43% of the total sample) expressed interest in belonging. About 11% of the nonmembers indicated that they used to belong to UFW, but had let their membership lapse. A total of 65% report either belonging to a farm labor organization or were interested in belonging.
[c] Of those who were aware of these boycotts, 52% participated in them.
[d] Of those who were aware of this boycott, 92% participated in it.
[e] Represents active involvement in at least 3 of the 4 items indicated.

Influences in Farmworkers' Support for the Farm Labor Movement

The survey of midwestern farmworkers documents their overwhelming support of the FLOC movement at the height of its struggle for union recognition. The quantitative data set permits further analysis of factors that influence their views. It should first be recognized, however, that several factors are *not* related to views about FLOC. These include farm work experience and also some demographic variables such as age and education. It is interesting to note that most living and working conditions also do not affect support for FLOC. These can be ruled out as directly influencing how midwestern farmworkers have responded to the farm labor movement. Those factors which *do* contribute to their support for FLOC are as follows.

(1) Knowledge of the farm labor movement: The survey shows that midwestern farmworkers have been fairly well informed about the farm labor movement. Several factors were found to be related to this knowledge (see Figure 4.1). Those farmworkers who were more informed were less socially isolated while in the Midwest. They were also more active in religious affairs. Both of these traits provide more opportunities to become aware of events. For example, there has been overt support of the farm labor movement by some Catholic parishes in the lower Rio Grande valley where many of the

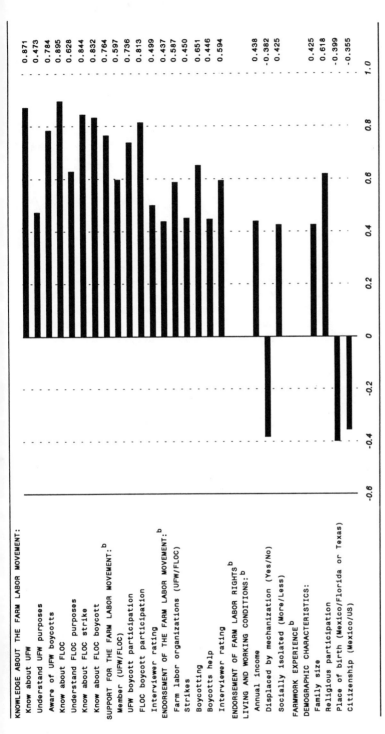

KNOWLEDGE ABOUT THE FARM LABOR MOVEMENT:						
Know about UFW						0.871
Understand UFW purposes						0.473
Aware of UFW boycotts						0.784
Know about FLOC						0.895
Understand FLOC purposes						0.628
Know about FLOC strike						0.844
Know about FLOC boycott						0.832
SUPPORT FOR THE FARM LABOR MOVEMENT:[b]						0.764
Member (UFW/FLOC)						0.597
UFW boycott participation						0.736
FLOC boycott participation						0.813
Interviewer rating						0.499
ENDORSEMENT OF THE FARM LABOR MOVEMENT:[b]						0.437
Farm labor organizations (UFW/FLOC)						0.587
Strikes						0.450
Boycotting						0.651
Boycotts help						0.446
Interviewer rating						0.594
ENDORSEMENT OF FARM LABOR RIGHTS[b]						
LIVING AND WORKING CONDITIONS:[b]						
Annual income						0.438
Displaced by mechanization (Yes/No)						-0.382
Socially isolated (More/Less)						0.425
FARMWORK EXPERIENCE[b]						
DEMOGRAPHIC CHARACTERISTICS:						
Family size						0.425
Religious participation						0.618
Place of birth (Mexico/Florida or Texas)						-0.399
Citizenship (Mexico/US)						-0.355

a Figures represent the relationship with a summary scale on the degree of knowledge about the farm labor movement, composed of the variables indicated in the first set of items. All figures represent Spearman's Rho correlation coefficient. Only correlations that are significant at the 0.05 level or less and that are stronger than 0.250 are reported ($n = 36$).
b A summary scale was correlated with knowledge about the farm labor movement. Specific variables in the scale which correlated with knowledge are indicated.

Figure 4.1: Influences in Farmworker Knowledge about the Farm Labor Movement[a]

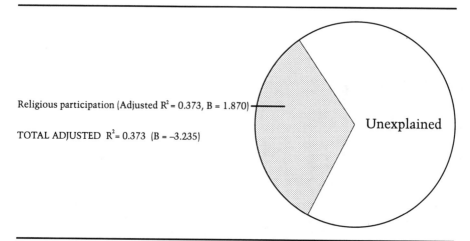

Religious participation (Adjusted R^2 = 0.373, B = 1.870)

TOTAL ADJUSTED R^2 = 0.373 (B = –3.235)

Unexplained

[a]Figures represent the results of stepwise regression using all variables that were significantly correlated with knowledge about the farm labor movement. Only items that are significant at the 0.05 level or less are reported. Figures represent the proportion of the total Adjusted R^2 explained by the model (n = 36).

Figure 4.2: Combined Influences in Farmworker Knowledge about the Farm Labor Movement[a]

farmworkers are based. Also, being active in religious affairs has provided farmworkers greater opportunity to interact with others. This has helped them to learn about events and to share thoughts with people beyond the immediate family and crew. The more informed farmworkers also have had larger families and greater incomes. However, they have been more displaced by mechanization, though they have not necessarily felt more threatened by such displacement. It is interesting to note that the more informed tended to be immigrants from Mexico.

When these factors are considered together, participation in religious activities turns out to have been the primary contributor to knowledge about the farm labor movement. As seen in Figure 4.2, this alone accounts for almost two-fifths of such awareness (adjusted R^2 = 0.373).

(2) Endorsement of the farm labor movement: The survey shows that midwestern farmworkers have overwhelmingly endorsed the farmworker movement when FLOC was at the height of its struggle.

There have been several factors that have contributed to this endorsement, as indicated in Figure 4.3. One is greater knowledge about the movement. As workers have become more informed, their endorsement has increased. Such endorsement seems to be based primarily on awareness about the organizations and activities of the farm labor movement. Our qualitative field research indicates that farmworkers feel deeply that the larger purpose of FLOC and the UFW is to help improve farmworkers' lives (see Barger and Reza 1985b, 1989). Another influence has been a commitment to basic labor rights for farmworkers. Also, Mexican immigrants, particularly those who have limited conversational ability in English, have more strongly endorsed the movement. The predominantly "Mexican" image of FLOC and the UFW may have appealed to their ethnic identity, particularly since they have been strangers and a minority in an "Anglo" land.

When these factors are considered together, a commitment to labor rights proves to have been a dominant influence, as seen in Figure 4.4. Immigrant status has been a clear secondary influence. Together, these two factors account for over 40 percent of farmworkers' endorsement of the farm labor movement (adjusted $R^2 = 0.414$). These findings indicate that support has been based on a commitment specifically to *labor* reform as well as a commitment to seeking new opportunities.

(3) Participation in the farm labor movement: The survey also shows that a substantial proportion of midwestern farmworkers were actively involved in the farm labor movement in 1983. Influences in this support have included both knowledge and endorsement of the movement, as indicated in Figure 4.5. This suggests that awareness and approval of FLOC and the UFW may have been preconditions for active support.

Being both less socially isolated while in the Midwest and more involved in religious activities have been related to support. Being based in Texas and Florida, where both the UFW and FLOC have been active in organizing farmworkers, has contributed to active support, too. These factors indicate that those who have been sympathetic to the farm labor cause are activated by wider opportunities for involvement. Since immigrating from Mexico and having limited ability in English have also been related, ethnic identity may have played an important role as well. Additionally, those with larger families have been more supportive of the farm labor cause, perhaps stimulated by a greater need for a stable and productive occupation.

When these influences are considered together, knowledge of the

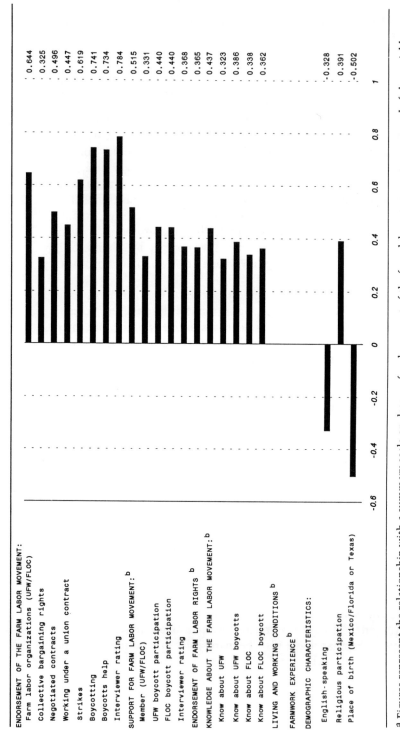

ENDORSEMENT OF THE FARM LABOR MOVEMENT:

Variable	Value
Farm labor organizations (UFW/FLOC)	0.644
Collective bargaining rights	0.325
Negotiated contracts	0.496
Working under a union contract	0.447
Strikes	0.619
Boycotting	0.741
Boycotts help	0.734
Interviewer rating	0.784

SUPPORT FOR FARM LABOR MOVEMENT:[b]

Variable	Value
Member (UFW/FLOC)	0.515
UFW boycott participation	0.331
FLOC boycott participation	0.440
Interviewer rating	0.440

ENDORSEMENT OF FARM LABOR RIGHTS [b]

Variable	Value
	0.368

KNOWLEDGE ABOUT THE FARM LABOR MOVEMENT:[b]

Variable	Value
Know about UFW	0.365
Know about UFW boycotts	0.437
Know about FLOC	0.323
Know about FLOC boycott	0.386
	0.338
	0.362

LIVING AND WORKING CONDITIONS [b]

FARMWORK EXPERIENCE[b]

DEMOGRAPHIC CHARACTERISTICS:

Variable	Value
English-speaking	-0.328
Religious participation	0.391
Place of birth (Mexico/Florida or Texas)	-0.502

a Figures represent the relationship with a summary scale on degree of endorsement of the farm labor movement, composed of the variables indicated in the first set of items. All figures represent Spearman's Rho correlation coefficient. Only correlations that are significant at the 0.05 level or less and that are stronger than 0.250 are reported ($n = 36$).

b A summary scale was correlated with endorsement of the farm labor movement. Specific variables in the scale which correlated with endorsement are indicated.

Figure 4.3: Influences in Farmworker Endorsement of the Farm Labor Movement[a]

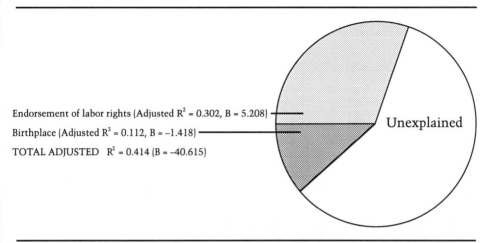

Endorsement of labor rights (Adjusted R^2 = 0.302, B = 5.208)

Birthplace (Adjusted R^2 = 0.112, B = –1.418)

TOTAL ADJUSTED R^2 = 0.414 (B = –40.615)

Unexplained

[a]Figures represent the results of stepwise regression using all variables that were significantly correlated with endorsement of the farm labor movement. Only items that are significant at the 0.05 level or less are reported. Figures represent the proportion of the total Adjusted R^2 explained by the model (n = 36).

Figure 4.4: Combined Influences in Farmworker Endorsement of the Farm Labor Movement[a]

movement alone accounts for over half of the active support among midwestern farmworkers, as seen in Figure 4.6. Those who have been actively involved in the movement have undoubtedly acquired greater knowledge. This finding, however, indicates that farmworkers in general have been basically predisposed in their support and have been motivated into action by specific awareness of the movement. Having a lack of English and having a larger family have been two important factors determining support. Again, these suggest that ethnic identity and greater need have been involved in motivating active support. Together, these three factors account for over two-thirds of the support for the farm labor movement among midwestern farmworkers (adjusted R^2 = 0.695).

In summary, the farmworkers' stories show the depth of feelings involved in the farmworkers' support for FLOC. Midwestern farmworkers are clearly convinced that FLOC is the most viable way for them to achieve better rights and conditions. This is coupled with feelings of being maltreated for too many years. FLOC has raised

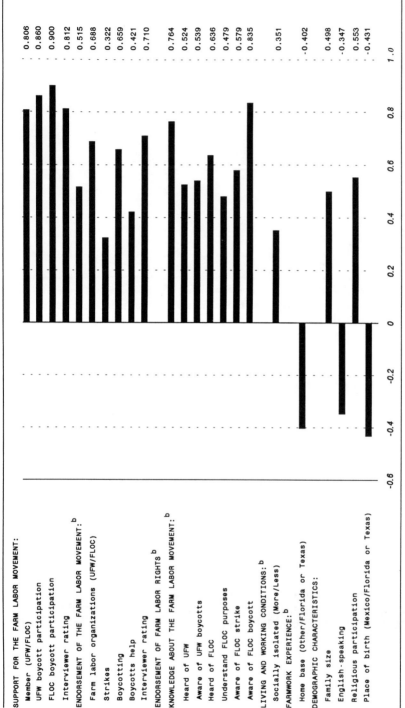

a Figures represent the relationship with a summary scale on degree of support for the farm labor movement, composed of the variables indicated in the first set of items. All figures represent Spearman's Rho correlation coefficient. Only correlations that are significant at the 0.05 level or less and that are stronger than 0.250 are reported ($n = 36$).

b A summary scale was correlated with support for the farm labor movement. Specific variables in the scale which correlated with support are indicated.

Figure 4.5: Influences in Farmworker Support for the Farm Labor Movement[a]

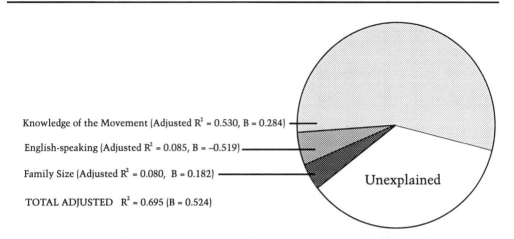

Knowledge of the Movement (Adjusted R^2 = 0.530, B = 0.284)

English-speaking (Adjusted R^2 = 0.085, B = –0.519)

Family Size (Adjusted R^2 = 0.080, B = 0.182)

TOTAL ADJUSTED R^2 = 0.695 (B = 0.524)

Unexplained

[a] Figures represent the results of stepwise regression using all variables that were significantly correlated with support for the farm labor movement. Only items that are significant at the 0.05 level or less are reported. Figures represent the proportion of the total Adjusted R^2 explained by the model (n = 36).

Figure 4.6: Combined Influences in Farmworker Support for the Farm Labor Movement[a]

their hopes for a just solution to their poor conditions and maltreatment. The survey of midwestern farmworkers indicates that these feelings have been widespread. This survey took place before FLOC had won contracts with Campbell Soup and Heinz. It not only indicates that the farmworkers have overwhelmingly endorsed FLOC but also that they have been *predisposed* to favor the movement. Just learning about FLOC and the UFW has generated positive attitudes.

It should be noted that there has been little systematic research on how farmworkers themselves view the farm labor movement. Howard (1974) raises the need to identify a social movement's base of support. Aside from public opinion polls, there has been insufficient focus on a movement's internal constituent population. Farm labor reform has been a major social issue for over a quarter of a century. But, to our knowledge, only two studies have systematically documented the representative views of farmworkers themselves about the movement, its goals, and methods. One is the 1983

Farmworkers attend a 1980 farm labor rally and mass at a Catholic church in San Juán, Texas. Many midwestern workers learned about FLOC in their home base areas from other farmworkers and from church and ethnic organizations. A 1983 survey of midwestern farmworkers documented widespread support for the FLOC movement at the height of its struggle with Campbell Soup. This study also demonstrated that farmworkers have been *predisposed* to support FLOC, and that just learning about the cause often generated their endorsement and active participation in the movement.

survey of midwestern farmworkers. The other is a survey of California farmworkers, which documents that there is a similar level of support for the farm labor movement across the United States (Barger and Reza 1985b, 1989).

Internal Forces in the FLOC Movement

Several sources provide insights into the internal forces that have enabled FLOC to achieve social reforms for midwestern farmworkers. We have reviewed the stories of several FLOC workers, and we have also examined the views of midwestern workers as a group. The summary of farmworkers' conditions in Chapter 2 and the history of FLOC discussed in Chapter 3 also provide important information. From these sources, we can identify nine internal forces which have helped FLOC achieve social reform, as indicated in Table 4.5. As we consider these in the context of the model of adaptation, we can distinguish both needs and resources.

Table 4.5: *Internal Forces in the FLOC Movement*

FARMWORKERS' NEEDS:
(1) Farmworkers' deprived conditions
(2) Farmworkers' powerlessness

FARMWORKERS' RESOURCES
(1) Farmworkers' motivations for reform
(2) Effective leadership
(3) A meaningful philosophy
(4) Achievable change goals
(5) Effective change methods
(6) A responsive organizational structure
(7) Farmworkers' support

Farmworkers' Needs

We have been able to identify two needs farmworkers have brought to the FLOC movement.

(1) Farmworkers' deprived conditions: One major set of obvious needs involves farmworkers' deprived subsistence conditions. Midwestern farmworkers have suffered poverty-level wages and substandard housing and sanitation facilities for decades. María Elena Ortega, for example, vividly remembers the converted chicken coops her family had to use for shelter. Many migrant families experience one health problem after another, which drain their meager resources. Child labor has been common since the families have been dependent upon the work of all members in order to survive. As with María Elena, children are in the fields from their earliest memory. Many farmworkers we have met over the years tell the same story. Almost all are dissatisfied about these conditions, and some speak with anger. Their deprived existence does not mean that they lack standards. Rather, the discrepancy between their conditions and those of other Americans produce feelings that range from defeat to frustration to bitterness.

Farmworkers' perceived needs for decent living and working conditions, then, have been a basic factor in their desire for farm labor reform. In their support for FLOC, they have had little to lose and much to gain.

(2) Farmworkers' powerlessness: Perhaps the most dire need of farmworkers has to do with their powerlessness to influence their conditions. The same disadvantages have been experienced by farm-

workers from generation to generation. Popular accounts, media documentaries, academic research, and government investigations have established these conditions for well over half a century. Yet farmworkers still suffer the same basic problems. Being disadvantaged and a minority group, they simply have not had the power to change these conditions on their own. They have remained dependent upon the goodwill and whims of others for their basic survival. Many like Baldemar Velásquez and Fernando Cuevas remember being angry and frustrated as children when their families were cheated and abused. "We were so helpless. We couldn't do anything about it," is a theme we have heard many times. One government report specifically concluded that the root cause of farmworkers' poor conditions has been their socioeconomic and political powerlessness (U.S. Senate Subcommittee on Migratory Labor 1970). Yet the same conditions have continued.

It should be noted that farmworkers' deprivations and powerlessness have had contradictory impacts on the FLOC movement. On the one hand, their marginal conditions have made many workers cautious about doing anything that would cause them to lose the meager subsistence they already have. On the other hand, their marginal conditions have provided a reason for actively seeking reforms. As the 1983 survey shows, however, most farmworkers have strongly endorsed FLOC as the most viable means for achieving positive changes. In many ways, they have realized that united they *do* have greater power.

Farmworkers' Resources

We have also been able to identify seven resources farmworkers have brought to the FLOC movement.

(1) Farmworkers' motivations for reform: As we have seen in their stories and in the survey, many midwestern farmworkers have exhibited strong convictions in support of FLOC, even when it has meant risking their livelihood. We have observed two factors which have motivated them to active involvement: worsening realities and raised expectations. On the one hand, a feeling that things were getting worse spurred, and continues to spur, many workers to action. Baldemar Velásquez states that a primary motivation for the 1978 strike by 2,300 farmworkers was a basic discontent. A number of events have led to this dissatisfaction. David Bermúdez, for example, reported that inflation in the previous decades had increased far beyond wages. In the 1983 survey, farmworkers reported a strong perception that they have experienced worse conditions than other

people in the Midwest. Many also felt threatened with displacement by mechanization. When mechanization did occur in the second year of the strike, it actually strengthened the motivation of many workers to get involved with the FLOC cause.

On the other hand, by 1978 many midwestern farmworkers had experienced an increase in their expectations. Most workers, for example, were familiar with the success of the United Farm Workers in California. The UFW's record had demonstrated that it was possible for farmworkers to influence their own conditions. Some midwestern workers have also told us that the success of the Warren strike had raised their hopes. When FLOC called for talks with the companies and growers in 1978, many workers believed there might really be an opportunity for meaningful changes. These expectations were dashed when the companies and growers ignored FLOC's call. Shortly thereafter, two thousand FLOC workers voted to strike, an action which ultimately led to farm labor reform in the Midwest. Similar hopes and frustrations are evident themes in the stories of many farmworkers with whom we have talked. The experience of worsening conditions and the disappointment of raised expectations appear to be clear motivations in the farmworkers' active support of FLOC.

(2) Effective leadership: Another resource for change has been the quality of the FLOC leadership. Baldemar Velásquez and Fernando Cuevas, in particular, have shown a deep conviction for farmworkers' rights and justice. They have also exhibited a vision about what can be accomplished and a sense of self-sacrifice in seeking these goals. Over the years, there has been some self-selection in the people who have been at the core of FLOC. We have observed a pattern of self-sacrifice in their commitment to the cause. They have also had a high level of tolerance and patience in following their vision throughout a long struggle with many obstacles.

In addition, FLOC leaders have shown a great deal of creativity in their efforts. For example, the Campbell boycott simply changed the rules in FLOC's relations with agribusiness. The traditional rules benefited those already in power. But the boycott took the issue to the larger court of public opinion, where popular values have supported the farmworkers' cause. Another example of creativity is the idea of three-way contracts, which has set a new precedent in labor history. The same is true of the idea of the Dunlop Commission, which acts as a private labor relations board transcending state and other boundaries. Such creativity is also evident in continuing FLOC efforts, like the building of cooperative ties with Mexican labor unions.

Another important trait of FLOC's leaders has been an ability to organize people and activities around the movement's goals. FLOC has had to use limited resources as effectively and efficiently as possible. During the strike, boycott, rallies, march on Camden, corporate campaign, conventions, farm elections, contract negotiations, contract administration, and membership development, activities had to be planned and coordinated. Whenever such events occurred, daily planning sessions were held every morning by the core staff. Activity and logistical tasks were identified and responsibilities assigned. Even more important, people had to be motivated to make the extra efforts and to bear the extra hardships in order to achieve needed reforms. The examples set by the leaders were important in this motivation, but they also challenged, encouraged, and supported people to give their best for the cause. Fernando Cuevas, David Bermúdez, and many other farmworkers have told us about being inspired to new actions by Baldemar Velásquez. Like José Hinojosa, many farmworkers also talk about Fernando Cuevas' convictions and efforts inspiring them to new efforts with FLOC.

At the core of those who have sustained the FLOC movement have been its leaders. They are leaders not because they have exercised formal authority but because others have chosen to follow them. This includes not only farmworkers but FLOC's many supporters in churches, labor unions, political offices, and local boycott committees. The quality of this leadership is recognized by the MacArthur Fellowship awarded to Baldemar Velásquez in 1989 and the Bannerman Fellowship awarded to Fernando Cuevas in 1990. It is even more evident in FLOC's achievements in farm labor reform.

(3) A meaningful philosophy: A meaningful and effective ideology has proven to be another internal force that has directed the FLOC movement. At the center of FLOC's vision has been a labor philosophy. This view looks at farmworkers literally as "workers." FLOC sees farmworkers as having been denied basic working rights and benefits, unlike other Americans. The farm labor movement, then, attributes much of farmworkers' problems to their own economic and political powerlessness. Others, they believe, have made key decisions that affect farmworkers' lives, and farmworkers have been denied a voice in determining their own conditions.

FLOC's philosophy has also emphasized social justice. This view sees farmworkers as human beings who deserve personal dignity and the right to pursue a better life for their families. Farmworkers generally hold the same basic values as others in American culture. As FLOC sees it, a major cause of their deprived conditions is the selfish accumulation of wealth by those with socioeconomic power. Farmworkers have seen crew leaders, growers, and agribusinesses exploiting the workers' labor for their own material gain. Greatest of all is the injustice of being subjected to the decisions and vested interests of others, with no meaningful voice in determining their own conditions.

The definition of the problem also serves to define the solutions. Given FLOC's views of farmworkers' problems, the solution is seen as winning the right to labor organizing and collective bargaining. The FLOC movement has thus emphasized the goal of direct negotiations between farmworkers and the growers and agribusinesses who benefit from their labor. This calls for farmworkers being equal parties in decisions that involve their labor and conditions. This does not mean they will get everything they want, of course. But they alone have the right to say what they want and what they are willing to give up.

(4) Achievable change goals: FLOC's ideology has provided the basis for a clear and achievable primary change goal. FLOC has sought to *reform* the agricultural system in the Midwest, not destroy it. It has sought to achieve for farmworkers those basic rights and benefits enjoyed by other American workers. FLOC has worked for farmworkers to share in core American opportunities and norms. It has also sought to achieve these ends through legitimate, nonviolent means, within the boundaries of basic American values. A specific objective in seeking this goal has been the three-way labor contracts. Other objectives to achieve reform have included building farmworkers into a cohesive movement organization, promoting leadership development among its members, mobilizing external support for the boycott, and building alliances with Mexican labor unions. Specific activities of the FLOC movement, from the march on Camden to the winter organizing of Dean Foods workers, have been guided by these goals and objectives. Maintaining a clear focus on achievable goals and objectives has helped FLOC maximize its energy and limited material resources.

(5) Effective change methods: FLOC has also been effective in its methods to achieve the reform goals. FLOC has been particularly successful at mobilizing both internal support among farmworkers and external support in the larger American society. Specific methods have included labor organizing, a workers' strike, a boycott, public demonstrations and marches, and a corporate campaign. FLOC has also used education campaigns to inform both farmworkers and the public of the issues and the legitimacy of its position. "We have consciously followed the lead of César Chávez, Mohandas Gandhi,

and Martin Luther King," Baldemar Velásquez says. "We are committed to the principle of nonviolence in all of our activities." As a reform movement, FLOC has followed those means that are basically legitimate. That is, FLOC has worked within the acceptable boundaries of the American value system. At the same time, it has sought to expand that value system to include farmworkers.

(6) A responsive organizational structure: Another resource has been FLOC's organizational structure and processes. There have been problems of burnout and turnover in the central staff. Out of necessity, however, FLOC's organization has been flexible over the years. The core leadership and staff have provided direction and continuity. But FLOC has regularly had to be fluid in its operations. Particularly in the period of the strike and boycott before winning contracts, human and material resources have had to be concentrated on the primary issue at the time. This has maximized the management of limited resources in achieving large-scale changes.

During major events like an organizing campaign or convention, FLOC has followed a system of daily debriefing meetings of central leaders and staff. The previous day's activities are reviewed and evaluated, and the coming day's activities are planned. This has kept people at all levels fully informed. It has also ensured that decisions result from effectively considering all relevant factors.

When it legally incorporated as a labor union in 1979, FLOC adopted a formal structure with a defined membership and officers with designated powers. As it is now, major decisions usually evolve in intense discussions among the core staff with the top leaders setting the tone and direction. Ordinarily, implementation of decisions has been decentralized, however. FLOC members have been able to provide input into decisions and activities through a number of forums. These include house and camp meetings, constitutional conventions, and various planning committees.

FLOC has continued to evolve its structure over the years. Organizing a constitutional convention, for example, takes a great deal of planning and coordination. In FLOC conventions, standard procedures and rules of order have been used to manage deliberations. These include having formal nominations and using resolution committees to prepare and present statements of the union's positions on key issues. Logistical arrangements are anticipated in advance, and people are assigned specific responsibilities. Regular staff meetings help coordinate activities throughout the event. As we have attended FLOC conventions, retreats, rallies, marches, and other events over the years, we have been impressed by the democratic processes involved. All participants generally have an opportunity to voice their ideas and views, and differences are usually discussed openly. The consensus process is the norm in making decisions. Where circumstances call for the leadership to make decisions on their own, this is done with a broad understanding of the issues and implications.

In recent years, a major activity has been contract administration. FLOC holds special workshops for its field staff to train them in their responsibilities. It has also developed activities such as house and camp meetings to educate workers about their contractual rights and to get input into contract negotiations. Special training sessions for camp representatives have also been organized to make the organization effective at the local level.

FLOC has achieved a remarkable level of organization over the years. It has been able to organize over five thousand farmworkers into an effective operational structure. This is a population that is particularly difficult to organize, since many are mobile, isolated, and disenfranchised. FLOC, however, has succeeded in uniting these people to work together for their common good. FLOC's structure is now more complex than in the early years. It has, however, continued to exhibit the qualities of flexibility and effectiveness as in the past.

(7) Farmworkers' support: A crucial internal force in the FLOC movement has been the support it has received from farmworkers themselves. As we have emphasized earlier, a social movement cannot succeed without a solid base of support in the group that it represents, particularly where it involves a minority group with goals of nonviolent reform. FLOC would have had little credibility without the endorsement and support of its constituents. A movement is a *social* phenomenon because it involves mass action by the group seeking change.

The overall level of internal support has important implications for a movement, its goals, and its methods (Gusfield 1970: 10; Howard 1974: 1). The degree to which a constituent population endorses and actively supports a movement can have an impact upon its credibility, effectiveness, and ultimate success. For example, at the height of the Campbell Soup boycott, the company charged that FLOC had no followers among farmworkers themselves. To test this assertion was one reason we conducted the 1983 survey (Barger and Reza 1984a, 1984b). On the other hand, the Teamsters in California have lacked a real support base among farmworkers (Walsh and Craypo 1979; Friedland and Thomas 1974). This has aroused political opposition and has even cost the Teamsters their "sweetheart" contracts with agribusinesses.

FLOC member Manuel Moreno participates at a strike line in Ohio during the summer of 1981. Manuel was permanently disabled when he was sprayed with methyl bromide, a powerful pesticide, which put him in a coma for several months and afterwards continued to cause periodic seizures. Though unable to work and left without income, he devoted his efforts to the FLOC cause. In appealing to field workers to join the strike, he would cite his condition as an example of how the growers and corporations cared little for farmworkers. The personal sacrifice and commitment of midwestern farmworkers like Manuel sustained the FLOC struggle during the Campbell strike and boycott.

The stories of midwestern farmworkers and the 1983 survey clearly indicate that FLOC has had a solid base in its constituent population. Midwestern workers went on strike. They worked on the boycott effort. They marched 560 miles to Camden. They voted overwhelmingly in farm elections to be represented by FLOC. They universally ratified new contracts. When the movement needed people to organize workers and events, complete necessary tasks, and show solidarity, there were always farmworkers who voluntarily got the job done. For all its other resources, FLOC could not have achieved its successes without the active and wholehearted support of midwestern farmworkers. In the long run, these are the people who have ultimately achieved farm labor reform.

The Internal Potentials of the FLOC Movement

As we have pointed out, one set of forces involved in systems adaptation is the internal potentials of a group involved in social change. It is hard to envision that FLOC could have achieved significant reforms without the important needs and resources midwestern farmworkers have brought to the movement.

Factors like leadership, ideology, organizational structure, and the support of midwestern farmworkers themselves have preselected what directions and reforms were possible for FLOC and have set the boundaries for making changes in the system. If farmworkers were not deprived and powerless, for example, FLOC would not have had the justice issues that were important in mobilizing the support of churches. Without effective leadership and a clear philosophy, FLOC would not have been able to organize farmworkers.

It is important to remember, however, that internal potentials do not exist in isolation. They are important in initiating changes in the group's external environment and in responding to external challenges. An example of this is the strong internal support for FLOC among farmworkers. With a secure support base, FLOC has been able to devote much of its limited resources to mobilize external allies and supporters. Some time and energy is necessary to maintain and expand its foundation among farmworkers, of course. Still, FLOC is able to use its limited resources efficiently in seeking reforms in its social environment. The strong internal support also establishes FLOC's credibility and moral credentials in dealings with external allies and opponents. FLOC can call upon help from external supporters assured that it legitimately represents midwestern farmworkers. Church, labor, and political leaders can cite this legitimacy in their support for the farm labor movement. Opponents also have to consider FLOC's legitimacy. For example, Campbell Soup eventually had to recognize that the farmworkers' support for FLOC was likely to persist. This undoubtedly influenced the company to assess the costs of long-term resistance to FLOC. FLOC's clear representation of midwestern farmworkers strengthened its bargaining position.

Midwestern farmworkers and FLOC have possessed essential internal potentials in achieving social reform. A reform movement, however, must also deal with external challenges. We must examine *both* internal and external forces to fully understand social change. With this in mind, we will now turn to those factors in FLOC's societal environment that have directed the movement's course.

CHAPTER 5

The Social Environment
of the FLOC Movement

Social change is not solely a matter of a particular group altering its own ways. The goals, needs, motives, and resources of a group can only partially explain change. As noted in the concept of social adaptation, forces external to the group also direct the course of change. Environmental conditions include both constraints and opportunities that operate upon a group's alternatives. These external conditions must also be examined if we are to have a comprehensive and balanced understanding of social change.

One major principle for those seeking social change is that they must "recognize the functional relationships that exist between issues, and between their community and the general social structure. They know that their problems are not peculiar to themselves and that their communities do not comprise little isolated worlds" (Alinsky 1969:62).

The social environment is particularly important in understanding reform movements involving minority and disadvantaged groups in pluralistic societies. There are three paradoxes in such situations. First, because the movement seeks to make social changes, it will automatically impact upon other social groups. Some of these groups will be threatened by any changes (Alinsky 1969:132). Thus the very existence of the movement will stimulate opposition to its goals. Some opponents are likely to be formidable, with vested economic and political interests.

The second paradox is that the movement is not trying to change the basic type of society. In fact, it accepts the general values and norms, even though it currently does not realize such standards. The group thus seeks to share in the opportunities and benefits of other segments in the society. In the civil rights movement, for example, African Americans have sought the same educational, employment, and other opportunities as Anglos. The group is therefore committed to seeking change through legitimate means.

The third paradox is that a minority and deprived group is only a small part of the whole society. Its disadvantaged conditions indicate that the group has not had the economic or political power to make desired changes on its own (Alinsky 1969:234–235; Katz 1974).

A reform movement by a disadvantaged minority group faces a formidable challenge. It seeks to make changes legitimately from a powerless base against established interests. To succeed against the very structures that have deprived the group involves two critical tasks:

On the one hand, *the group must mobilize the support of other segments of society*. Since it cannot effect changes on its own, it must call on others to help counterbalance its powerlessness.

On the other hand, *a reform movement must overcome opposition to its goals*. This can be done in several ways. One is to reduce any threats perceived by an opponent and thus eliminate the source of opposition. Another means is to render the opponents ineffective by neutralizing their legitimacy and socioeconomic power. A third means is to make any opposition too costly in economic and political terms.

In the balance, then, a major challenge for a reform group is to mobilize enough external support to neutralize opposition (Alinsky 1969, 1971; Zald and Ash 1966; Zald and McCarthy 1979a, 1979b; McCarthy and Zald 1977; Freeman 1979; also see Wallace 1956). As we have seen, the FLOC movement was successful in meeting this challenge against great odds. We will now look more closely at those external forces involved in the FLOC movement and how they influenced the directions of events. We will first examine the opposition to FLOC, then the support FLOC received from other segments of the society, including the general public. We will assess how these forces impacted on the FLOC movement and also how FLOC impacted on them.

Opponents of the FLOC Movement

The FLOC movement has faced a number of opponents in its struggle for improved farmworker rights and conditions. One Catholic nun from Wisconsin, for example, condemned FLOC as undermining the American family farmer. Several officials of a union that had organized workers in Campbell processing plants also made negative statements. Since there was so much support from many Catholic organizations and labor unions, however, such opposition had little impact. In general, there were two major opponents to the FLOC movement. One was composed of midwestern growers who used farm labor to produce specialty crops. The other consisted of the large corporations which processed and marketed foods from these crops.

Growers

Some of the most bitter opposition to FLOC has come from the Ohio tomato growers whose operations were the focus of farmworker strikes and pickets. In its early years, FLOC focused its efforts on those growers with whom farmworkers had direct contact. This is understandable since that was the level at which farmworkers most directly experienced maltreatment. The early focus aroused strong reactions by growers. Over the years of the Campbell strike, there were many cases of growers' hostility. As we have seen, one grower sprayed a FLOC picket line with pesticides. Another drove his pickup truck into a picket line, injuring several farmworkers. Hoping to avoid dealing with FLOC, Campbell's growers followed the company's mandate and mechanized their tomato harvest. Some even dropped their tomato operations.

Not all growers have been hostile, of course. But the bitterness of some is understandable, even though we may disagree with their reactions. Many family farmers operate with a high overhead and debt load. Their economic survival is therefore easily threatened by organized disruption of their operations. FLOC's activities also impinged upon farmers' strong identity of self-sufficiency and independence. While their feelings may be understandable, the actions of some growers were extreme. Spraying picket lines with dangerous chemicals and burning crosses in front of strikers' quarters are destructive reactions. Such actions certainly validated farmworkers' claims of discrimination and maltreatment (Johnson 1976; McDonagh 1955; Moore 1965; Perry and Snyder 1971).

The effects of grower hostility toward FLOC were at times formidable. FLOC leaders and workers had a hard time finding work from any grower, even those producing specialty crops for corporations other than Campbell Soup. This blacklisting made it difficult for many farmworkers to support themselves and their families. The growers were also integrated into local communities and so gener-

ated widespread animosity toward FLOC and its workers. Farmworkers reported being refused service and receiving verbal abuse in
many stores in the area. The social atmosphere in the strike area
was thus tense and hostile.

It is interesting to note that the attitudes of many growers have
changed since the contracts with FLOC were signed. They have
found that the three-way contracts also give them a stronger voice
in deciding their own conditions. They are now in a position to argue for higher rates for their products. They receive larger acreage,
and their credit ratings have improved. Some have also received sup-
plemental funds to improve migrant housing.

Campbell Soup

Another FLOC opponent was the Campbell Soup Company, which
was the focus of an eight-year strike and boycott. Early in the conflict, the company created a special office to deal with the farm labor
issue. This office produced a steady stream of statements over the
years, in response to FLOC charges. As we have seen, Campbell at
first denied any connection with farmworkers. It stated that its relations were with the growers, and it could not interfere with the
internal operations of these subcontractors. In other efforts, the company donated funds to migrant social service agencies in the strike
area. It also urged its growers to improve farmworker housing and
other conditions.

Eventually, Campbell Soup agreed to formal meetings with FLOC.
In these first meetings, however, it tried to focus on improving migrant conditions, rather than discussing possibilities for labor negotiations. Finally, however, the company agreed to labor negotiations
with FLOC. As indicated earlier, the company then pressured its
growers to form associations and become a party to the agreements.
It also participated in the establishment of the Dunlop Commission
as a private labor relations board.

The opposition of Campbell Soup was a serious obstacle to
FLOC's achieving its goals. The company had considerable assets to
fight the FLOC movement, compared to FLOC's limited resources.
Campbell was able to mandate mechanization of tomato harvests
and mounted publicity campaigns against FLOC. In general, however, FLOC usually took the initiative, introducing new issues and
charges into the conflict. Campbell's energies were largely expended
in *re*acting to FLOC.

Once labor contracts were a reality, FLOC leaders report, Campbell Soup generally proved to be a responsible and cooperative party.

For example, Campbell worked with its pickle growers to phase out the sharecropping system. The company was also cooperative in re-negotiating contracts with FLOC when the first ones were due to expire.

FLOC leaders report that Heinz has always been a cooperative business associate. One reason for this is that there was no history of conflict with Heinz, which remained on the sidelines during FLOC's struggle with Campbell. Also, Heinz undoubtedly desired to avoid the extended and unproductive conflict experienced by Campbell Soup. So after the Campbell issue was settled, Heinz readily entered into the negotiations with FLOC and signed contracts. We have observed that most Heinz representatives with whom we have had contact have shown more social awareness, but it is hard to say whether this has been a cause of the company's cooperative attitude. It is clear, however, that FLOC, as its leaders have reported, has experienced productive relations with Heinz since the first official contact between the two parties in 1987.

Effects of the Opposition

FLOC was eventually successful in achieving its goals. However, it took eight years of conflict to overcome the combined opposition of Campbell Soup and its growers. FLOC workers encountered hostilities on many levels. In the fields, many growers and crew leaders were abusive to FLOC organizers and to farmworkers sympathetic to FLOC. In the local communities, stores refused to serve them and the Putnam County, Ohio, sheriff's forces harassed FLOC strikers. On a national level, FLOC and its supporters devoted considerable energies to the boycott. Many FLOC workers suffered abuse and deprivation during this time, though they now look back with pride at their perseverance.

It must be remembered, however, that Campbell Soup and its growers were only a part of the farmworkers' social environment. Other segments of the American environment were supportive to FLOC. They contributed their socioeconomic power to overcoming the opposition and to achieving reforms for farmworkers.

Supporters of the FLOC Movement

Over the eight years of the Campbell strike and boycott, FLOC was able to mobilize a broad range of allies and supporters, as indicated in Table 5.1. Groups who helped FLOC achieve fundamental farm

Table 5.1: *Types of Groups Supporting FLOC during the Campbell Soup Strike and Boycott*[a]

AFL-CIO, state councils of Indiana and Ohio
American Federation of State, County, and Municipal Employees,
　　state councils of Michigan, New York, Ohio, and Oregon
American Federation of Teachers, Local 3950
American Friends Service Committee
American Postal Workers Union, Indiana
Archdioceses of Cincinnati, Detroit, St. Paul/Minneapolis, and
　　Columbus
Bowling Green State University Student Government Association
Brothers of the Holy Cross, South Bend
Chicano/Latino Student Culture Center, Minneapolis
Christian Church (Disciples of Christ) Regional Assembly, South Bend
Church Federation of Greater Indianapolis
Communication Workers of America, Local 11505
Consumers League of Ohio
Council of Churches, Indiana and Ohio
Democratic Party, Oregon
Detroit City Council
Indiana State Council of the National Organization of Women
League of United Latin American Citizens, Corpus Christi
National Association of Farm Workers Associations
National Lawyers Guild, Executive Board
Notre Dame University student body
United Auto Workers, Executive Board
United Methodist Church, Board of Church and Society
United Methodist Church, Conferences of Northern Illinois and
　　New York
United Church of Christ, Southern California Conference
United Farm Workers of America

---

[a] In all, over 200 religious, labor, and other organizations formally endorsed FLOC and/or the boycott of Campbell Soup. In addition, FLOC estimates that more than 1,200 public and private schools dropped participation in the Campbell labels program, in support of the boycott.

labor reforms include religious organizations, organized labor, political figures, local support committees, and the general public.

Religious Organizations

Many kinds of religious organizations became involved in supporting FLOC issues. The National Farm Worker Ministry (NFWM) has one of the longest records of supporting the farm labor movement.

Religious supporters at the 1991 FLOC convention include (*left to right*) Olgha Sandman, executive director of the Illinois Farm Worker Ministry, Sister Pat Drydyk, executive director of the National Farm Worker Ministry, Millie Moser Smith, Church Women United, and Cynthia Ikuta, United Church of Christ. The support of religious organizations has been important in the success of the FLOC movement. The visible presence of church leaders on FLOC strike lines and at rallies was an inspiration to FLOC workers. Church endorsements of the boycott served to legitimize the FLOC cause, and exerted considerable moral pressure on Campbell Soup to recognize its social responsibilities to farmworkers.

For example, the NFWM and its affiliates in several states circulated an informational newsletter to keep general supporters informed about issues and boycotts. They provided transportation for farmworker leaders to attend meetings with the heads of organizations considering endorsement of boycotts. They also actively participated in organizing workers and supporters in Texas and Florida.

Many other religious organizations have also supported FLOC. Interdenominational organizations like the Indiana Council of Churches, the Ohio Council of Churches, and the National Council of Churches formally endorsed the Campbell boycott in support of the FLOC cause. A number of Catholic bishops across the country also endorsed FLOC. Numerous local churches and synagogues, orders of Catholic nuns, and national denominational groups like the Christian Church (Disciples of Christ) actively advocated the Campbell boycott. Protestant and Catholic agencies provided funds for specific farm labor activities. They also held fund-raising activities, and collected food and other goods for strikers. They informed their members about the boycott issues through church bulletins and newsletters. The presence of nuns, priests, and ministers in strike lines and demonstrations acted as an effective deterrence to violence. Also, after rallies and demonstrations, local churches would frequently hold religious services for the FLOC workers and their supporters.

Perhaps one of the most moving acts of religious support occurred in the summer of 1983. As already indicated, FLOC workers had marched 560 miles from Toledo, Ohio, to Campbell's headquarters in Camden, New Jersey. At the end of the march, a large mass for the farmworkers was held at the Camden Catholic cathedral. During the service, fifteen priests washed the feet of the marchers. This event was an inspiration to both the farmworkers and their supporters.

The support by religious groups had a number of impacts. The endorsements were an important source of encouragement to the FLOC workers. Also, the funds the groups raised and food they provided helped sustain the strikers, who were sacrificing much of their annual earning time for their cause.

Perhaps the most important impact was the *moral* force the religious community brought to the issue. Most important, the backing of religious groups gave FLOC considerable credibility. The social pressure exerted by this support was critical since it tarnished Campbell's popular image. The company could not really attack or neutralize this religious force without further affecting its own credibility. Campbell Soup was hard-pressed to counter the legitimacy religious groups gave to the boycott. An excellent example of this occurred when the the Church Federation of Greater Indianapolis openly endorsed the boycott in front of Campbell's corporate representative. Such actions were powerful statements that continually put the company on the defensive. It is important to note that the Archdiocese of Boston and the National Council of Churches played an important role in getting Campbell Soup to talk directly with FLOC.

The religious support also had a moral effect on the FLOC farmworkers. As said before, the funds and food collected directly contributed to the well-being of the workers. Yet the visible presence of the religious community conveyed that the workers' desire for dignity and justice was valid. This encouraged the workers in the legitimacy of their cause and stimulated them to further their sacrifices and efforts. The support of religious leaders and organizations was perhaps the most effective among FLOC's allies because of the social impact of its moral force.

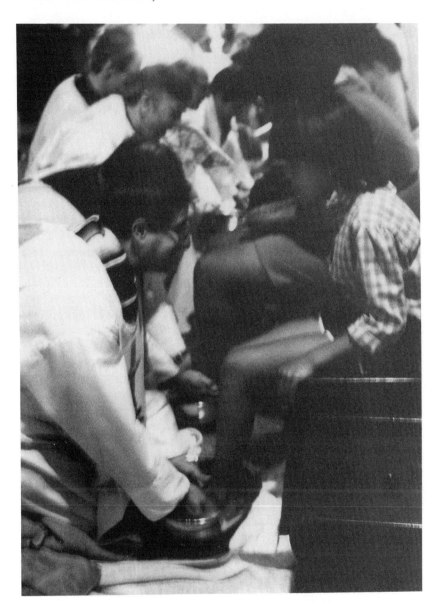

A mass was held in Camden, New Jersey, in 1983 for FLOC farmworkers who had marched 560 miles to the headquarters of Campbell Soup to present their grievances. Perhaps one of the most moving events in the FLOC movement was when about fifteen priests washed the feet of the farmworkers during the mass. This event inspired both farmworkers and supporters to new commitments to FLOC's cause.

Organized Labor

Another group of FLOC allies was organized labor. Large international unions took strong stands of support for FLOC. These included prominent unions such as the United Auto Workers (UAW) and the American Federation of State, County, and Municipal Employees (AFSCME). Many labor unions identified the FLOC cause with their own history. Senior union officials can remember when child labor, poverty wages, hazardous working conditions, and other social ills were common among their own ranks. A labor movement had successfully eliminated these problems, just as the FLOC movement was seeking to do. Union leaders were therefore sympathetic to FLOC's philosophy of labor organizing, equal bargaining powers, and negotiated contracts to resolve workers' problems. Union locals and international boards formally endorsed FLOC, donated strike funds, organized members for rallies, and actively informed their members of the boycott.

One example of significant labor support is that given by the United Auto Workers (UAW) in Central Indiana. UAW Region 3 officials like Dallas Sells and Bill Osos came to FLOC's aid on a number of occasions. They sponsored a luncheon for Baldemar Velásquez and other FLOC leaders so that they could meet with the heads of major unions in the area. They arranged for a briefing on the FLOC strike and boycott at a regional convention. The local UAW Community Action Program (CAP) Council, led by Ed Yates, printed tens of thousands of fliers and newsletters for FLOC supporters. Many locals in UAW Region 3 actively informed their members of the boycott, particularly where the Campbell labels program in area schools were concerned. The UAW took the initiative in demonstrating their solidarity with FLOC, and this had a major impact in the central Indiana area.

Organized labor thus had several impacts in support of FLOC. They helped to materially support FLOC, and they enlisted thousands of their members as active boycotters. They also enhanced the legitimacy of FLOC as a labor movement.

Political Figures

FLOC supporters have also included political groups and politicians. For example, prominent public figures such as the Reverend Jesse Jackson, Governor Richard Celeste of Ohio, and Senator Neal Zimmers, also of Ohio, stood behind FLOC's goals. A number of city councils around the country passed resolutions in support of FLOC and the boycott. Local civil rights leaders in Ohio took clear stands with FLOC, participating in rallies and farmworker conventions. All this political backing provided further legitimacy for the FLOC cause.

Local Support Committees

As indicated in the history of FLOC, another set of important supporters were the local volunteer committees organized across the country. These groups represented FLOC on a local level. Local support committees were formed and operated primarily on their own, but they were directly linked to FLOC. FLOC would set objectives, like convincing schools not to participate in the Campbell labels program. It would put out calls for help with the boycott, the corporate campaign, fund-raising, and lobbying political figures. FLOC organized retreats for the support committees to inform them of current issues and to develop and coordinate strategies. Also, to keep supporters informed, FLOC issued regular boycott newsletters. In addition, the FLOC staff and support committees were in regular touch by telephone and visits. FLOC leaders were often able to attend events organized by local supporters, bringing a personal presence for the cause.

The local support committees were entirely made up of volunteers. They came from many backgrounds and included teachers, lawyers, union members, church workers, and students. The supporters were sympathizers with the FLOC cause and generally informed themselves about the issues. They organized efforts to lobby local churches and unions to support the boycott, sponsored rallies, and raised money and goods for the striking farmworkers. The particular committee structures and activities varied widely, and supporters exercised considerable initiative in how they contributed to FLOC's efforts. Each group drew upon the particular strengths of their own members, resources, and settings.

The Indianapolis Farm Worker Support Committee was one such volunteer group (Barger and Reza 1985a, 1987). It was founded in 1980 by FLOC sympathizers who were teachers, social workers, clergy, former farmworkers, and union members. In addition to public education activities, the committee was instrumental in enlisting the first statewide labor organization (the Indiana AFL-CIO) and the first statewide religious organization (the Indiana Council of Churches) in support of the FLOC cause.

An example of support committee activities was a project to encourage local schools not to participate in the Campbell labels pro-

gram. The labels program provided educational and athletic equipment to schools and churches, in exchange for a designated number
of labels from the company's products. In 1981, FLOC decided the
program provided a highly visible opportunity to raise the boycott
issues. The Indianapolis support committee had previously worked
with the Catholic school system, and all schools in the archdiocese
dropped the labels program. In response to the FLOC initiative, the
committee decided to encourage public schools not to participate in
the labels program. An initial survey of local schools was conducted
to identify which ones were involved with the program.

Drawing upon personal experience of its members, the committee
focused on parent-teacher groups as the most effective point of in-
tervention. The general goal was to win over public support by informing people about the issues in a manner that was relevant to
those being addressed. Committee members who were teachers and
parents felt that little cooperation was likely to be received from
school boards, superintendents, or principals. Parent groups, however, were more likely to be responsive if appropriately approached.
Since labels were actually collected by parents anyway, a focused
effort to inform them of the issues was likely to be most effective.
A multichannel approach was devised to reach parents by crosscut-
ting many different community settings. The main effort focused on
using the internal communication channels of community-based
organizations to reach parents. Local teachers' associations, interfaith church organizations, labor unions, and other community
groups were approached. Each was asked to help inform their members about the issues, particularly parents with children in schools
collecting labels (which were identified). An effort was also made to
inform the community at large. Press releases were issued, and appearances were made on radio and television talk shows concerned
with religious and minority affairs.

In the spring of 1982, a follow-up survey of all local schools re-
vealed that significant changes had occurred, as indicated in
Table 5.2. In the central city schools, 43 percent of those schools
collecting labels had dropped the program. This proved to be a sta-
tistically significant change. Furthermore, awareness of the boycott
issue had risen from 9 percent in the fall to 82 percent in the spring.
Most important, however, was that over half (52 percent) of those
schools which had learned about the boycott issue had stopped collecting labels. The success of targeting the labels program indicates
the responsiveness of Americans to farm labor issues. It also indicates that much of the American public is predisposed to supporting
the farm labor cause, once they learn of the issues.

Table 5.2: *Changes in Participation in the Campbell Labels School Program*[a]

PARTICIPATION November 1981	39%
PARTICIPATION April 1982	23%

[a]$X^2 = 36$, with 1 df, p = .002. Figures represent the reduced participation in the Campbell labels program by the 79 Indianapolis central city primary schools, as a result of the applied project in support of the farmworkers' boycott (Barger and Reza 1985a).

In summary, many groups came to the aid of the FLOC cause. These groups represented a broad spectrum of the American society. They enlisted support for FLOC at home, church, work, and school. There was widespread support for FLOC in different segments of society. This was particularly true where the boycott against Campbell Soup was concerned. Members from almost all social segments in the country were involved. Such support was critical to the success of the FLOC movement.

A Public Survey on Farm Labor Reform

The support of distinct social groups is important in establishing the legitimacy of a movement like FLOC. However, this does not mean that the social segments such groups represent share the views of their leaders. Church and union leaders who endorsed FLOC, for example, may have erroneously assumed that their members held the same convictions. On the other hand, some leaders may have hesitated to take a stand on the issues because they erroneously assumed their members did not agree with certain social actions. There is a need, then, to understand the views of the general population. Social reform can affect many people across the larger society. We need to know how much different individuals actually support such changes.

This is particularly important where a reform movement includes public actions like a consumers' boycott. Boycotts have been an important part of the farm labor movement, where both the UFW and FLOC are concerned. As we have seen, the major rationale was that the combined socioeconomic power of millions of individuals can counterbalance the powerlessness of farmworkers. This in turn can overcome the economic and political power of the large agribusinesses. A consumers' boycott can be effective for two reasons. One is economic, where the targeted unit is financially jeopardized by reduced income. Much of this comes from reduced sales. It may also include lower prices paid by wholesalers and retailers, who are trying to reduce their own losses. The other reason boycotts can be effective is social. The targeted organization can lose popular and political support, as a result of the controversy in which it is involved. This can undermine conditions that may favor its operations. The UFW and FLOC thus argue that their boycotts have acted as a democratic vote in the marketplace. It sends a clear message to agricultural corporations that they must respect such societal norms as "justice" and "self-determination."

The endorsements of religious, labor, and other leaders are important in a consumers' boycott. The structure of their organizations they lead can be used to inform their members about the boycott and its issues. Also, they can use clearly defined organizational goals and philosophies to motivate their members to action. Church groups, for example, can appeal to a sense of "dignity" and "humanitarianism," and unions can raise the issues of "workers' rights." The success of a boycott, however, ultimately depends on the active support of individuals within the larger society. Religious and labor leaders, for example, may endorse certain social actions. But many consumers may not be members of these organizations or may not be swayed by their philosophies.

For a movement to depend on widespread popular support of its cause calls for three considerations. One is how to organize those rationales which best mobilize popular participation. A second is how to inform the population at large that a boycott exists and what the issues are. The third is how much the general populace is actually likely to participate in such a social action. The question that remains is how effective FLOC has been in these areas.

In order to document the representative views held by the general public concerning the FLOC issues, a public telephone survey was conducted in Indiana in 1982 (Barger and Haas 1983). A total of 385 people were interviewed, with an overall response rate of 70 percent.[1]

In the analysis of the survey data, four sets of factors concerning public views about the FLOC movement were examined. The first was people's *knowledge about farmworkers*. We were also interested in *knowledge about the farm labor movement*, about FLOC, its goals, and its methods. Another factor was public attitudes about the farm labor movement, particularly the degree of *endorsement* of FLOC, its goals, and its methods. The fourth factor concerned people's *active support* for the farm labor movement, particularly in terms of participation in boycotts in support of the farmworkers'

Table 5.3: *Popular Knowledge about Farmworkers* [a]

Think there are 5,000–10,000 farmworkers in the state [b]	24%
Think 85%–95% of farmworkers are migrants	10%
Think Texas or Florida is a primary home base for farmworkers	42%
Think most farmworkers are Mexican Americans	40%
Think at least 90% of farmworkers are U.S. citizens [c]	18%
Think 75%–85% of noncitizen workers are in the U.S. legally [d]	18%
KNOWLEDGEABLE ABOUT FARMWORKERS [e]	6%

[a] Figures represent awareness of the background and characteristics of midwestern farmworkers on the items indicated, based on responses to open-ended questions (n = 385).

[b] Records of the Indiana State Board of Health indicate that there were about 8,000 farmworkers in the state in 1982.

[c] This includes those born in the U.S. or naturalized citizens.

[d] Undocumented workers are estimated to be only a small proportion of midwestern farmworkers. Undocumented farmworkers tend to concentrate in border states like California and Texas and may even displace Mexican Americans into the migrant stream.

[e] Represents an awareness of at least 4 of the 7 items indicated.

cause. Other factors were also examined to determine how they collectively influence views about the farm labor movement. The survey findings indicate that the public has had several views that have important implications for the farm labor movement in the Midwest.

Knowledge of Farmworkers

The public has not been very aware of the backgrounds of farmworkers (Table 5.3). Only 24 percent of the respondents were able to give a reasonably accurate estimate of how many farmworkers were in the state. Less than half (40 percent) knew that most farmworkers in the state are Mexican Americans. In general, the public was only aware of about 6 percent of the six items measured.

Awareness that farmworkers experience disadvantaged conditions, however, has been more pronounced (Table 5.4). The majority of people correctly perceived that farmworkers have worse conditions than other people in Indiana. For example, 54 percent thought farmworkers experience more child labor, 61 percent believed they have substandard housing and sanitary facilities, and 56 percent

Table 5.4: *Popular Knowledge about Farmworker Conditions*[a]

Think farmworkers have a low annual income ($10,000 or less)	52%
Think farmworkers have substandard housing and sanitation facilities	61%
Think child labor is high among farmworkers	54%
Think farmworkers have poor education	58%
Think farmworkers have high exposure to hazardous pesticides	66%
Think farmworkers have high rates of diseases and health problems	55%
Think farmworkers are subjected to discrimination and prejudice	56%
KNOWLEDGEABLE ABOUT FARMWORKER CONDITIONS[b]	60%

[a] Figures represent those who stated farmworkers experience worse conditions than other people in Indiana, based on responses to closed questions (except the item on annual income, which was based on an open-ended question). The scale represents a sum of the variables indicated, measuring the degree of awareness. No relationship between variables is necessarily assumed ($n = 385$).
[b] Represents an awareness of at least 4 of the 7 items indicated.

thought they are subjected to discrimination and prejudice. The respondents were generally aware of about 60 percent of the seven conditions included. Even though the public may not have understood who farmworkers are, people seemed aware that farmworkers suffer deprived conditions.

Knowledge of the Farmworker Movement

The survey indicates that the public has had mixed knowledge about the farm labor movement, as indicated in Table 5.5. A strong majority of around two-thirds knew about the United Farm Workers or its former grape and lettuce boycotts. But less than a third were aware of FLOC or the Campbell Soup boycott, which represent the movement in their region. When these four items are considered together, the respondents were aware of about half (67 percent) of the organizations and events that represent the farmworker movement.

Endorsement of the Farmworker Movement

The survey indicates that there has been widespread popular endorsement of the farmworker movement. People strongly endorsed

Table 5.5: *Popular Knowledge about the Farm Labor Movement*[a]

Have heard of the United Farm Workers (UFW)	69%
Have heard of the Farm Labor Organizing Committee (FLOC)	32%
Have heard about the former UFW boycotts of grapes and lettuce	66%
Have heard about the FLOC boycott of Campbell Soup	22%
KNOWLEDGEABLE ABOUT THE FARM LABOR MOVEMENT[b]	67%

[a]Figures represent awareness of the farm labor movement on the items indicated (n = 385).
[b]Represents an awareness of at least 2 of the 4 items indicated.

basic labor rights for farmworkers (Table 5.6). These include minimum-wage earnings (90 percent), workers' compensation for job-related injuries (84 percent), and unemployment insurance (64 percent). They also endorsed the right to sue employers who violate occupational safety regulations (77 percent) and supported first choice of new mechanized jobs (58 percent) and job retraining (76 percent) when mechanization displaces workers. In general, there was an average endorsement of 82 percent of the eight rights considered in the survey.

An overwhelming majority of the public has also specifically approved of the farmworker movement (Table 5.7). Some 80 percent approved of organizations like FLOC and the UFW. Support was also expressed for their main goals, including collective bargaining for farmworkers (73 percent) and labor negotiations (78 percent). About half (48 percent) also approved of public boycotts, one of the main methods the movement has used to achieve its goals. The respondents on the average approved of 74 percent of the six items considered. This indicates that there has been a strong popular sympathy with the general purposes of the movement.

Active Support of the Farmworker Movement

The survey further indicates that there has been moderate public support of the farmworker movement, which was measured by participation in the UFW and FLOC boycotts (Table 5.8). About 10 percent of the Indiana public said they participated in the former UFW boycotts of table grapes and lettuce. These included about 15 percent of those who were aware of these boycotts. On the other hand, 2 percent said they were participating in the FLOC boycott of Camp-

Table 5.6: *Popular Endorsement of Farm Labor Rights*[a]

Earnings that average at least minimum wage rates	90%
Payment of full wages every payday[b]	83%
Workers' compensation for job-related injuries	84%
Unemployment insurance	64%
Access to restroom facilities in the fields	91%
Sue employers who violate occupational safety regulations	77%
First choice of new jobs created by agricultural mechanization when this eliminates old jobs	58%
Retraining programs for workers displaced by agricultural mechanization	76%
ENDORSEMENT OF FARM LABOR RIGHTS[c]	82%

[a]Figures represent approval of the farm labor movement on the items indicated (n = 385).
[b]This is in contrast to the common practice of withholding part of a worker's pay until the end of the season as a "bonus" for continuing work when piece-rate earnings are low.
[c]Represents a positive attitude toward at least 5 of the 8 items indicated.

Table 5.7: *Popular Endorsement of the Farm Labor Movement*[a]

Approve of the legal rights to labor organizing and collective bargaining for farmworkers	73%
Approve of organizations like UFW and FLOC trying to improve farmworkers' conditions and rights	80%
Agribusinesses whose products involve farmworkers' labor should negotiate with FLOC/UFW	78%
Approve of farmworkers' boycotts as a means to improve their conditions	48%
Schools should be informed about boycott issues before participating in the Campbell labels program	81%
Endorsement of basic labor rights for farmworkers[b]	82%
ENDORSEMENT OF THE FARM LABOR MOVEMENT[c]	74%

[a]Figures represent approval of the farm labor movement on the items indicated (n = 385).
[b]This figure represents those who endorse at least 5 of the 8 basic labor rights indicated in Table 5.6.
[c]Represents a positive attitude toward at least 4 of the 6 items indicated.

Table 5.8: *Popular Support for the Farm Labor Movement*[a]

Participated in the UFW boycotts of grapes and lettuce[b]	10%
Participated in the FLOC boycott of Campbell Soup[c]	2%
ACTIVE SUPPORT FOR THE FARM LABOR MOVEMENT[d]	11%

[a] Figures represent active support of the farm labor movement by participation in farmworker boycotts, the main means available to the general public ($n = 385$).
[b] Of those who were aware of these boycotts, 15% participated.
[c] Of those who were aware of this boycott, 8% participated.
[d] Represents an active involvement in at least 1 of the 2 items indicated.

bell Soup, 8 percent of those who were aware of it. There was an average participation of 11 percent in the boycotts of these two movement organizations. This suggests that much of the popular sympathy for the farm labor movement was largely latent and was not actively mobilized.

It should be noted, however, that the UFW's initial victories were gained with a popular participation of 12 percent in its original grape boycott and 11 percent in its lettuce boycott (L. Harris 1975). So even a modest proportion of public participation in boycotts can be effective because of the economic and social pressure exerted on targeted organizations. Such participation can also apply pressure on legislative and government officials to act on the issues involved. One of the most significant impacts of a successful boycott is that it provides broad legitimacy to a cause.

Influences in Popular Views about the Farmworker Movement

The survey data set was further analyzed, using Spearman's Rho correlation coefficients and stepwise regression analysis, to identify those factors which influence popular knowledge, endorsement, and active support of the farm labor movement:

(1) Knowledge of the farmworker movement: The data set was first examined to identify those factors that are *not* related to knowledge of the farmworker movement. As indicated in Figure 5.1, awareness of farmworkers' backgrounds and conditions and the demographic characteristics of ethnicity and socioeconomic status are not influences in this knowledge.

Only four demographic variables were related to knowledge, and all of these were weak or moderate influences. People who are older, currently or formerly married, more active in their religious group,

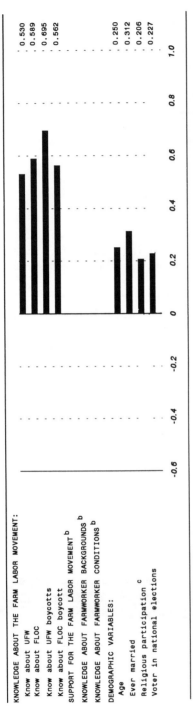

KNOWLEDGE ABOUT THE FARM LABOR MOVEMENT:	
Know about UFW	0.530
Know about FLOC	0.589
Know about UFW boycotts	0.695
Know about FLOC boycott	0.562
SUPPORT FOR THE FARM LABOR MOVEMENT [b]	
KNOWLEDGE ABOUT FARMWORKER BACKGROUNDS [b]	
KNOWLEDGE ABOUT FARMWORKER CONDITIONS [b]	
DEMOGRAPHIC VARIABLES:	
Age	0.250
Ever married	0.312
Religious participation [c]	0.206
Voter in national elections	0.227

-0.6   -0.4   -0.2   0   0.2   0.4   0.6   0.8   1.0

[a] Figures represent the relationship with a summary scale on knowledge about the farm labor movement, composed of the variables indicated in the first set of items. All figures represent Spearman's Rho correlation coefficient. Only correlations that are significant at the 0.05 level or less and that are stronger than 0.200 are reported ($n = 385$).

[b] A summary scale was correlated with knowledge of the farm labor movement. Specific variables in the scale which are correlated with knowledge are indicated.

[c] Frequency of participation in religious activities was coded from responses to a closed question as follows:

    1= Hardly ever

    2= Several times a year

    3= Several times a month

    4= Once a week or more

Figure 5.1: Influences in Popular Knowledge about the Farm Labor Movement[a]

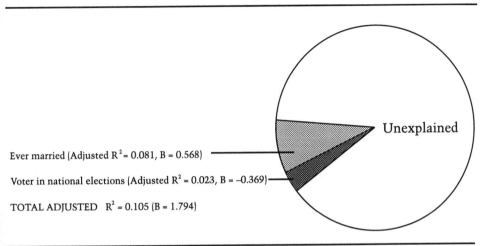

Ever married (Adjusted R^2 = 0.081, B = 0.568)

Voter in national elections (Adjusted R^2 = 0.023, B = –0.369)

TOTAL ADJUSTED R^2 = 0.105 (B = 1.794)

Unexplained

[a]Figures represent the results of stepwise regression using all variables that were significantly correlated with knowledge about the farm labor movement. Only items that are significant at the 0.05 level or less are reported. Figures represent the proportion of the total Adjusted R^2 explained by the model (n = 385).

Figure 5.2: Combined Influences in Popular Knowledge about the Farm Labor Movement[a]

and vote in national elections were generally more aware of the farm labor movement. These findings suggest that young adults less involved with social institutions have had less exposure to information about the farmworker movement.

When these variables were considered together, as indicated in Figure 5.2, only marital status and voting in national elections proved significant. These are only slight influences, however, accounting for only 11 percent of people's knowledge. In general, any lack of awareness about the farm labor movement seems rather evenly distributed across most segments of society.

The survey indicates that people become most informed about farmworker events through the mass media. A similar survey conducted in California, it should be noted, indicates that in-house publications, like newsletters of church and labor organizations, are effective channels for informing people about the farm labor cause (Barger 1987).

(2) Endorsement of the farmworker movement: When the data set was examined to identify factors *not* related to endorsement, several items were evident. As indicated in Figure 5.3, these include awareness of farmworkers' backgrounds and knowledge of FLOC or of particular boycotts. It is interesting to note that neither socioeconomic background nor political activity were related to endorsement. It should also be noted that knowledge of the farm labor movement is not related to endorsement.

A few factors, however, are moderately related to positive attitudes about the movement. These include awareness of farmworkers' deprived conditions and knowledge of the UFW boycotts. Youth, education, and living in more urban areas are also related to endorsement.

When these variables were considered together, as indicated in Figure 5.4, all except urban setting proved to have a moderate combined influence in popular endorsement of the farmworker movement. Youth is the most clear influence, with awareness of the farmworkers' conditions and knowledge of the UFW having slight influence. Together, these factors account for about 20 percent of the attitudes about the movement. These results indicate that the strong popular endorsement of the farmworker cause has been evenly distributed across most segments of society.

Widespread endorsement of the farm labor movement is clear in the survey results. This endorsement, however, seems to be based more in general social values rather than in specific farmworker issues.

(3) Active support of the farmworker movement: Figure 5.5 indicates that active support of the farm labor movement has also cut across most segments of society. No particular social characteristic identifies boycotters, except for living in urban areas. Given that the public has been generally sympathetic to the farm labor cause, two factors are moderately involved in participation in farmworker boycotts: endorsement of boycotts in support of the farm labor cause and awareness of previous UFW boycotts. It should also be noted that knowledge of farmworkers and their conditions is not related to support since people are generally not well informed.

When these variables were considered together, as indicated in Figure 5.6, endorsement of boycotts and knowledge of UFW boycotts were moderate influences in active support. Together, they account for about 11 percent of the participation. The lack of distinguishing social characteristics indicates that boycotting in support of the farmworkers' cause has also been distributed across different segments of society.[2]

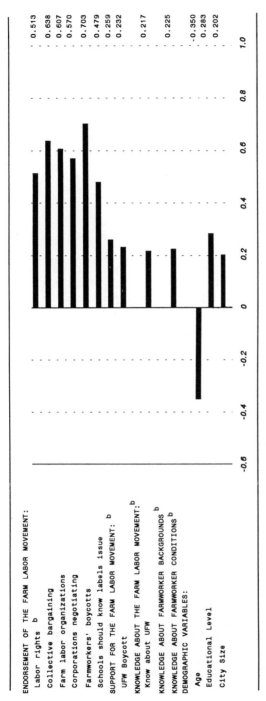

a Figures represent the relationship with a summary scale on endorsement of the farm labor movement, composed of the variables indicated in the first set of items. All figures represent Spearman's Rho correlation coefficient. Only correlations that are significant at the 0.05 level or less and that are stronger than 0.200 are reported ($n = 385$).

b A summary scale was correlated with endorsement of the farm labor movement. Specific variables in the scale which correlated with endorsement are indicated.

Figure 5.3: Influences in Popular Endorsement of the Farm Labor Movement[a]

ENDORSEMENT OF THE FARM LABOR MOVEMENT:

Labor rights [b] — 0.513
Collective bargaining — 0.638
Farm labor organizations — 0.607
Corporations negotiating — 0.570
Farmworkers' boycotts — 0.703
Schools should know labels issue — 0.479

SUPPORT FOR THE FARM LABOR MOVEMENT: [b]

UFW Boycott — 0.259
— 0.232

KNOWLEDGE ABOUT THE FARM LABOR MOVEMENT: [b]

Know about UFW — 0.217

KNOWLEDGE ABOUT FARMWORKER BACKGROUNDS [b]
KNOWLEDGE ABOUT FARMWORKER CONDITIONS [b] — 0.225

DEMOGRAPHIC VARIABLES:

Age — -0.350
Educational Level — 0.283
City Size — 0.202

-0.6   -0.4   -0.2   0   0.2   0.4   0.6   0.8   1.0

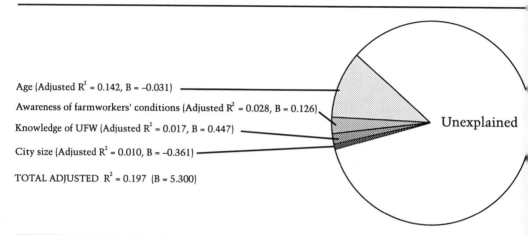

Age (Adjusted R^2 = 0.142, B = –0.031)

Awareness of farmworkers' conditions (Adjusted R^2 = 0.028, B = 0.126)

Knowledge of UFW (Adjusted R^2 = 0.017, B = 0.447)

City size (Adjusted R^2 = 0.010, B = –0.361)

TOTAL ADJUSTED R^2 = 0.197 (B = 5.300)

Unexplained

[a]Figures represent the results of stepwise regression using all variables that were significantl[y] correlated with endorsement of the farm labor movement. Only items that are significant a[t] the 0.05 level or less are reported. Figures represent the proportion of the total Adjusted [R²] explained by the model (n = 385).

Figure 5.4: Combined Influences in Popular Endorsement of the Farm Labor Movement[a]

The main factor which appears to stimulate predisposed sympathizers to active support is simple awareness of the boycotts' existence. There is a significant pool of people who have already boycotted in support of the farm labor cause and are therefore likely to do so again. This seems to have been the case with former UFW boycotters who participated in the FLOC boycott of Campbell Soup (Spearman's Rho = 0.278).

It should be noted that there has been little information on popular views concerning the farm labor movement. Two public opinion polls have shown that a majority of Americans have favored the UFW cause and that about 12.5 percent had actively boycotted grapes and lettuce in support of the UFW (Field 1985; L. Harris 1975). We are aware of only two attempts to systematically document the representative views of the American public about the farmworker movement, its organizations, and its goals and means. One of these is the 1982 public survey in Indiana (Barger and Haas 1983). The other is a 1986 public survey of the California public,

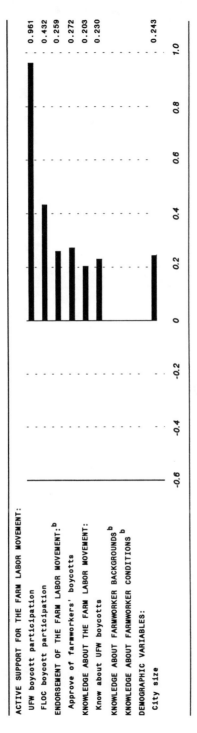

ACTIVE SUPPORT FOR THE FARM LABOR MOVEMENT:

UFW boycott participation	0.961
FLOC boycott participation	0.432
ENDORSEMENT OF THE FARM LABOR MOVEMENT: [b]	0.259
Approve of farmworkers' boycotts	0.272
KNOWLEDGE ABOUT THE FARM LABOR MOVEMENT:	0.203
Know about UFW boycotts	0.230
KNOWLEDGE ABOUT FARMWORKER BACKGROUNDS [b]	
KNOWLEDGE ABOUT FARMWORKER CONDITIONS [b]	
DEMOGRAPHIC VARIABLES:	
City size	0.243

-0.6   -0.4   -0.2   0   0.2   0.4   0.6   0.8   1.0

[a] Figures represent the relationship with a summary scale on support for the farm labor movement, composed of the variables indicated in the first set of items. All figures represent Spearman's Rho correlation coefficient. Only correlations that are significant at the 0.05 level or less and that are stronger than 0.200 are reported ($n = 385$).

[b] A summary scale was correlated with support for the farm labor movement. Specific variables in the scale which correlated with support are indicated.

Figure 5.5: Influences in Popular Support for the Farm Labor Movement[a]

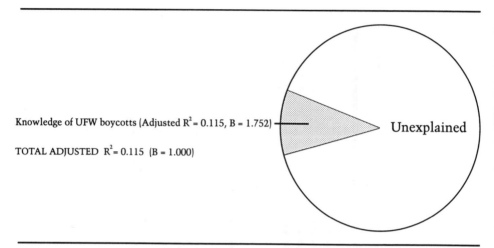

Knowledge of UFW boycotts (Adjusted R^2= 0.115, B = 1.752)

TOTAL ADJUSTED R^2= 0.115 (B = 1.000)

[a]Figures represent the results of stepwise regression using all variables that were significantly correlated with support for the farm labor movement. Only items that are significant at the 0.05 level or less are reported. Figures represent the proportion of the total Adjusted R^2 explained by the model ($n = 385$).

Figure 5.6: Combined Influences in Popular Support for the Farm Labor Movement[a]

which indicates there is widespread popular support for the farm labor movement on the West Coast as well as in the Midwest (Barger 1987).

Social Values in Popular Support for the Farmworker Movement

Widespread endorsement of the farm labor movement is clear in the results of the Indiana public survey. As indicated, this endorsement seems to be based more in *general social values*, rather than in knowledge of specific farmworker issues. Social values can be a powerful force in mobilizing groups to action (Alinsky 1969 : 152– 154). In more than twelve years of field work with the farm labor movement, several social values have been consistently expressed by church leaders, labor officials, teachers, lawyers, college students, and many others from all walks of life. Four of these stand out as dominant American values, which are consistent with the survey findings: human dignity, social justice, working rights, and the democratic process.

One dominant theme among supporters of farm labor reform is *human dignity* (Alinsky 1969:175). People believe that farmworkers deserve to be treated with respect and recognition of their human worth. This has also been a major value evident in the civil rights and women's rights movements in recent American history. There is clear popular approval for people who are trying to provide the best for their families.

Social justice is another dominant theme among supporters of the farm labor movement. Farmworkers are seen as a hardworking people who are trying to provide for their families' well-being and who have the right to seek better opportunities for themselves. This is contrasted with the discrimination and exploitation that keeps them from realizing their potentials. As in the civil rights movement, many Americans believe disadvantaged people should have the chance to achieve better conditions for themselves. The forebears of most Americans left their homelands seeking new opportunities for a better life. While American history has not always reflected full equality and justice, equal opportunity to fulfill one's potentials is seen as a basic right for all, including farmworkers.

Another value expressed is that farmworkers deserve basic *working rights*. Many believe that farmworkers do not labor under conditions which are standard for other American workers. The survey clearly documents widespread and strong popular endorsement of specific labor rights for farmworkers. These include fair wages, safe working conditions, fringe benefits, and clear procedures for resolving grievances, to which all American workers are entitled. This, of course, is the primary goal of the farmworker movement.

Another theme among farmworker supporters is a belief in the *democratic process*, the right of people to participate in the affairs of society which affect their well-being. This has been a dominant value since the American Revolution and is a major issue in the civil rights movement. The argument that farmworkers have been denied a voice in determining their own conditions has struck a common chord of sympathy among many supporters.

It is important to remind ourselves that FLOC represents a *reform* movement, not a revolutionary one. The goal is for farmworkers to *share* the same basic rights and conditions as other American workers, not to replace or destroy the system. Also, FLOC's methods are not only nonviolent, but are basically legitimate in terms of standard American norms.

The widespread popular support for FLOC indicates that its cause has tapped a set of core American values. These values led Americans from many backgrounds to see farmworkers' conditions as unacceptable. They have also led people to judge Campbell Soup as being at fault for its part in perpetuating these conditions. Few people believed the company had intentionally exploited farmworkers. But there was a common view that Campbell substantially benefited from farmworkers' labor and that the corporation had little human regard for the consequences to these people. Once FLOC raised these issues, the company's vocal denials of any involvement with midwestern farmworkers projected the image of its being hard and uncaring. Its opposition to dealing directly with FLOC as the representative of these workers made it appear to be stubborn and inflexible in a matter of human concern. Campbell Soup, in other words, was seen as violating basic American norms. It was popularly judged as deviant, not only for fostering such conditions but in particular for resisting reforms to correct them.

FLOC's boycott of Campbell Soup provided people from all walks of life with a ready sanction which they could use in their everyday settings. The drop in sales associated with the boycott, together with financial difficulties in the industry, exerted economic stress on Campbell's operations. Perhaps an even stronger sanction was the social pressure of the boycott. When church organizations and other social groups endorsed the boycott, FLOC, on the one hand, gained legitimacy, and Campbell, on the other hand, had its corporate image tarnished. Campbell was continually responding to inquiries and protests, and its corporate leaders had their prestige within the American business community challenged. The end result is that basic American values were upheld as standards that apply to business institutions as well as to individual members of the society.

FLOC's success has been based largely on the fact that there has been a broad range of *predisposed* allies and supporters. In some ways, knowledge that a boycott exists in itself seems to motivate people to participate. The strong public endorsement of the farm labor movement, though, appears to be based more on popular social values rather than on understanding the specific farm labor issues involved. FLOC has been effective in mobilizing popular support for its cause. Though not necessarily by conscious plan, FLOC has appealed to several basic American values in motivating people to take stands on its behalf. The responsiveness of many Americans has been evident in a wide variety of social segments. Many endorsements of FLOC and the boycott were even made spontaneously, as

Table 5.9: *External Forces in the FLOC Movement*

ENVIRONMENTAL CONSTRAINTS:
(1) The structure of the agricultural system
(2) The local Anglo communities
(3) Lack of public awareness

ENVIRONMENTAL OPPORTUNITIES:
(1) Agribusinesses' corporate structures
(2) Predisposed allies and supporters

boycotters urged others to boycott. This responsiveness has generated considerable legitimacy for FLOC's goals and methods.

The widespread popular support for FLOC's cause exerted considerable economic and social pressure on Campbell Soup. It also encouraged the FLOC farmworkers in their struggle. The outcomes certainly indicate that the rationale of the boycott was valid. The combined power of thousands of individual Americans *has* counterbalanced farmworkers' powerlessness and overcome the socioeconomic power of large agribusinesses. The extensive social support for FLOC was perhaps the most critical force in achieving farm labor reforms for midwestern farmworkers.

External Forces in the FLOC Movement

Several sources provide insights into those forces in FLOC's social environment that have contributed to social reforms for midwestern farmworkers. We have reviewed the opposition to and support for FLOC, and we have examined public views concerning the farm labor movement. The history of FLOC in Chapter 3 also provides useful information. These sources help identify five environmental forces that have directed the course of the FLOC movement, as indicated in Table 5.9. These include both constraints and opportunities.

Environmental Constraints

We have been able to identify at least three constraints in the social environment of midwestern farmworkers that have influenced the direction of the FLOC movement.

(1) The structure of the agricultural system: The most obvious obstacle to farm labor reform was the structure of the agricultural system itself. This structure had isolated and impoverished midwestern farmworkers for generations. It had also denied them a voice in determining their own conditions. We do not believe that there were conscious intentions to deprive farmworkers. However, where specialty crops were concerned, the system nevertheless had that effect. The system was dominated by the large food-processing corporations, which received most of the benefits. Perhaps the strongest trait of the agricultural system which FLOC faced was an "inertia factor." That is, the system developed its own manner of functioning and then stayed the course for decades. To make reforms, FLOC had to mobilize enough energy to overcome the direction in which the system was "naturally" heading.

The large food-processing corporations were a specific obstacle to farm labor reforms. The companies had considerably more socioeconomic power and resources to resist change than farmworkers did to initiate change.

The growers represented another specific constraint in the system. The inflexibility and hostility of many growers became perhaps the most overt resistance encountered by FLOC. Some FLOC leaders point to the fragile economic situation of farmers in explaining this reaction. The farmers themselves have generally been constrained by the high overhead costs and debt load of the agricultural system. So many reacted bitterly and in a few cases violently, to a further threat to their well-being.

(2) The local Anglo communities: Another obstacle that FLOC had to overcome was opposition from the local Anglo communities. The Anglo members of the rural areas of northwestern Ohio, including law enforcement officers and some politicians, were strongly opposed to FLOC. Personal and business ties to growers, a general conservatism, and sometimes racism contributed to negative views of FLOC. Incidents reflecting these views include cross burnings and beatings of farmworkers; also, the local press continually posed a negative image of FLOC (Valdés 1984). Local Anglo attitudes proved to be a deep-seated barrier to the success of the FLOC movement.

(3) Lack of public awareness: Another environmental limitation to the FLOC movement was a lack of public awareness about farm labor issues. Support of the general public was crucial to the success of the boycott. Many people have had a vague perception that farmworkers experience deprived conditions. Yet few have any real understanding of those conditions or of the issues in the farm

labor movement. In winning popular support for the boycott, then, FLOC had to inform people about farmworkers and the reasons for social actions. It should be noted that this did not prove to be a major constraint.

Environmental Opportunities

We have also been able to identify at least two environmental opportunities that have made an impact on the direction of the FLOC movement.

(1) Agribusinesses' corporate structures: Interestingly enough, the corporate infrastructures of agribusiness itself proved to be a benefit to the FLOC movement. For example, the interlocking boards of directors and mutual investments of big business made Campbell Soup vulnerable to the corporate campaign strategy.

The success of the boycott was also enhanced by several corporate traits of Campbell. For example, the company has had high public visibility. Its resistance to recognizing farm labor issues conflicted with its positive public image. In many cases, as we often observed during the boycott, this created a negative reaction among consumers.

Another trait that made Campbell Soup vulnerable to the boycott was its product line. It is easy for people who are conscious of the boycott not to purchase an item that is as highly visible as a can of soup with a distinctive label. An "invisible" product, like sewer pipe or electrical wiring, would probably not be as vivid in the public's mind nor so easy to boycott.

The profit margin of Campbell's line of products proved to be still another susceptible point. Because the food-processing industry has lower profits than many other businesses, the impacts of a boycott can be swift and heavy. Profits are directly affected, of course, when people do not buy the product. But boycotts also affect wholesale prices, so that a company receives less income even from those items it does market.

Also, contributing to the success of the boycott was the hierarchical structure of the corporation. In a centralized structure, key decisions are made at the top level. Such a structure may have initially insulated top Campbell executives from social pressure. However, once they decided to deal with FLOC, it proved to be an advantage for the farm labor cause. Baldemar Velásquez notes that the decision to deal with FLOC as the representative of farmworkers came from the top level of Campbell management. This decision was quickly implemented at all levels of the company. A centralized authority thus contributed to more productive relations with the farm labor movement.

Economy of scale, another corporate trait, also became an accessible point for FLOC. The idea is that it is easier and more cost-effective to manage one system than many. After Campbell decided to work with FLOC, economy of scale proved to be an advantage for the movement. One reason the company exerted pressure on its growers to form associations to collectively negotiate with FLOC was because it was easier to deal with one organization than with many individuals. In such a system, only one grower bargaining unit and one master contract needed to be administered. Campbell also reportedly provided unionized farms with more acreage in an effort to encourage growers to work with FLOC. Not only has economy of scale worked to the advantage of Campbell Soup but also to FLOC and in the long run, even the growers.

(2) Predisposed allies and supporters: Perhaps the major environmental opportunity for the success of the FLOC cause was the broad range of predisposed allies and supporters. As we have seen, FLOC was able to mobilize a wide variety of social groups and individuals to support its cause. These supporters crosscut all segments of society. Many people actively supported the boycott once they learned of the issues. As already indicated, the public was *predisposed* to support farm labor reform. This support seemed to be based on popular values rather than on knowledge of specific farm labor issues.

FLOC's widespread popular support applied considerable economic and social pressure on Campbell Soup. It also encouraged the FLOC farmworkers in their struggle. The outcomes certainly indicate that the rationale of the boycott was valid. The combined power of thousands of individual Americans *did* counterbalance farmworkers' powerlessness to overcome the socioeconomic power of large agribusinesses. The extensive social support for FLOC was perhaps the most critical force in achieving farm labor reforms for midwestern farmworkers.

The Social Environment of the FLOC Movement

As we have indicated, a second major force in systems adaptation is the societal environment for change. This is particularly true of reform movements of disadvantaged groups that seek changes through legitimate channels. We have seen that FLOC faced seemingly powerful opposition. Yet these constraints did not prove to be lasting.

In contrast, the depth of societal support for FLOC's cause was not evident in the beginning. Yet the cumulative social, political, and economic power generated tipped the scales in favor of midwestern farmworkers. It overcame the opposition and focused the course of farm labor affairs in new directions. FLOC has gained substantial social and moral legitimacy by the widespread support it has been able to mobilize. Together with the internal support of farmworkers, this has made FLOC an unquestioned force in farm labor affairs.

It is perhaps a credit to the ultimate democratic nature of American society that those in need do not necessarily stand alone once they voice their plight. As indicated, no disadvantaged minority group can hope to succeed in achieving reforms on its own. It is when there is little hope for realizing reforms that a movement turns to violence and revolution to achieve change. But substantial support for the farm labor cause *has* existed in other segments of American society. This has made the difference for midwestern farmworkers. In the final outcome, the American system has been flexible and effective enough to ensure needed farm labor reforms have been possible. The fact that midwestern farmworkers now enjoy more labor rights and a greater human dignity reflects positively on the American society as a whole.

CHAPTER 6

FLOC and Social Reform

The model of systems adaptation has led us to examine those internal and external forces which have directed the course of social change. The model also emphasizes how these forces *interact* in providing the energy and direction for change. For example, we have seen that there has been a large predisposition in the American public to support FLOC. Yet if FLOC had not had the internal support base among midwestern farmworkers, it would have lacked the credibility to mobilize external support. From another perspective, even with external support, FLOC would have been severely constrained if it had not had the internal support of farmworkers themselves.

We would now like to consider what changes have been produced by this interaction in the FLOC case. Change itself is not necessarily adaptive. It is rather those changes which positively enhance the functioning and vitality of the group that are adaptive. In order to assess the adaptive nature of changes in the FLOC case, we need to review the actual outcomes of social reform.

Social Reforms of the FLOC Movement

When the first FLOC contracts were signed in 1986, the socio-economic system in which midwestern farmworkers existed was changed. All other outcomes of the FLOC movement basically stem from this primary change. Production, price structures, and the roles of agribusinesses, growers, and farmworkers have been restructured. The new three-party structure and the private labor relations commission are perhaps the most creative contributions of the FLOC movement to the agricultural system in the Midwest.

Table 6.1: *Internal Reforms of the FLOC Movement among Midwestern Farmworkers*

(1) Improved working conditions
(2) Organization into a larger social structure
(3) New feelings of security
(4) Personal growth

The most important change, from FLOC's point of view, is that midwestern farmworkers now have a more equal role in the agricultural system. They have a direct voice in determining those conditions that affect their lives and well-being. Following the 1978 strike, FLOC worked for eight years to achieve this basic right for midwestern farmworkers. Since the contracts were signed in 1986, FLOC has worked to implement their workers' new rights and benefits.

FLOC has thus achieved important changes that affect midwestern farmworkers in a number of ways. Following the general systems model of adaptation, we will first review the major internal developments within the population of midwestern farmworkers. We will then examine the important reforms in the external social environment of these workers.

Internal Changes

As indicated in Table 6.1, four principal changes resulting from the FLOC movement can be identified among midwestern farmworkers:

(1) Improved working conditions: On an immediate level, FLOC workers now enjoy considerably improved conditions. Since the 1978 strike, their wage rates have almost doubled. Workers like David Bermúdez see their increased earnings and higher standard of living as essential rights. Isaías Alfaro reports his wages have increased by 19 percent under the FLOC contracts. He says that in other regions where he works his wages are 30 percent lower, and he has begun to think of how the farm labor movement may be effective there. Additional benefits include workers compensation and unemployment insurance.

Other conditions have improved as well. Many camps have new housing and sanitary facilities, and others are now better maintained. FLOC workers are guaranteed their jobs from year to year.

New migrant houses were built by Scott Osier, a Michigan pickle grower who worked with FLOC to pioneer a cooperative housing program. The FLOC contracts have brought many significant new benefits for midwestern farmworkers, including more stable employment, higher earnings, and elimination of the sharecropping system and child labor in the pickle industry.

Conditions of employment are clarified before farmworkers go to work on a contract farm. Farmworkers are also provided with a full accounting of their earnings and withholdings at the end of the season. FLOC workers are covered by a clear grievance procedure, which ensures that no worker is subject to arbitrary treatment. They are learning more about their rights under the labor contracts. They are also becoming more informed about their general civil and legal rights, such as minimum wage regulations, unemployment insurance, and child labor standards. FLOC farmworkers are seeing their occupation with a new perspective and now feel farm labor deserves greater regard and rewards than they have experienced in the past.

A particularly important change has been the elimination of the sharecropping system in the pickle industry. The new contracts have phased out this kind of arrangement that puts the workers at so many disadvantages. FLOC pickle workers are no longer subject to higher taxes and Social Security payments, which many have not understood. They are now employees, receiving regular benefits like other American workers.

These new standards are guaranteed by contract. In the 1991 season, five thousand farmworkers were covered by FLOC contracts. When asked how things are different now, their responses show a new level of understanding about their legal status and a new sense of self-worth. FLOC's achievements have established significantly higher standards for farmworkers' rights and benefits. Even farmworkers not under contract have realized higher wages and better benefits, since unionization has had many positive carryover effects for nonunion workers (Roach and Roach 1981). As important as these improved working conditions are, we wish to emphasize that the reforms achieved by FLOC have had even greater impacts in the personal lives and identity of midwestern farmworkers.

(2) Organization into a larger social structure: As a result of the FLOC movement, midwestern farmworkers are now more organized as a social group. Before FLOC, their social networks were limited primarily to individual families and crews. FLOC workers are now additionally part of a clearly defined labor organization. They have clear roles as union members, camp representatives, field organizers, and officers. They have a larger identity and a structure for interacting with each other on a broader basis. They have direct ties to thousands of other farmworkers. They also have a broader and more cohesive structure for interacting with other parties in the agricultural system. As a part of FLOC, they even have direct access to the top levels of the agricultural system.

This new structure is evident in many FLOC activities. Several thousand farmworkers, for example, were directly represented at the 1988 and 1991 FLOC conventions. At training sessions for camp representatives, workers have been able to compare experiences and aspirations with each other. They are learning that many others share their own goals and concerns. Many are gaining ideas that have worked with others to try out with their own crews. Numerous FLOC workers are broadening their social relationships with each other as well. For example, new friendships and *compadrazgo* (godparent) relationships have been established as FLOC members have worked together. Interpersonal relations have also been developed and strengthened at FLOC dances and fiestas.

The workers' roles in FLOC are still evolving. FLOC is working to build a membership that actively participates in the organization. Many workers are still learning how they can best function in this new social structure. But we have observed a new identity emerging, where people are seeing themselves as *FLOC* workers rather than

Fernando Cuevas, Sr., briefs FLOC workers about the contract provisions
with a Heinz representative at a joint camp meeting. Fernando explains
these provisions are guaranteed "like a law." Through such events, FLOC
workers have seen cooperative relations with growers and the corporations.
When camp representatives attend meetings with reps from other crews,
their social awareness and networks have been broadened. Some camp reps
have become FLOC organizers and board members. FLOC farmworkers in
general have demonstrated a new sense of security and confidence in dealings with growers and companies.

just farmworkers. Baldemar Velásquez notes that there are many ad-
justments to be made. "Given the democratic forum of FLOC," he
says, "the workers will make these for themselves."

(3) New feelings of security: A significant personal change we
have observed in FLOC farmworkers is a new sense of security and
stability. One important source of these feelings is the grievance
procedure in the FLOC contracts. One example is the case where a
grower demanded that everyone load their own cucumbers, instead
of hiring a loading crew. When the workers filed a complaint, the
grower raised pay rates to cover the additional work. "Before," one
worker says, "we wouldn't have been able to say anything at all."

Many FLOC farmworkers have reported a feeling of security as a
result of the contract provisions. On a daily basis, as José Hinojosa
says, "the bosses can't treat us any way they want. They can't
threaten to fire us if we don't do whatever they want. We now have
the grievance." Lupe Franco also emphasizes that they now have a
forum to express their complaints: "For example, if we wanted

smoke alarms in our cabins in case of fire, we have a way to tell the grower what we want." But the workers' attitudes have led to even more fundamental changes, beyond just making complaints. As José says, "We can now work together with the grower to make things better."

The contracts also include other provisions that have generated new feelings of security. FLOC workers now receive a full disclosure of conditions of employment, including the time period, place, pay rates, and work activities. The worker knows exactly what to expect in terms of both benefits and responsibilities. Another provision is a seniority clause. This states that currently employed workers will be given preference for jobs in the following year. FLOC workers can now count on at least some jobs and wage rates in their annual cycle. Furthermore, these are guaranteed for three years. As a result, the farmworkers are better able to plan on a basic income with which to support their families. As Lupe says, "We know for sure what we can earn. We didn't have any security like this before the contracts." There is a clear awareness that their new rights and benefits are guaranteed by a contract. As FLOC staff members put it, "It's like a law."

On many occasions, FLOC has taken other steps that have contributed to a growing sense of security among its members. For example, Lupe notes how FLOC organized relief for workers when their earnings were severely limited by the 1988 drought. FLOC has also helped families get back to their home areas when a family death or other crisis has occurred. And FLOC has helped many workers get medical care, legal advice, and other assistance when needed, even in the home-base areas.

(4) Personal growth: Another significant impact of FLOC we have observed is the personal growth in those who have become involved in FLOC. When people become involved in social reform, they typically break out of a shell of isolationism and broaden their interest in how their community is related to larger events and issues (Alinsky 1969:167).

Fernando Cuevas is a primary example. Before becoming involved in FLOC, he was a successful crew leader. When he joined FLOC, his life changed in many ways. He educated himself about American business and national and international events in order to better understand the farmworkers' situation. Additionally, Fernando developed effective organizing skills. He also learned how to address church, labor, and other groups to build support for the boycott. Furthermore, he has been active in negotiating labor contracts and in training FLOC organizers and worker representatives. Fernando has

FLOC Vice President Fernando Cuevas, Sr., *(on the right)* listens to Heinz grower Tom Sachs address the 1991 FLOC convention. Behind him is his oldest son, Fernando, Junior (holding a FLOC flag), who is a FLOC organizer. Fernando reports how he and his family have grown through their involvement with FLOC over the years.

sometimes expressed a feeling of not being fully prepared for his leadership role. Yet over the years, we have seen him develop his skills and convictions, and we have seen these inspire others to become more involved in FLOC. All in all, he has proved to be a major figure in the FLOC movement.

Whole families of people involved in the FLOC movement have experienced growth. For example, Fernando's family has developed along with him. His wife and children were active in helping other strikers. His oldest son Fernando (Junior) helped put on skits by the "FLOC kids" at rallies. By eighteen, he was a field organizer. The elder Fernando talks about how his children used the democratic procedures they learned with FLOC to challenge his role as the ultimate authority in the family. As a result, family decisions became a process involving all members. Fernando credits these developments for a more satisfying family life.

While Fernando provides a highly visible case, we have observed a similar process of the growth in many FLOC farmworkers over the years. When they become involved in the farm labor cause, they start developing as individuals. Their vision broadens beyond their own immediate needs. They start caring about what happens to farmworkers in general and to other disadvantaged groups. They become more aware of political processes and of national and international events. Some start studying the Bible and reading works by Martin Luther King and Gandhi. We find this process of personal growth to be one of the most exciting impacts of the FLOC movement.

(5) Other internal changes: The FLOC movement has experienced other important internal developments. One such development is FLOC's new organizational structure to more effectively administer labor contracts. This includes maintaining computer records of workers' home addresses and Social Security numbers, hours worked, pay rates, and incentive earnings. It also entails procedures for investigating grievances and negotiating solutions between workers and growers. Another area of development is more involvement for workers in contract negotiations and implementation. Camp meetings and the social training of camp representatives are steps in this direction. Another area concerns effective use of new financial and personnel resources. For example, FLOC has developed *Nuestra Lucha* (Our Struggle), a newspaper for its members to keep them informed about current issues and events. Also, staff members now keep individual records to help guide them in the use of their time and energy.

In summary, FLOC farmworkers are experiencing significant economic, social, and personal changes as a group. The new rights, conditions, broader social integration, greater stability, and personal growth have many important long-term benefits. FLOC workers can now expect to lead healthier lives. This is assured by greater access to medical care, more sanitary living conditions, and better nutrition that comes with a higher income. Workers can also expect their children to receive more education, as families no longer have to rely on their children's labor to survive. In general, FLOC farmworkers can now turn much of their energy from just surviving to achieving more stable and productive lives, like those of most other American workers.

External Changes

FLOC has also achieved significant changes in the external socioeconomic environment of midwestern farmworkers. When FLOC signed contracts with Campbell Soup and Heinz, the whole agricultural system in the Midwest was changed. The new three-way structure is an innovative contribution of the FLOC movement in several

Table 6.2: *External Reforms of the FLOC Movement on Farmworkers' Sociocultural Environment*

(1)   New relations with agribusiness
(2)   A new process for conflict resolution
(3)   Integration into the American socioeconomic system

ways: it has created the basis for new relations with agribusiness, it provides a new process for addressing problems, and in a larger perspective, it enables farmworkers to actively participate in the system.

As indicated in Table 6.2, three major changes, which are outcomes of the FLOC movement, can be identified in the larger societal structure of midwestern farmworkers:

(1) New relations with agribusiness: Since 1986, FLOC's relations with food-processing corporations have been considerably altered. With the FLOC contracts, Campbell Soup, Heinz, and Dean Foods operate in a different business and social context. They can no longer consider their own production, marketing, and profit goals alone. The system has been opened for the active participation of farmers and farmworkers as equal partners.

Baldemar Velásquez comments on FLOC's relations with Campbell Soup after the contracts were signed. "Now that they have accepted us," he says, "we have a legitimate dialogue, and they are willing to work with us." Relations with Heinz have been particularly cooperative. An example is the FLOC-Heinz program of drought relief in the summer of 1988. We have also noted a positive atmosphere in camp meetings organized by FLOC organizers, Heinz field agents, and Heinz growers. It should be noted that Campbell Soup and Heinz were both instrumental in getting their growers to sign contracts with FLOC. The corporations, of course, have much to gain by working with FLOC. Not only do they avoid labor conflict, but they can now rely on a more stable source of produce. Relations with Dean Foods are still developing, but FLOC leaders anticipate their cooperation in working together for the good of the whole industry.

FLOC's relations with growers have also changed dramatically since the first contracts were signed. Juanita Reyes, a camp rep and FLOC board member, in considering her thirteen years with FLOC, says, "The cooperative relationships between growers and workers has been an important change." As already noted, the hostility of the growers in the beginning was a major obstacle to the FLOC movement. Even when Campbell was willing to negotiate with FLOC, many of its growers were not.

Since contracts were signed with FLOC, however, the role of the growers has changed considerably. They no longer directly control the conditions of farmworkers. They now have to face their workers as equals in the bargaining process, and as one camp rep put it, "There's a lot more communication between farmers and workers now." The formation of associations of growers who supply Campbell, Vlasic, Heinz, and Dean has had several positive effects. FLOC can now deal with a collective body rather than having to negotiate with each individual farmer. Baldemar Velásquez reports that the new structure has served to diffuse hostilities and to generate constructive interactions. Two examples are the use of the grievance procedure to reach solutions that are satisfactory to all parties and the cooperative efforts to build modern housing in farmworker camps.

There have been several occasions of real cooperation with farmers. One example involves a farmer who encouraged his workers to vote for FLOC in the union elections held in 1985. When Campbell Soup cut his acreage in apparent retaliation, FLOC made a strong effort to have the full quota restored. In another example, Scott Osier, a Michigan Vlasic grower, pioneered with FLOC and Campbell to phase out the sharecropping arrangement. Other farmers have worked with FLOC, too, in providing sanitary facilities in the fields and otherwise helping to improve the working conditions.

The growers have received a number of benefits from the restructured agricultural system. As equal participants in contract negotiations, they have more bargaining power for achieving their own goals. In addition, the contracts guarantee set earnings for the three years. This strengthens not only their credit ratings for farm loans but their general economic and psychological security as well. The grievance procedure guarantees fair treatment for the growers as well as the farmworkers. This is evident in the case of a tractor driver who complained to FLOC that he was fired. When an organizer investigated the matter, he found the grower had been falsely accused and that the complaints from other workers had forced the driver to quit. As a result of this incident, the workers' relations with that grower were considerably strengthened. Another benefit is that growers are guaranteed a stable labor supply to work their specialty crops. One Michigan grower emphasized this point when he addressed farmworkers at a FLOC fiesta. "We growers want the same people to come back each year. They are more efficient and productive workers." He went on to ask for FLOC's help in this area.

The farmers can also enjoy greater economic security from securing the three-year term of contracts and from having a more stable work force. FLOC workers express a sense of obligation from working under contracts. When drought reduced the earnings of FLOC workers in 1991, for example, one camp rep was asked by the grower if his crew was planning to leave and seek work elsewhere. He replied, "No. The people in this camp won't leave. We signed a contract, and we'll keep picking until the contract's up." Also, as we have already reported, some leaders of the grower associations have made trips with FLOC to meet with union officials in Mexico. They have seen that it is to their advantage as well to contain any company efforts to export crop production.

These new relations were dramatically illustrated when the heads of the growers' associations addressed the 1991 FLOC convention. Roger Hanes, an Ohio Vlasic grower, told the farmworkers, "You have much to be proud of. You have earned dignity and worth. We will be going into the new employment status [eliminating sharecropping], and we will work together for better housing. With patience and cooperation, we will work together to shape the future."

The new atmosphere of cooperation between the companies, growers, and FLOC farmworkers is also evident in the joint meetings in the camps. The three parties come together to inform the workers about pay rates, incentive payments, union dues, and work conditions as stipulated in the contracts. Another visible effort has been the cooperative ventures to improve housing and other migrant conditions.

One effect of these new relations is that FLOC farmworkers now have a more positive image of the companies and many of the growers. During the strike and boycott, the larger food-processing companies and growers were generally seen as the enemy. Some farmworkers are still suspicious of growers. But FLOC leaders tell them, "We have already won. We can afford to be gracious now." The more positive attitudes stem, we believe, from the fact that many FLOC workers now see the companies and growers as their equals. In a deeper sense, this reflects a new perception by the farmworkers of *themselves.*

(2) A new process for conflict resolution: Another major change in the agricultural system is a formal process for addressing problems among the three major parties involved. The grievance procedure included in the contracts provides a clear means for resolving conflicts. When farmworkers experience a problem, it is taken to the camp representatives and organizers. The matter is investigated, and if warranted, the problem is then taken to the grower. Likewise, if the grower encounters a problem, he raises it with the FLOC

Wally Wagner, a Campbell's tomato grower who used to be a strong opponent of FLOC, addresses farmworkers at the 1991 convention. He noted
how farmers and workers now understand each other better and how relations have become cooperative. The three pickle growers who also addressed the convention noted how there was open communication. They
also noted that by working together they could make the elimination of the
sharecropping system succeed. All the farmers noted how the grievance procedure in the contracts was an effective means for resolving conflicts. The
growers have benefited along with the farmworkers from the changes initiated by the three-year FLOC contracts. Their credit ratings for farm loans
have been improved, their bargaining position with the corporations has
been strengthened, and they can rely on a more stable and productive work
force.

organizers. If the matter is not resolved, the complaint is submitted
in writing to a third party for resolution. In the old system, how a
problem was resolved was dependent upon the character of the individuals concerned. Too often, conflicts led to unjust abuses. A
grower or crew leader, for example, could simply fire anyone with
whom he had a disagreement. Now the grievance procedure provides
a fair and constructive means for resolving problems for all parties
concerned.

On a larger scale, the major means for resolving problems involves
the Dunlop Commission. The commission functions as a private
labor relations board whose authority is guaranteed in the contractual agreements signed by all three parties. This body was
formed early in the negotiations between FLOC and Campbell
Soup. Its jurisdiction has since been expanded to include all of
Campbell tomato, Vlasic pickle, Heinz pickle, and Dean pickle

operations. The commission's primary function is mediation, acting as a go-between to facilitate a meaningful dialogue that transcends state boundaries, companies, and levels of production from the fields to the factories.

When necessary, the Dunlop Commission is also empowered to arbitrate conflicts, making decisions which are binding on the parties involved. The commission, for example, is the final board of appeal in the grievance procedure. It was also the final authority in setting up representation procedure for union elections in 1985. FLOC wanted a union checkoff process. In this approach, a crew comes under the union contract when a majority of workers sign cards authorizing FLOC to represent them. The commission, however, ruled that there had to be formal elections. FLOC abided by this decision. After winning many elections and establishing its legitimacy, FLOC was later able to use a checkoff procedure.

The creative element of the Dunlop Commission is that it provides by private contractual agreement many of the labor rights earlier denied farmworkers. Farmworkers are specifically excluded from many national and state labor laws. They are further subjected to a confusing variety of state laws and regulations as they migrate in their annual cycles. The Dunlop Commission simply sidesteps these obstacles. Its boundaries of authority are independently set by contractual agreement among the parties involved. The Dunlop Commission has functioned effectively in generating constructive relations among FLOC, the growers, and the corporations. All three parties involved have shown respect for the commission and its responsibilities. In talking about the reforms achieved by FLOC, for example, Baldemar Velásquez states, "We would not have been able to achieve all this without the Dunlop Commission." He believes the commission members have performed their responsibilities in a fair and just manner. Also, he believes the commission provides a *structure* for constructively resolving differences.

Both FLOC workers and the farmers appear to appreciate the new arrangements. Janie Reyes, a FLOC camp rep, says the grievance procedure has generated more open communication and cooperation with the farmers. Tom Sachs, a Heinz grower, told FLOC workers at the 1991 convention, "The three-way agreement is in its sixth year now and is doing well. We were apprehensive at first, but communication is open and we know each other better. We have a formal grievance procedure, and we both know what to expect." At the same convention, Baldemar Velásquez also emphasized the constructive relations with farmers: "As we venture into the new world created by the ending of sharecropping, we will rely heavily on the feeling of trust and the process for equitable problem-solving. By talking with each other, we can solve 90 percent of our problems." He notes that "it is a process based on equality and respect between the growers and workers for reaching mutual solutions to problems in the camps and fields. In the last two years, we have had good face-to-face dialogue, and we have not had to use the [formal] grievance procedure at all."

Other means for resolving problems have been the study groups set up by the original contractual agreements. All three parties are involved in these study groups. They are thus collectively involved in examining issues like pesticide hazards, housing needs, health care and safety, and day care for children. For example, as a result of one study group's efforts, FLOC and selected growers received federal grants for model housing programs for migrants with Campbell Soup providing matching funds.

The grievance procedure, the Dunlop Commission, and joint study groups have all provided constructive means for resolving problems. Before, unilateral action and socioeconomic power were the basis for addressing conflicts. But these means probably contributed to more conflict rather than to problem solving. The new structure, however, is a critical reform in farm labor affairs that can be fair and beneficial for all parties concerned.

(3) Integration into the American socioeconomic system: As we have noted, the agricultural system in the Midwest has been reorganized to include FLOC farmworkers in decisions that influence their own conditions. They do not have an absolute power, of course, but for the first time they are in a position to decide for themselves what they will demand and what they will concede. This change has the most far-reaching implications for farm labor reform in the Midwest and underlies most of the successes of the FLOC movement that we have already considered.

The larger American socioeconomic system has also been affected by the FLOC movement. FLOC workers are now more integrated into the national structure in a number of ways. FLOC's leaders recognize that farmworker issues are related to larger social issues and structures, and they have actively built alliances with other groups. Through FLOC, midwestern farmworkers are now linked with other labor organizations, religious bodies, political parties, federal and state agencies, and other segments of the American society. These ties are even extended into the international arena, where relations with the Mexican unions are concerned. Such networks enable

Farmworker delegates listen to Baldemar Velásquez at the 1988 FLOC convention. FLOC has provided the means for midwestern farmworkers to become more integrated into American society and to contribute to the national well-being. Through FLOC, they have gained ties to numerous church, labor, political, and other organizations, rather than being isolated on the fringes of society. They can better provide for their families' education, health care, and other needs. Furthermore, they can be more productive taxpayers, rather than depending on tax-supported social services. Finally, through their increased buying power, they can help support the American economy and the jobs of other American workers.

FLOC to mobilize social and economic forces in support of the farmworkers' cause. They continue to ensure that farmworkers are not isolated on the fringes of society.

FLOC workers are now in a position to contribute more to the national well-being. For example, they can be more productive taxpayers and can be less dependent on tax-supported social services. They can better support their families' education, health care, and other needs. They already contribute their labor in producing food for other Americans. Now they can also contribute their greater purchasing power to supporting the American economy and the jobs of other workers. Whenever any individual or group experiences discrimination, as farmworkers have, they are denied the fulfillment of their potentials. This also denies their potentials to the larger society. As farmworkers are more included in the social system, other Americans can benefit from their talents and abilities.

This greater integration is perhaps the most far-reaching impact of the FLOC movement. Ultimately, each FLOC farmworker is tied with other members of the American society. As we will see, all of us benefit by farmworkers being more comprehensively included into the American system.

(4) Other external changes: The FLOC movement has made many important changes in the farmworkers' larger socioeconomic environment, many of which have also benefited other Americans. Not all the impacts have been positive for midwestern farmworkers, of course. Perhaps the most unfortunate outcome is the loss of a number of farmworker jobs in tomatoes. Originally, Campbell Soup clearly mandated mechanization of the tomato harvest as a means of undermining the FLOC strike. This significantly reduced the need for workers, compared to hand picking. Mechanization also costs the growers and companies, since the yields per acre and the quality of the tomatoes have been greatly reduced. It should be noted, however, that mechanization was already a fact of life in agribusiness. Other crops that were labor intensive have also experienced mechanization, including sugar beets and cherries. FLOC has been conscious of this trend and has not necessarily opposed it. Indeed, FLOC leaders note that stoop labor in hot and muddy fields is far from ideal work. Yet they have taken the position that farmworkers should be treated justly in the process. FLOC's position is that displaced farmworkers should be given the first choice of mechanized jobs. Any remaining workers should be retrained for other work. This position is not unlike that taken by other labor unions.

There are several external efforts of the FLOC movement that are still in progress. For example, some segments of the agricultural system have not yet been affected by the FLOC movement. So FLOC intends to continue organizing pickle and tomato operations and to continue addressing the sharecropping issue. There are also mushrooms, strawberries, and other table-crop industries to be organized. FLOC leaders note that many of the same people involved in pickles are also involved in working these other crops. These workers are already familiar with FLOC; so this should facilitate organizing.

The FLOC movement has come a long way. Yet FLOC's leaders are looking ahead. Each new success positively affects both midwestern farmworkers and the American society. FLOC's vision is far-reaching, and there are still many reforms needed in the agricultural system. Still, as José Hinojosa says, "FLOC started something good."

The System Has Changed

The model of adaptation poses that the basic process of social change is reorganization of the system, not just a shift in a trait. This is what has occurred in the case of the FLOC movement. The overall impact of FLOC is that the *system* has changed. This has occurred on two levels: the internal economic, social, and personal experiences of FLOC workers have been greatly improved, while the larger socioeconomic structure in which farmworkers function has also been restructured. Changes in each level have been in conjunction with the changes in the other, and the resulting reorganization of the system has largely been to the farmworkers' benefit.

In summary, reform has taken place. The FLOC movement has set new precedents for farmworkers in general, just as the UFW set precedents for FLOC. Each achievement establishes new standards for farmworker rights and benefits and opens the way for other agricultural industries like greenhouse vegetables and tree nursery operations. FLOC has also set precedents for other industries. The three-way contracts, for example, provide effective alternatives for multiparty enterprises.

Another step taken by FLOC, which has broad implications, is the development of cooperative international labor relations. The alliance FLOC is building with Mexican unions has far-reaching impacts for farm laborers. Collaborative ties can combine their mutual bargaining strength for organizing Campbell tomato operations in both countries. This protects each union from being played against the other. Growers have also been involved in this strategy. These relations can help prevent the exporting of child labor and other social problems to third world countries where labor is cheaper but the workers are severely disadvantaged. Such relations can also help maintain the productivity of domestic agriculture by preventing the exporting of food production.

The reforms achieved by FLOC can be beneficial for all concerned. FLOC workers have certainly benefited from the changes. There are new standards for how farmworkers are to be treated and rewarded for their contributions. They are no longer anonymous figures who are cycled through labor tasks. They now have clearer working rights, and more stable and beneficial conditions. The growers also have more stable conditions with three-year contracts and a dependable labor force. Too, the larger food-processing corporations can expect a more consistent supply of table crops. The larger American society can also benefit, as FLOC workers contribute their greater productivity and purchasing power, and as they assume greater responsibilities as citizens and taxpayers. We would like to quote Baldemar Velásquez again on his assessment of these reforms: "These changes should have been made a long time ago."

CHAPTER 7

Social Adaptation of Midwestern Farmworkers

We have had two purposes in examining the farm labor movement in the Midwest. One has been to document the story of FLOC, its goals, activities, and achievements. The second has been to explain *why* and *how* FLOC has been successful in reforming the farm labor system.

We have posed a model of systems adaptation to guide us in understanding social change in the FLOC case. As we have said, *adaptation* is a process of change made by a population in its interaction with its environment that enhances its survival and continuation. This model calls for us to assess both the internal and the external forces evident in the FLOC movement. In particular, the concept of adaptation emphasizes the *process* involved in social change. We have therefore examined the interaction of these forces in reorganizing the system toward particular outcomes. The ultimate measure of adaptive success is how much a change contributes to the well-being and continuation of a group. The systems model of change, then, can help us better understand the FLOC case. The FLOC case, in turn, can help us better understand social change.

The main issue we have investigated, then, is the adaptation of midwestern farmworkers. More specifically, we have sought to understand how the FLOC movement has been adaptive for these workers. We would now like to briefly examine the FLOC story on two levels. First, we would like to summarize FLOC as a social movement and the reforms it has initiated. On a larger level, we would like to evaluate the FLOC movement as an example of social adaptation.

FLOC as a Social Reform Movement

The deprived socioeconomic conditions of farmworkers have been documented for much of the twentieth century. These people work hard to help produce food for the rest of the nation, a product that is at least as valuable to our society's well-being as petroleum. For their labor, however, farmworkers have suffered poverty-level wages, substandard housing, child labor, exposure to dangerous pesticides, and among the poorest health in the country.

We have explored several possible solutions to resolving the problems that farmworkers experience. One is for farmworkers to leave their occupation and find other employment. However, we have seen that this only opens their positions to be filled by others, who then suffer the same conditions. Another alternative is for those who benefit the most by the system, the large agricultural corporations, to pass on benefits to farmworkers. Historically, however, this has happened very rarely. Another solution is to enact laws and regulations safeguarding farmworkers' well-being. But the legal record has been mixed and ineffective. We have seen that farmworkers have been excluded from key labor laws, and even where they are covered, standards are reduced and provisions are not enforced. A fourth possible solution is public assistance. This has only addressed basic survival needs, however. Public assistance programs drain societal resources and do not resolve the basic problem of powerlessness and disenfranchisement. We have argued that the primary challenge is to make farm labor a positive and productive occupation.

Historically, the only alternative that has significantly improved farmworkers' conditions and has achieved for them the same working rights as other Americans has been the farm labor movement. This social movement has been led by the United Farm Workers (UFW) in California and by the Farm Labor Organizing Committee (FLOC) in the Midwest. Both groups represent the efforts of farmworkers to achieve meaningful changes in the socioeconomic order in which they are involved.

As we have seen, FLOC represents a reform movement. It has sought to reorganize the socioeconomic system to be more beneficial to the group it represents. It has not sought to destroy or replace that system. Rather, FLOC's purpose has been to *include* farmworkers in the basic norms and structures of the American society. It has sought for them to share in the opportunities enjoyed by other American workers. Even at the height of the Campbell Soup boycott, FLOC never wished to ruin the company. To do so would simply eliminate the jobs of its members. FLOC, then, has generally accepted the basic norms and organizational premises of the larger society.

FLOC's methods have always focused on reform. Its efforts to achieve change have been within the legitimate boundaries of the existing social order. These have included strikes, boycotts, and public demonstrations. Such methods are completely legal and have been traditional since the Boston Tea Party. FLOC has continually been careful about the legal basis of its activities. For example, when setting up strike picket lines along tomato fields, FLOC workers were careful to remain in the legal right of way.

FLOC demonstrates all the characteristics of a social movement. It has been based upon a constituent group, from which it arises and whose cause it advocates. Certainly the support of midwestern farmworkers was a critical component in FLOC's credibility, effectiveness, and ultimate success. As we have seen, it is likely that greater expectations and lower realizations combined to motivate FLOC workers to sustain the strike for eight years.[1]

Charismatic leaders are generally associated with social movements, and this is the case for FLOC. Baldemar Velásquez has had influence with both farmworkers and supporters, for example, because others have been inspired by him and have chosen to follow him.[2] The ideology of a social movement is also important in directing its course. FLOC's philosophy has emphasized labor rights and social justice in explaining both farmworkers' problems and solutions. Another factor in the development and direction of mass action is the movement organizations involved. As indicated earlier, FLOC has developed a successful structure for promoting reform over the years of its struggle. Resource mobilization is a major challenge for all reform movements, and FLOC has been successful in winning and organizing external support for its cause and for containing and neutralizing its opposition.

A number of forces have operated to drive and direct the FLOC movement. One level of the adaptive process involves the internal potentials of a group. The needs and resources that a group brings to a change situation can be critical in its adaptation.

As we have seen, one need in the FLOC movement has been the necessity for farmworkers to break out of deprived conditions. Many midwestern workers have risked their meager livelihood to support FLOC. One reason is their belief that FLOC offers the only real alternative to improve their families' well-being. A second need has been to overcome their powerlessness to change their deprived conditions. This has perhaps been the most severe deprivation they have experienced, for without any direct means to change their conditions there was no valid hope that their lives could ever improve. Such needs would normally be considered a hindrance to meaningful changes, but guided by innovative leadership, they actually proved to be a positive resource. As already indicated, Baldemar Velásquez stated many times during the strike and boycott, "What have we got to lose? We would only go back to what little we had." This statement reflects a basic view among midwestern farmworkers who have come to see FLOC as the most viable means for meeting these needs.

We have also seen that FLOC has been able to draw upon a number of internal resources in achieving reforms for midwestern farmworkers. While they may have lacked material means, FLOC workers have had important social and psychological resources to pursue the movement's goals. Driven by new hopes and frustrations, FLOC workers have proved to have strong motivations in seeking changes.

One major resource has been FLOC's effective leadership. We have noted that the leadership of Baldemar Velásquez and Fernando Cuevas has not been based on formal authority but rather on the fact that others have chosen to follow them. They have demonstrated the deep convictions and self-sacrifice which have inspired others to devote their efforts to the FLOC cause. They have also proven to be creative leaders, guiding FLOC's strategies and activities to keep the initiative in farm labor reform. Instead of playing by the traditional rules in farm labor affairs, for example, the boycott took the issues to the society at large where popular values have supported the farmworkers' cause. The three-way contracts, a private labor relations board in the Dunlop Commission, and new relations with labor organizations in Mexico are other examples of the creativity of the FLOC leaders. It should be noted that FLOC has actively been trying to develop new leaders by training organizers and camp reps.

Another resource has been a meaningful philosophy, which has explained farmworkers' problems and solutions in terms of labor rights and social justice. Over the years, FLOC's philosophy has continued to evolve as new issues and challenges have developed. FLOC has also maintained clear and achievable goals, particularly the right of farmworkers to have an active role in deciding their own working conditions. It should also be noted that FLOC's goals have been both practical and ideal. FLOC has sought significant social reforms involving moral issues, but these reforms have been attainable.

FLOC's change methods have also been effective. Using nonviolent means like the strike, the 560-mile march to Campbell's headquarters, and in particular, the popular boycott of Campbell Soup eventually resulted in the achievement of FLOC's main goals.

FLOC's responsive organizational structure proved to be a valuable resource. FLOC faced a number of problems in maintaining a cohesive organization to deal with a wide variety of challenges. But it was always able to reorganize around each challenge and to maintain its initiative and continuity in seeking reforms. Its organizational structure has evolved to include such diverse operations as labor organizing, contract administration, membership development, and alliance building with other groups like the Mexican unions.

An essential resource for the whole FLOC movement has been the support of the midwestern farmworkers themselves. The ability of a group of mobile and marginal people to unite in a formal organization might surprise some observers. Yet the record shows that this is exactly what has happened. The solid base of support and participation by over five thousand farmworkers is what characterizes FLOC as a *social* movement. As Fernando Cuevas says, "That's what social change is all about. It's the changes made by the people who are on the bottom, oppressed by systems like the multinational agribusiness industry that gets ninety-two cents of every food dollar while we get two cents. It's being involved. It's organizing to stand up for our rights and self-determination." This active support has been critical for both FLOC's purpose and its credibility. Its strong internal base, in fact, has allowed FLOC to devote considerable energy to mobilizing external resources.

Another level of the adaptive process involves the challenges in a group's external environment, including the larger socioeconomic setting of a particular group. External challenges consist of both constraints and opportunities for making effective changes.

We have indicated that FLOC has faced strong constraints in seeking reforms. A major obstacle to the FLOC movement was the structure of the agricultural system in the Midwest. Where specialty crops are concerned, this system has isolated and impoverished farmworkers for generations. To overcome the inertia of this system required considerable energy and effort. Also, since a movement is dedicated to making social changes, it will inevitably arouse opposition by threatening vested interests. This was the case with Campbell Soup, which like other food-processing corporations, received most of the benefits from the system. Corporations such as Campbell Soup had considerably more resources to resist change than

FLOC did to initiate change. The Ohio growers presented more obstacles. Their fragile economic situation was threatened by the FLOC movement, and many reacted bitterly. Reorganizing the agricultural system itself was FLOC's major reform goal, and for this, it faced strong opposition. Other barriers included the local Anglo communities that identified strongly with the growers, and a general lack of public awareness of farmworkers' conditions and their underlying causes.

FLOC's socioeconomic environment, however, has provided critical opportunities that have been instrumental in its ability to achieve its goals. These included some opportunities to tap into the corporate structure of Campbell Soup. Furthermore, the company's public visibility, product line, and lower profit margins made it susceptible to a popular boycott. Even its hierarchical structure and economy of scale proved to be benefits, once Campbell decided to accept FLOC.

Perhaps the greatest factor in FLOC's success was the predisposed support it found in the American society. As we have noted, the FLOC movement has involved a disadvantaged minority group that typically lacks the socioeconomic power to restructure society, particularly since it is dedicated to the use of legitimate means. So FLOC has needed the support of other segments in the society to counterbalance farmworkers' relative powerlessness and to overcome opposition. FLOC proved to be highly successful in mobilizing external socioeconomic resources in support of its cause. Several thousand religious, labor, civic, and other groups endorsed FLOC and the boycott, giving FLOC considerable legitimacy. The popular participation in the boycott eventually proved to be an overwhelming economic and social force on Campbell Soup. This support was critical in neutralizing and containing opposition and in FLOC's eventual success in achieving social reform.[3]

Neither internal potentials nor external challenges exist in isolation, as we have argued. The ultimate outcome of change is guided by how these forces interact. These interactions in the FLOC case have been complex, but they have been the driving force in directing social reform. For example, farmworkers' severe socioeconomic conditions enabled them to outwait the corporations and growers for eight years. They had little to lose and much to gain. These same needs also provided a basis for appealing for the support of other Americans. The farmworkers' deprived conditions contradict basic American values regarding social justice. This contradiction undoubtedly motivated Americans from every social background to boycott Campbell products in support of the FLOC cause.

Another example of these complex interactions involves the unresponsive attitude of the corporations and growers. In 1978, they simply ignored FLOC's call for a dialogue. This apparent scorn helped motivate farmworkers to strike. The workers realized that their deprived conditions would not be voluntarily addressed by those who controlled the agricultural system. It also made FLOC leaders realize that the existing system benefited those in power. Their call for the strike and boycott changed the "rules" to benefit the farmworkers. FLOC's ideology of labor rights and social justice provided a legitimate basis for calling upon the support of Americans. At that point, the lack of agribusinesses' responsiveness also motivated many Americans to boycott. The nature of the interactions between FLOC workers and the company-grower opposition thus stimulated considerable support from both midwestern farmworkers and the American public. This external support further encouraged FLOC workers in their determination to continue the struggle.

In the long run, it has been the *combination* of internal and external forces that has directed the course of the FLOC movement and ultimately enabled FLOC to achieve its goals. Some factors have constrained FLOC, and others have enhanced its effectiveness. Some forces have been stronger than others. But the net result is that in the balance all have been involved in FLOC's success in achieving social changes. And all have to be considered collectively in understanding the events of the FLOC movement. It is the whole interaction of these forces that have led to significant reforms for midwestern farmworkers.

The basic process of change is the reorganization of the system in which a group exists. In the FLOC case, the socioeconomic system in which midwestern farmworkers exist has clearly been reorganized. FLOC is now an established factor in farm labor affairs. Reorganization can occur at two levels. A group can alter its internal characteristics, and it can also alter its external conditions. Both levels of reorganization are evident in the case of the FLOC movement. We would like to turn now to a deeper assessment of this reorganization and how it reflects the adaptation of midwestern farmworkers.

FLOC and Social Adaptation

FLOC is an excellent example of a social reform movement that has been successful in achieving a number of important goals. We have argued, however, that social changes are not necessarily adaptive in themselves. We still need to address the larger issue of how adaptive the changes have been for midwestern farmworkers. The model of adaptation calls for assessing outcomes in terms of how much they contribute to a group's survival and continuation. In the long term, continuation of the group as a viable social unit is the ultimate measure of adaptation. This, though, can take generations to assess. So a number of intermediary measures have been used, such as the evaluation of a group's health. The rationale of such measures is that patterns which contribute to the immediate well-being of a group enhance its long-term chances of viable continuation.

Farmworker Adaptation

We see two overall sets of changes resulting from the FLOC movement and would now like to evaluate how they reflect the well-being and ultimate adaptation of midwestern farmworkers.

(1) Greater self-determination: Farmworker self-determination is a fundamental reform achieved by FLOC in the agricultural system in the Midwest, and many other changes emerge from this one major change. Through FLOC, we have seen, farmworkers can now exercise greater control over their life situation. This basic change has enabled them to achieve other changes. They have now gained more clearly defined working rights, higher wages, more stable work opportunities, better sanitary facilities in the camps and fields, better nutrition, reduced exposure to hazardous pesticides, and greater access to health care. As Fernando Cuevas says, "That's why we fight for a platform that puts the growers and the food corporations at the table with us as equals. We want a fair day's wage for our work. We want the dignity of feeding, clothing, and educating our children from the fruits of our own work." Because they can now speak directly for themselves, FLOC farmworkers are no longer anonymous figures who are cycled through labor tasks.

There are a number of adaptive benefits from these changes. FLOC workers can now enjoy greater occupational stability, greater confidence and security in their work situation, personal growth, and a higher standard of living. These developments foster more productive and healthier lives for both themselves and their children. The immediate improvements in their living and working conditions can only have positive effects.

FLOC workers are now a part of an organized social group that is concerned with their well-being and is able to influence their conditions. Furthermore, this new structure will enable them to *continue* making adaptive changes in the years ahead. The FLOC movement has brought about new conditions that can maximize the quality of the farmworkers' lives for generations. This ongoing self-determination, then, has important implications for the long-term well-being of midwestern farmworkers.[4]

(2) Greater integration into the American socioeconomic system: Another fundamental change in the lives of FLOC farmworkers, as we have seen, is that they are more integrated into the American socioeconomic system. They are less marginal members of society and now more actively participate in social institutions. They are formally associated with FLOC, which ties them more directly with each other. As they compare conditions and consider contract provisions, they gain a broader perspective of farm labor and have established new social relationships in this arena. They are also more formally linked to other segments of the agricultural scene, particularly the growers and large agribusinesses. These links, however, are more as equal partners, and they can more directly contribute their input into the system. We have also noted how FLOC workers are better integrated into the larger American socioeconomic system. Through FLOC, they are linked to labor, religious, and other organizations. With more stability and a higher standard of living, farmworkers can be more active on another level. They are freer to participate in educational, medical, political, and other social institutions. As more productive members of society, they can also contribute their greater purchasing power to the national economic system, which indirectly links them to other American workers.

This greater integration has far-reaching implications for the quality of life experienced by FLOC workers. They can lead more fulfilling and meaningful lives as their marginality is reduced. This is even more true for their children, who are better able to pursue educational and other opportunities. We can thus expect FLOC workers and their families to experience a more positive lifestyle and a more lasting well-being.

In summary, we conclude that the FLOC movement is having an adaptive impact in the lives of midwestern farmworkers. Their well-being is a direct result of the reforms they have been able to achieve through FLOC.

It should be noted that the FLOC movement has provided the predominant means for achieving adaptive reforms for midwestern farmworkers. From time to time, an individual farmer may have shown goodwill and given certain farmworkers greater benefits. Sometimes legislation and regulations may have addressed particular farmworkers' problems. In addition, some social programs have certainly helped meet migrants' survival needs. But the system which has structured farmworkers' deprived conditions has not been basically changed by such events. Adaptive reorganization of the system itself has primarily been achieved by the farm labor movement in the Midwest.

The systems model of change reminds us that adaptation occurs within the context of time. Since the first contracts in 1986, FLOC workers have realized a number of adaptive changes. Yet FLOC leaders recognize that these achievements are only initial ones. They are seeking further advantages for those workers already under contract through programs like leadership development for its members. They are also seeking the basic advantages for workers not yet under contract, in the Midwest and other regions. There is still much to be done in fulfilling their goals. In this sense, the adaptation of midwestern farmworkers is still in progress. The long-term adaptive benefits of the FLOC movement are likely to increase over the coming years.

Adaptive for All

We also believe that the FLOC movement has been adaptive for the rest of us. We have indicated that FLOC's achievements have brought some advantages for farmers and the large food-processing corporations. In particular, they can expect greater stability and productivity from FLOC workers.

From a larger view, farmworkers are a part of the broader American socioeconomic system, and it is a system that changes, not just traits. So we would like to note how the FLOC movement has adaptive advantages for our society as a whole.

A social system is composed of many interacting components. This means that changes in one part of a system will automatically impact on other parts. FLOC has managed to restructure the American socioeconomic system to achieve more benefits for its constituent group. This also means that the larger system is restructured for *all* of us, not just for farmworkers. There are several reasons why we believe FLOC reforms can be beneficial for the American society as a whole.

(1) A more constructive social balance: A social movement can serve to restore an optimal balance in the larger society. A principle underlying the civil rights movement, for example, is that the American society has been seriously imbalanced by discrimination.

There has been a need to restore a functional integration among its member groups, for the good of us all. Whenever a significant proportion of a society is disaffected, the whole system is more unstable. Such imbalance has costs for everyone in the society, not just the disaffected group. This cost can be economic, in such forms as lost productivity and social services for the disadvantaged. In the case of violent protests, there is a loss of property and sometimes lives. There are also serious social costs. Societal stresses and strained ties between groups can seriously undermine the ability of the whole society to function effectively.

In such cases, social reform can help restore a balance that is in the long run constructive for the whole system as well as for the disaffected group. This is the case of the FLOC movement. The deprived conditions of farmworkers have costs for other Americans. For example, health benefits that other Americans have as a normal part of their jobs have to be provided to farmworkers through our taxes. Instead of contributing to the national tax base, deprived people are a drain upon it. Also, with low incomes used primarily to meet survival needs, they are not significant consumers. They cannot contribute to the economic growth of the nation nor to the gainful employment of other Americans. FLOC has altered the course of these problems where midwestern farmworkers are concerned. They now have the promise of being contributing members of the society in which we all live.

(2) Reinforcement of social norms: Another benefit of a reform movement is that it can reinforce social norms, which help the society function more effectively. Every society must encourage social bonds among its members in order to operate together as a more cohesive unit. On the other hand, a society must also contain and resolve internal factionalism that can jeopardize its basic structure and continuity.

Shared values are one way to build efficient interaction among a society's members. People and groups can expect certain behavior from each other, without expending energy to analyze and negotiate every activity. Values also serve as societal symbols that encourage unity. The FLOC movement has drawn upon such basic American norms as individual freedom, self-reliance, and social justice. The participation of so many Americans in a popular boycott has had two effects. It has effectively extended these values as applicable to farmworkers. Also, by including farmworkers in such norms, FLOC supporters have declared such values to be cohesive for the whole society.

(3) Social control of societal institutions: Dominant social values impose limits on personal behavior and call for sanctions to enforce these values. A value on individual life, for example, constrains acts that endanger another, whether a murder or drunken driving, and violators can receive serious penalties. Social values and sanctions, however, also operate on an institutional level. For example, an industry that dumps toxic wastes into water systems can be fined for endangering public health. Both values and their sanctions have an adaptive purpose in maintaining the well-being of a society as a whole.

We argue that a social movement can serve as a means of social control of societal institutions, to maintain an adaptive balance in a society (see Zald 1978). The FLOC movement in many ways has served this purpose with the agricultural industry. As we have seen, Americans have been predisposed to support the farm labor movement, and we have posed several values to explain this predisposition. In supporting FLOC, Americans have in practice stated that central values apply to agricultural corporations as well as to individual growers. Participation in the Campbell boycott proved to be an effective sanction imposed on agribusiness to enforce institutional compliance with norms like working rights and social justice for farmworkers. Societal institutions are therefore put on notice that they must conform to dominant values, as well as on an individual level.

(4) Greater realization of the society's potentials: Perhaps the most important contribution a social movement can make is to enable all members of a society to contribute to its collective well-being. During the 1983 march to Campbell's headquarters in Camden, New Jersey, Baldemar Velásquez addressed a rally in Philadelphia. He called the farmworkers' children up front. He pointed out how one child might become a doctor and discover a new cure for cancer. Another might be a scientist and develop a pollution-free source of energy. Another might be a teacher and nurture the love of learning in our children. He argued how each child had such potentials.

The greatest problem with discrimination is that it denies people the right to fulfill their potentials. For the individuals concerned, the tragedy is that they cannot achieve the most meaningful lives of which they are capable. But the larger society is also a loser. The potentials of each person are lost for us all, whether that person could be a doctor, scientist, teacher, or taxpayer. One of the most significant contributions of the FLOC movement, then,

Baldemar Velásquez addresses a rally in Philadelphia during the 1983 march on Campbell's headquarters. He called the farmworker children to come up front. He pointed to the children and indicated how one might be the scientist who discovers a cure for cancer, how another might be a teacher who can develop the love of learning in our children, and how each one had a potential for greatness. But, Baldemar said, these children would never realize their potentials as long as they had to suffer discrimination and deprived conditions. He emphasized that the loss of their potentials is also a loss for *all* Americans. FLOC's achievements, however, could help these children become contributing members of society, and thus enhance the adaptiveness of this society, for all.

has been to provide the opportunity for midwestern farmworkers and their children to be more productive members of the American society. Having achieved this for farmworkers, FLOC has also enabled them to contribute more to our collective well-being as a society.

Systems Adaptation

We have seen how the systems model of adaptation helps us understand cases of social change. In the FLOC case, we have examined the internal and external forces that have initiated and directed social reforms for midwestern farmworkers. We have considered these reforms as the reorganization of the socioeconomic system in which FLOC workers exist. And we have evaluated these changes as measures of adaptation of midwestern farmworkers.

Lessons about Social Change

Now we would like to review the systems model of adaptation and examine how the FLOC case can help us better understand social change. There are two important lessons about social change that the FLOC movement emphasizes. One concerns forces in social change, and the other involves the process of change.

(1) Forces in social change: In order to have a comprehensive and balanced understanding, we must consider the internal potentials and the external environmental challenges involved as a group faces social change. As we have seen in the FLOC case, the potentials a group brings to a change situation stem from its needs and resources. The challenges in its environmental setting include constraints and opportunities for change.

In essence, a group's internal potentials set the alternatives for change, and the external challenges determine which among these alternatives are most likely to contribute to the group's well-being. The FLOC case illustrates that *both* internal and external forces must be examined. Neither can explain the case of change on its own. Some forces may be strong, and others may be moderate, but all interact to initiate and direct the course of change.

(2) The process of change: The FLOC case also illustrates the process of change. By this, we mean not only the sequence of events in a case of change but how forces interact to initiate and direct change. There are two points to note here. First, we have seen that it is how internal and external forces *interact* that explains which changes occur and how these changes happened.

Second, change involves the *reorganization* of the system. As we have tried to emphasize in the FLOC case, it is a *system* that changes, not just traits. "System" infers interacting components, and in a social system there are many people, groups, traits, and forces involved. One trait cannot change without directly or indirectly impacting on other components of the system. So we must consider how the whole system is affected by the collective interaction of its parts.

We also wish to note again that change in itself is not necessarily adaptive. There has to be some *measure* of whether the changes contribute to the well-being and continuation of the group. This also involves the *time* frames considered. For example, in the 1983 survey of midwestern farmworkers, we observed that those people who actively supported FLOC had higher stress levels. At that time, four years into the Campbell strike and boycott, we might have concluded the FLOC movement was maladaptive. Examining FLOC workers after six years of working under union contracts, however, we have observed a new sense of security, confidence, and personal growth. So we now conclude that the changes achieved by FLOC have been adaptive. Since the larger system has been restructured and since FLOC is now a major force in farm labor affairs, we also conclude that these adaptive developments are likely to continue.

We believe that the systems model of adaptation provides an excellent conceptual structure for understanding social change. It has proven to do so in the FLOC case. Furthermore, we believe that the FLOC movement provides an empirical test of this systems model. We therefore offer it as a basis for understanding other examples of social change, in which case the model can be further tested and refined.

Hasta la Victoria

One last lesson in the FLOC story is that there is a need to better understand what sociocultural change is and how it works. There are many people who daily are trying to make us change. Politicians, businesspeople, scientists, teachers, revolutionaries, and many others want to change our lives. Yet these people typically do not have much understanding of social change. Even where intentions are noble, the consequences of their efforts can range from disastrous to ridiculous.

As we consider the example of the FLOC case and its lessons for social adaptation, we can identify two important policy principles regarding social change. The first is this:

Self-determination is a productive and stable means of social reform for both a disadvantaged group and for the larger society.

The members of any particular social group are in the best position to judge what changes are best for themselves. We need to ask who is making the decisions as well as who is receiving the benefits and who is bearing the costs of those decisions. Others may provide valuable insights and support, but when outsiders make decisions for a group, they will not experience the consequences in the lives of that group's members. When FLOC farmworkers gained the right to negotiate what *they* wanted to gain and would be willing to give, the results have been improved socioeconomic conditions, new health and educational opportunities for their families, and a new sense of security and confidence. We have also seen that self-determination for FLOC farmworkers has had significant benefits for other Americans as well. The adaptive benefits of the FLOC movement can best be understood as we consider the impacts on all levels concerned. This leads to the second important principle of social change:

> *All components of a system need to be examined in order to understand the potential impacts and benefits of change.*

Both the process of change in the FLOC movement and the resulting reforms have involved many different segments of the American socioeconomic system. We have argued that it is systems that change, not just traits or groups. We need to examine all levels of a socioeconomic system in order to understand the potential impacts and benefits of change. Public and private policies must consider the whole socioeconomic system in which changes are being made and must evaluate the adaptive impacts at all levels. A final lesson in the FLOC case, then, is that those who wish to make constructive changes in our society need to understand social change itself.

In closing, we would like to restate the two purposes we have had in examining the farm labor movement in the Midwest. First, we have documented the story of FLOC, its goals, activities, and achievements. To do this, we have drawn upon over ten years of field work, surveys, interviews, and participation. Second, we have tried to explain *why* and *how* FLOC has been successful in reforming the farm labor system. The systems model of adaptation has helped us to organize this effort. We have examined the internal and external forces evident in the FLOC movement. Also, we have examined the processes involved in social change. The systems model of adaptation has helped us to better understand social change in the FLOC case, while the FLOC case in turn has helped us to better understand social change.

For these lessons in social change and social reform, we thank Baldemar Velásquez, Fernando Cuevas, and the FLOC farmworkers, all of whom have not accepted anything less than the justice and dignity they deserve. As we look forward to a better society for us and for our children, we want to remember that FLOC's slogan of "*Hasta la Victoria*," "Onward to Victory," is for all of us.

Notes

Chapter 1: Social Reform and Adaptation

1. "Alfredo" is a composite character. He is based primarily on one FLOC farmworker whom we know well. But we have added events from two other migrant workers whom we also know, in order to illustrate the range of conditions which farmworkers experience.

Chapter 2: Midwestern Farmworkers

1. All direct quotations are from personal interviews unless otherwise indicated.

Chapter 4: The Internal Potentials of the FLOC Movement

1. Since over 90 percent of Midwestern farmworkers are Mexican Americans, it was decided to focus on this group. Respondents were selected by a stratified sampling design based on states (Indiana, Ohio, and Michigan), migrant labor camps for tomato workers (an estimated 52, 160, and 48 camps, respectively), and residential units within camps (an average of 17 housing units per camp, or an estimated 4,420 units). The figures used to develop the sampling design were based on estimates provided by the state agencies that license migrant camps.

The standardized and pretested questionnaire used in the survey took an average of seventy-seven minutes to administer. Nearly all interviews (92 percent) were conducted in Spanish at the respondents' preference. Four individuals were deleted from the analysis because they did not meet the criteria for the defined study group (married, Mexican American).

Statistical reliability checks verified that there were no significant differences in response patterns according to interviewer. There were also no differences according to the state in which interviews were conducted nor the home-base area from which the respondents came. These tests indicate that the survey sample could be treated as representative of one population.

The maximum 90 percent confidence interval for the survey data is plus or minus 13 percent; that is, there is a 90 percent probability that the responses will not vary from those of the larger research population by more than 13 percent (and as little as 0 percent). Where there is missing data of more than 10 percent of the sample on a particular item, this is indicated in the tables. Participant observation for twelve years with farmworkers and the FLOC movement contributed to greater depth of interpretation of the quantitative findings.

We are grateful to the Project Development Program of Indiana University at Indianapolis for its support of the research project. We particularly wish to thank Mary Qualls Grossman and José Castro for helping with the interviewing and Rosio Yaselli for her help with the data analysis.

Chapter 5: The Social Environment of the FLOC Movement

1. The research population was defined as adult members of residential households in Indiana. According to the 1980 census, 93 percent of the households in Indiana have telephones. To ensure that each household had an equal chance of being contacted, a statewide random-digit dialing method was used to select residential telephone numbers. When a household was contacted, one respondent eighteen years of age or older was further randomly selected by age rank. The general purposes of the study and respondents' rights were then explained, and they were asked permission to be interviewed. The interview consisted of administering a pretested standardized questionnaire of both open-ended and closed questions. The interviews averaged twenty minutes.

The actual response rate of those contacted was 72 percent. A few of the randomly generated telephone numbers were never answered. It could not be determined whether these were residential telephones in service, or business, public telephone, or other numbers. Also, two procedures were adopted to save survey costs: certain long-distance telephone zones in the state were undersampled, and some individuals in multiple-adult households were also undersampled. In the data analysis, statistical weights were computed to compensate for these undersamplings.

When the survey sample was compared with the 1980 census, it matched the adult population of Indiana closely in terms of key demographic characteristics: sex, age, ethnic group, education, occupation, and household income. The sample can therefore be taken as representative of adults in Indiana. Several sets of variables reflecting the same general phenomena were combined into scales, though there was no assumption that the component items were necessarily related to each other. For example, in summarizing knowledge about farmworkers' conditions, a general understanding about their annual income is not necessarily related to knowledge about their educational level. Also, in summarizing knowledge about the farm labor movement, knowing about the UFW cannot presume knowing about FLOC. The scales were therefore constructed by simply summing the component variables, without regard to the internal consistency of responses. The data set was then analyzed to determine patterns of public views concerning the farm labor movement and to identify those factors which influence these views.

There is a 95 percent confidence interval of a maximum of plus or minus 5 percent for responses; that is, there is a 95 percent probability that responses will not vary from those of the total research population by more than 5 percent.

The survey was directed by Barger and Dr. Ain Haas, Department of Sociology at Indiana University at Indianapolis. We are grateful to the Indiana Council of Churches, the Indiana Catholic Conference, and the Project Development Program of Indiana University at Indianapolis for their support of the research project. We particularly wish to thank Reverend Harold Statler, Dr. Desmond Ryan, Reverend Patrick Cameron, Father Edward Moszur, and Sister Catherine Doherty for their involvement and support in the project. Vicki Cummings Copenhaver was responsible for project administration, and Sandy Davidson served as interview director.

2. Part of the lack of many significant associations may be related to the small numbers in the sample who participated in the UFW and FLOC boycotts (thirty-eight for the UFW boycotts, and seven for the FLOC boycott).

Chapter 7: Social Adaptation of Midwestern Farmworkers

1. We are confident that relative deprivation has been an important factor in motivating midwestern farmworkers to actively support the FLOC movement. However, we do not have the direct evidence to empirically prove this. There are a number of indications that realities worsened for midwestern farmworkers and that expectations rose by the time of the original strike in 1978. On the one hand, farmworkers' frustrations had increased over the preceding years concerning such factors as the reduction of their real earnings and displacement by mechanization. On the other hand, their hopes had been raised by such events as the successes of the United Farm Workers in California and the Warren strike. Many workers were bitterly disappointed when these hopes were not realized. It is clear that midwestern farmworkers *were* motivated to support FLOC en masse. During the strike and the farm elections, these workers consistently demonstrated an overwhelming support for FLOC, its goals, and its methods. Without the support of its constituent group for the eight years of the strike and boycott, FLOC's successes would have been unlikely.

2. It is hard to say what the nature of "charisma" actually is in social movements. Baldemar Velásquez has shown absolute conviction about farmworkers' rights and justice. His self-sacrifice and his creativity have stimulated others to become involved in FLOC. His followers have included church, labor, and other supporters as well as farmworkers. Other leaders have also been important in building FLOC. For example, Fernando Cuevas

has been a dedicated and tireless figure in organizing farmworkers. The breadth of FLOC's followers, in fact, is one measure of the effectiveness of its leaders.

3. It should be noted that there has been one environmental factor that has not been an obvious force in the FLOC movement—the state. Majka and Majka (1982), in an analysis of the UFW movement, emphasize the role of the state in suppressing or sustaining social reforms. They argue that protest by subordinate groups can initially force concessions from a government. However, the state usually mediates conflicts so that further protest is unnecessary or inappropriate, by absorbing the issues into government agencies. In the long run, the political interests of dominant groups are maintained. This places groups seeking reforms in a dilemma. The original reasons for protest are undercut, and yet they have to devote substantial resources to protect gains, which in the long term places poor groups at a disadvantage. The Majkas' argument has some merit for understanding the UFW case. We have not found these circumstances very evident in the FLOC movement, however. Government officials and agencies, like the Putnam County Sheriff's Department, were sometimes involved at the local level. And there was an investigation of farm labor conditions by the Ohio Senate. But the state and federal governments were generally aloof to the conflict. In this sense, of course, it could be argued that they were a force for those in power, since they exerted no pressure on changing the existing system.

However, the Majkas note exceptions to the state serving the interests of dominant groups. The more reform efforts are sustained by disadvantaged groups, they argue, the less the state is able to control changes. In some cases, the struggle can dominate the development of state structures and win a structural shift in power. This was evident with the labor movement in the 1930's and the civil rights movement in the 1960's and 1970's, for example. The Majkas argue that where democratic processes are established, mechanisms for influence of reforms are more possible. These are the circumstances evident in the FLOC movement, we believe.

4. It should be noted that not all midwestern farmworkers have benefited from the FLOC movement. There are still many workers, who are not covered by FLOC contracts, who continue to work cherry, apple, asparagus, mushroom, shrubbery, and other crops. It should be noted, too, that there have been some benefits to nonunion workers as a result of the FLOC movement, such as increased wages and improved sanitation facilities. But these benefits are irregular, and there are no guarantees that they will be continued. More important, these farmworkers have no voice in their own conditions. They are still dependent upon growers, canneries, politicians, and other vested interests for whatever conditions they experience.

Bibliography

Aberle, David F.
  1967   *The Peyote Religion among the Navaho.* Aldine.
Acosta, Phyllis B., Robert Aranda, Jane Lewis, and Marsha Reid
  1974   "Nutritional Status of Mexican American Preschool Children in a Border Town." *American Journal of Clinical Nutrition* 27: 1359–1368.
Acuña, Rodolfo
  1988   *Occupied America: A History of Chicanos.* 3d ed. Harper and Row.
Alinsky, Saul D.
  1969   *Reveille for Radicals.* Random House.
  1971   *Rules for Radicals.* Random House.
Alland, Alexander, Jr.
  1967   *Evolution and Human Behavior.* Natural History Press.
  1970   *Adaptation in Cultural Evolution.* Columbia University Press.
  1972   "Cultural Evolution." *Social Biology* 19:227–239.
  1975   "Adaptation." *Annual Review of Anthropology* 4:59–73.
Alland, Alexander, Jr., and Bonnie McCay
  1973   "The Concept of Adaptation in Biological and Cultural Evolution." In *Handbook of Social and Cultural Anthropology.* John J. Honigmann, ed. Rand McNally.
Allen, Robert E., and Timothy J. Keaveny
  1988   *Contemporary Labor Relations.* 2d ed. Addison-Wesley.
Allen, Steve
  1966   *The Ground Is Our Table.* Doubleday.
Arensberg, Conrad M.
  1978   "Theoretical Contributions of Industrial and Development Studies." In *Applied Anthropology in America.* Elizabeth M. Eddy and William L. Partridge, eds. Columbia University Press.

Ash, Roberta
     1972   *Social Movements in America.* Markham.
Bakersfield Californian
     1984   "Stirling Took Ride to Hearing from Grower's Lawyer: Ethical
               Questions Arise in Wake of ALRB Counsel's Disclosure." *Bakers-
               field Californian* (April 29): A2.
Barger, W. K.
     1977   "Culture Change and Psychosocial Adjustment." *American Eth-
               nologist* 4(3): 471–495.
     1982   "Cultural Adaptation." *Anthropology and Humanism Quarterly*
               7(2–3): 17–21.
     1987   "California Public Endorses the United Farm Workers." *La Red*
               105: 4–6.
Barger, W. K., and Ain Haas
     1983   "Public Attitudes Toward Mexican-American Farmworkers in
               the Midwest." *La Red* 63: 2–4.
Barger, W. K., and Ernesto Reza
     1984a   "Views of Midwestern Farmworkers Concerning the Farm Labor
               Movement." *La Red* 78: 2–7.
     1984b   "Midwestern Farmworkers Support the Farm Labor Movement."
               Science for the People 16(5): 11–15.
     1985a   "Processes in Applied Sociocultural Change and the Farmworker
               Movement in the Midwest." *Human Organization* 44(3): 268–
               283.
     1985b   "Views of California Farmworkers Regarding the Farm Labor
               Movement." *La Red* 91: 3–5.
     1987   "Community Action and Sociocultural Change: The Farmworker
               Movement in the Midwest." In *Collaborative Research and So-
               cial Change.* Donald D. Stull and Jean J. Schensul, eds. Westview
               Press.
     1989   "Policy and Community-Action Research: The Farm Labor Move-
               ment in California." In *Making Our Research Useful: Case Stud-
               ies in the Utilization of Anthropological Knowledge.* John van
               Willigen, Barbara Rylko-Bauer, and Ann McElroy, eds. Westview
               Press.
Barnett, Homer G.
     1953   *Innovation: The Basis of Cultural Change.* McGraw-Hill.
Barnett, S. E., and R. L. Call
     1979   "Student Community Dental Experience with Migrant Farm
               Worker Families and the Rural Pool." *American Journal of Public
               Health* 69: 1107-1113.
Barth, Frederick
     1956   "Ecological Relationships of Ethnic Groups in Swat, North Paki-
               stan." *American Anthropologist* 58: 1079-1089.
Bleiweis, Phyllis R., R. C. Reynolds, L. D. Cohen, and N. Butler
     1977   "Health Care Characteristics of Migrant Agricultural Workers in

Three North Florida Counties." *Journal of Community Health* 3:32–43.

Borjas, George J., and Marta Tienda
1985   *Hispanics in the U.S. Economy.* Academic Press.

Braidwood, R. J.
1967   *Prehistoric Man.* Scott, Foresman.

Burnaway, Michael
1976   "Functions and Reproduction of Migrant Labor." *American Journal of Sociology* 81(5): 1050-1087.

Buss, Fran Leeper
1985   *Dignity: Lower Income Women Tell of Their Lives and Struggles.* University of Michigan Press.

Cardenas, Gilbert
1976   "Los Desarraigados: Chicanos in the Midwestern Region of the United States." *Aztlán* 7:153–186.

Carlson, Alvar W.
1976   "Specialty Agriculture and Migrant Laborers in Northwestern Ohio." *Journal of Geography* 5:292–310.

Catholic Universe Bulletin
1984   "Chavez Renews Grape Boycott, Old Alliances." *Catholic Universe Bulletin* (November 9):17.

Chase, H. Peter, V. Kumar, J. M. Dodds, and H. E. Sauberlich
1971   "Nutritional Status of Preschool Mexican-American Migrant Farm Children." *American Journal of Disease in Children* 122: 316–324.

Chávez, César
1976   "California Farm Workers' Struggle." *Black Scholar* 7:16–19.
1985   "Deukmejian Has a Bitter Crop for Farm Workers." *Philadelphia Enquirer* (July 10):9A.

Cleveland Plain Dealer
1986   "Farm Workers, Campbell Soup Agree to Contracts." *Cleveland Plain Dealer* (February 20):14.

Clifton, James A., ed.
1970   *Applied Anthropology: Readings in the Uses of the Science of Man.* Houghton Mifflin.

Cockburn, T. Aidan
1971   "Infectious Diseases in Ancient Populations." *Current Anthropology* 12:45–62.

Cockcroft, James D.
1986   *Outlaws in the Promised Land: Mexican Immigrant Workers and America's Future.* Grove Press.

Coffey, Joseph D.
1969   "National Labor Relations Legislation: Possible Impact on American Agriculture." *American Journal of Agricultural Economics* 51:1072–1073.

Cohen, Yehudi A.
  1971   "Adaptation and Evolution." In *Man in Adaptation: The Institutional Framework*. Yehudi A. Cohen, ed. Aldine.
Coles, Robert
  1970   *Uprooted Children: The Early Life of Migrant Farm Workers*. University of Pittsburgh Press.
Columbia Broadcasting System
  1960   "Harvest of Shame." Television documentary.
Coye, Molly Joel
  1985   "The Health Effects of Agricultural Production: I. The Health of Agricultural Workers." *Journal of Public Health Policy* 6(3): 348–370.
Craddock, Brian R.
  1979   *Farmworker Protective Laws*. Motivation Education and Training, Inc.
Dahrendorf, Ralf
  1964   "Toward a Theory of Social Conflict." In *Social Change*. Amitai Etzioni and Eva Etzioni, eds. Basic Books.
Daniel, Cletus E.
  1981   *Bitter Harvest: A History of California Farmworkers, 1870–1941*. University of California Press.
Davies, John E.
  1977   *Pesticide Protection: A Training Manual for Health Personnel*. U.S. Environmental Protection Agency.
Day, Mark
  1971   *Forty Acres: Cesar Chavez and the Farm Workers*. Praeger.
Denny, William M.
  1979   "Participant Citizenship in a Marginal Group: Union Mobilization of California Farmworkers." *American Journal of Political Science* 23:330–337.
DiMarco, N.
  1974   "Stress and Adaptation in Cross-Cultural Transition." *Psychological Reports* 35:279–285.
Dubos, Rene
  1965   *Man Adapting*. Yale University Press.
Dunn, Frederick L.
  1968   "Epidemiological Factors: Health and Disease in Hunter-Gatherers." In *Man the Hunter*. Richard L. Lee and Irvin DeVore, eds. Aldine.
Education Commission of the States
  1979   *Migrant Health*. Interstate Migrant Education Task Force.
Field, Mervin
  1985   "Public's Opinion Split on UFW Grape Boycott." *Bakersfield Californian* (September 8):E3.
Freeman, Jo
  1979   "Resource Mobilization and Strategy." In *The Dynamics of So-*

cial Movements. Mayer N. Zald and John D. McCarthy, eds. Winthrop.

Fresno Bee
1984   "Chavez Renews Grape Boycott." *Fresno Bee* (July 12):6.

Friedland, William
1969   "Labor Waste in New York: Rural Exploitation and Migrant Workers." *Transaction* 6(4):48–53.

Friedland, William, and Dorothy Nelkin
1972   "Technological Trends and the Organization of Migrant Farm Workers." *Social Problems* 19:504–521.

Friedland, William, and Robert T. Thomas
1974   "Paradoxes of Agricultural Unionism in California." *Society* (May–June):54–62.

Fuller, V., and B. Mason
1977   "Farm Labor." *Annals of the American Academy of Political and Social Sciences* 429:63–80.

Galarza, Ernesto
1964   *Merchants of Labor: The Mexican Bracero Story.* McNally and Loftin.
1970   *Mexican-Americans in the Southwest.* McNally and Loftin.
1977   *Farm Workers and Agri-Business in California, 1947–1960.* University of Notre Dame Press.

Galasch, H. F., Jr.
1975   "Minimum Wages and the Farm Labor Market." *Southern Economic Journal* 41:480–491.

Geertz, Clifford
1963   *Agricultural Involution.* University of California Press.
1972   "The Wet and the Dry: Traditional Irrigation in Bali and Morocco." *Human Ecology* 1:23–40.

Geschwender, James A.
1968   "Explorations in the Theory of Social Movements and Revolutions." *Social Forces* 47(2):127–135.

Goldfarb, Ronald
1982   *Migrant Farm Workers: A Caste of Despair.* Iowa State University Press.

Gomez-Quiñones, Juan
1982   *Development of the Mexican Working Class North of the Rio Bravo: Work and Culture among Laborers and Artisans, 1600–1900.* Popular Series No. 2, Chicano Studies Research Center Publications, University of California, Los Angeles.

Gomez-Quiñones, Juan, and Luis Leobardo Arroyo
1978   *Orígenes del Movimiento Obrero Chicano.* Serie Popular Era, Mexico.

Good Neighbor Commission
1977   *Texas Migrant Labor.* Good Neighbor Commission of Texas.

Gusfield, Joseph R., ed.
   1970   *Protest, Reform, and Revolt*. Wiley.
Harper, David, Bobby Mills, and Ronald Farris
   1974   "Exploitation in Migrant Labor Camps." *British Journal of Sociology* 25(3): 283–295.
Harris, Louis
   1975   "Chávez Favored 6 to 1 by Public in Farm Dispute." *Long Beach Press Telegram* (October 20): 6.
Harris, Marvin
   1966   "The Cultural Ecology of India's Sacred Cattle." *Current Anthropology* 7: 51–60.
Hightower, Jim
   1978   *Hard Tomatoes, Hard Times*. Schenken.
Hoffman, Cecil
   1978   "Empowerment Movements and Mental Health: Locus of Control and Commitment to the United Farm Workers." *Journal of Community Psychology* 6(3): 216–221.
Holmberg, Allen R.
   1958   "The Research and Development Approach to the Study of Change." *Human Organization* 17: 12–16.
Howard, John R.
   1974   *The Cutting Edge: Social Movements and Social Change in America*. Lippincott.
Indiana Advisory Committee
   1974   *Indiana Migrants*. U.S. Commission on Civil Rights.
Jacobson, Mark L., M. A. Mercer, L. K. Miller, and T. W. Simpson
   1987   "Tuberculosis Risk among Migrant Farm Workers on the Delmarva Peninsula." *American Journal of Public Health* 77: 29–32.
Jenkins, J. Craig
   1985   *The Politics of Insurgency*. Columbia University Press.
Jenkins, J. Craig, and C. Perrow
   1977   "Insurgency of the Powerless: Farmworker Movements (1964–1972)." *American Sociological Review* 42(2): 249–268.
Johnson, Thomas M.
   1976   "Sociocultural Factors in the Intergroup Perception of Health Problems: A Case of Grower Attitudes Toward Their Migrant Labor." *Human Organization* 35: 79–83.
Katz, Daniel
   1967   "Group Processes and Social Integration: A Systems Analysis of Two Movements of Social Protest." *Journal of Social Issues* 23(1): 3–22.
   1974   "Factors Affecting Social Change: A Social Psychological Interpretation." *Journal of Social Issues* 30(3): 159–180.
Kaufman, Mildred, Eugene Lewis, Albert V. Hardy, and Joanne Proul
   1975   "Florida Seasonal Farm Workers: Following a Nutritional Study." *Journal of the American Dietetics Association* 66: 605–609.

Khare, R. S.
1962   "Ritual Purity and Pollution in Relation to Domestic Sanitation." *Eastern Anthropologist* 15:125–139.
Killian, Lewis M.
1964   "Social Movements." In *Handbook of Modern Sociology*. Robert E. L. Faris, ed. Rand McNally.
Kimball, Solon T.
1978   "Anthropology as a Policy Science." In *Applied Anthropology in America*. Elizabeth M. Eddy and William L. Partridge, eds. Columbia University Press.
Kiser, George C., and Martha Woody Kiser
1979   *Mexican Workers in the United States: Historical and Political Perspectives*. University of New Mexico Press.
Kushner, Sam
1975   *Long Road to Delano*. International Publishers.
Larson, Lora Beth, J. M. Dodds, D. M. Massoth, and H. P. Chase
1974   "Nutritional Status of Children of Mexican-American Migrant Families." *Journal of the American Dietetic Association* 64: 29–35.
Levy, Jacques
1975   *César Chávez: Autobiography of La Causa*. W. W. Norton.
Lewontin, Richard C.
1978   "Adaptation." *Scientific American* 239(3):212–230.
London, Joan, and Henry Anderson
1970   *So Shall Ye Reap*. Crowell.
Los Angeles Times
1984a   "Chavez Launches a New Global Grape Boycott." *Los Angeles Times* (July 21, sec. 4):5.
1984b   "Woman Is Named New Farm Labor Board Chief." *Los Angeles Times* (July 26, sec. 4):2.
Majka, Linda C.
1981   "Labor Militancy among Farm Workers and the Strategy of Protest: 1900–1979." *Social Problems* 28(5):533–547.
Majka, Linda C., and Theo J. Majka
1982   *Farm Workers, Agribusiness, and the State*. Temple University Press.
Maquet, Jacques
1964   "Objectivity in Anthropology." *Current Anthropology* 5:47–55.
Marx, Karl
1904   *The Critique of Political Economy*. 1859. Reprint. International Library.
Mazess, Richard B.
1975   "Biological Adaptation: Aptitudes and Acclimatization." In *Biosocial Interrelations in Population Adaptation*. Elizabeth S. Watts, Francis E. Johnston, and Gabriel W. Lasker, eds. Aldine.
1978   "Adaptation: A Conceptual Framework." In *Evolutionary Mod-*

els and Studies in Human Diversity. Robert J. Meier, Charlotte M. Otten, and Fathi Abdel-Hameed, eds. Mouton.

McCarthy, John D., and Mayer N. Zald
  1977   "Resource Mobilization and Social Movements." *American Journal of Sociology* 82(6): 1212–1241.

McDonagh, E. C.
  1955   "Attitudes Toward Ethnic Farm Workers in Coachella Valley." *Sociology and Social Research* 40: 10–18.

McElroy, Ann, and Patricia K. Townsend
  1979   *Medical Anthropology in Ecological Perspective.* Westview Press.

McGill, Nettie Pauline
  1929   *Children in Agriculture.* U.S. Children's Bureau.

McWilliams, Carey
  1939   *Factories in the Field.* Little, Brown.
  1944   *Ill Fares the Land.* Little, Brown.

Meier, Matt S., and Feliciano Rivera
  1972   *The Chicanos: A History of Mexican Americans.* Hill and Wang.

Meister, Dick, and Anne Loftis
  1977   *A Long Time Coming: The Struggle to Organize America's Farm Workers.* Macmillan.

Miller, James G.
  1978   *Living Systems.* McGraw-Hill.

Mooney, James
  1965   *The Ghost Dance Religion and the Sioux Outbreak of 1890.* University of Chicago Press.

Moore, Truman E.
  1965   *The Slaves We Rent.* Random House.

Moran, Emilio
  1979   *Human Adaptability.* Duxbury Press.

Morrison, D. E.
  1971   "Some Notes Toward Theory on Relative Deprivation." *American Behavioral Scientist* 14(5): 675–690.

Murphy, Raymond J., and James M. Watson
  1971   "Level of Aspiration, Discontent, and Support of Violence: A Test of the Expected Hypothesis." In *The Black Revolt.* James A. Geschwender, ed. Prentice-Hall.

Murphy, Robert F., and Julian H. Steward
  1956   "Tappers and Trappers: Parallel Process in Acculturation." *Economic Development and Cultural Change* 4: 335–353.

Murrillo, Nathan
  1971   "The Mexican American Family." In *Chicanos.* Nathaniel N. Wagner and Marsha J. Haug, eds. C. V. Mosby.

National Broadcasting Company
  1980   "The Migrants." Television documentary.

National Rural Health Care Association
  1985   *The Occupational Health of Migrant and Seasonal Farmworkers*

in the United States: Report Summary. National Rural Health Care Association.

New York Times
1986   "Campbell Soup Accord Ends a Decade of Strife." *New York Times* (February 24):B7.

Nicholas, Ralph W.
1973   "Social and Political Movements." *Annual Review of Anthropology* 2:63–84.

Orlove, Benjamin S.
1980   "Ecological Anthropology." *Annual Review of Anthropology* 9:235–273.

Packer
1984   "ALRB Policy Allows General Counsel to Question Levied Specifications." *Packer* (July 28):6.

Parsons, Talcott
1964   "A Functional Theory of Change." In *Social Change*. Amitai Etzioni and Eva Etzioni, eds. Basic Books.

Partridge, William L., and Elizabeth M. Eddy
1978   "The Development of Applied Anthropology in America." In *Applied Anthropology in America*. Elizabeth M. Eddy and William L. Partridge, eds. Columbia University Press.

Perry, Joseph B., Jr., and Eldon E. Snyder
1971   "Opinions of Farm Employers Toward Welfare Assistance for Mexican American Migrant Workers." *Sociology and Social Research* 55:161–169.

Pollock, George H.
1961   "Mourning and Adaptation." *International Journal of Psycho-Analysis* 42:341–361.

Pratt, M.
1973   "Effect of Mechanization on Migrant Farm Workers." *Social Casework* 54:105–113.

President's Commission on Migratory Labor
1951   *Report of the President's Commission on Migratory Labor*. President's Commission.

Rappaport, Roy
1968   *Pigs for the Ancestors*. Yale University Press.
1971   "The Flow of Energy in an Agricultural Society." *Scientific American* 224(3):116–132.

Reavis, Dick J.
1978   *Without Documents*. Condor.

Reining, Conrad C.
1962   "A Lost Period of Applied Anthropology." *American Anthropologist* 38:149–152.

Reno, Lee P.
1970   *Pieces and Scraps: Farm Labor Housing in the U.S.* Rural Housing Alliance.

Roach, Jack L., and Janet K. Roach
  1981   "Organizing the Poor." In *The Solution to Social Problems*. 2d
          ed. Martin S. Weinberg, Earl Rubington, and Sue Keifer Ham-
          mersmith, eds. Oxford University Press.
Rochin, Refugio I.
  1977   "New Perspectives on Agricultural Labor Relations in Califor-
          nia." *Labor Law Journal* 28(7): 395–402.
Ross, Fred
  1989   *Conquering Goliath: César Chávez at the Beginning*. El Taller
          Gráfico Press/United Farm Workers.
Rubel, Arthur
  1966   *Across the Tracks: Mexican Americans in a Texas City*. Austin:
          University of Texas Press.
Rudd, Peter
  1975   "The United Farm Workers Clinic in Delano, California: A Study
          of the Rural Poor." *Public Health Reports* 90(4): 331–339.
Sable, Martin H.
  1987   *Mexican and Mexican-American Agricultural Labor in the
          United States: An International Bibliography*. Haworth Press.
Sacramento Bee
  1984   "UFW's Chavez Announces New Grape Boycott." *Sacramento
          Bee* (July 12):A3.
Sahlins, Marshall D., and Elmer R. Service
  1960   *Evolution and Culture*. University of Michigan Press.
Samora, Julian
  1971   *Los Mujados: The Wetback Story*. University of Notre Dame
          Press.
  1977   *A History of the Mexican-American People*. University of Notre
          Dame Press.
San Francisco Chronicle
  1984a   "New Direction Seen for ALRB." *San Francisco Chronicle* (Au-
          gust 19):6.
  1984b   "Cesar Chavez's Fall From Grace." *San Francisco Chronicle* (Oc-
          tober 21):8.
  1984c   "State Farm Labor Board Sues Its Attorney in Power Struggle."
          San Francisco Chronicle (November 27):12.
  1985   "ALRB Official's Ouster Demanded: Church Leaders' Charges."
          San Francisco Chronicle (October 22):8.
San Jose Mercury News
  1984   "Cesar Chavez: Is Anyone Following the Leader?" *San Jose Mer-
          cury News West Magazine* (August 19):6–8.
Schensul, Jean J.
  1985   "Systems Consistency in Field Research, Dissemination, and So-
          cial Change." *American Behavioral Scientist* 29(2): 186–204.
  1987   "Knowledge Utilization: An Anthropological Perspective." *Prac-
          ticing Anthropology* 9(1): 6–8.

Schensul, Stephen L., and Jean L. Schensul
  1978   "Advocacy and Applied Anthropology." In *Social Scientists as Advocates: Views from the Applied Disciplines*. George Wender and George McCall, eds. Sage.
Schwartz, Harry
  1945   *Seasonal Farm Labor in the United States*. Columbia University Press.
Schwartz, Theodore
  1962   "The Paliau Movement in the Admiralty Islands, 1946–1954." *Anthropological Papers of the American Museum of Natural History* 49:207–421.
Scott, Alan
  1990   *Ideology and the New Social Movements*. Unwin Hyman.
Scruggs, Otey M.
  1988   *Braceros, "Wetbacks," and the Farm Labor Problem: Mexican Agricultural Labor in the United States, 1942–1954*. Garland Publishing.
Shenkin, Budd N.
  1974   *Health Care for Migrant Workers: Policies and Politics*. Ballinger.
Siewierski, Marie
  1984   *Determination and Assessment of Pesticide Exposure*. Elsevier.
Smelser, N. J.
  1963   *Theory of Collective Behavior*. Free Press.
Smith, T. L.
  1970   "Farm Labor Trends in the U.S., 1910–1969." *International Labor Review* 102(2):149–169.
Snow, David, E. Burke Rochford, Steven K. Worden, and Robert D. Benford
  1986   "Frame Alignment Processes." *American Sociological Review* 51(5):464–481.
Solis, F.
  1971   "Socioeconomic and Cultural Conditions of Migrant Workers." *Social Casework* 52:308–315.
Sosnick, Stephen H.
  1978   *Hired Hands*. McNally and Loftin, West.
Steinbeck, John
  1988   *The Grapes of Wrath*. 1938. Reprint. Viking Press.
Stern, J. J.
  1970   "The Meaning of 'Adaptation' and Its Relation to the Phenomenon of Natural Selection." In *Evolutionary Biology*. Vol. 4. Theodosius H. Dobzhansky, ed. Appleton-Century-Crofts.
Steward, Julian H.
  1955   *Theory of Culture Change*. University of Illinois Press.
Stini, William A.
  1975   *Ecology and Human Adaptation*. Brown.
Tax, Sol
  1958   "The Fox Project." *Human Organization* 17:17–19.

Thompson, Laura
  1965   "Is Applied Anthropology Helping to Develop a Science of Man?"
          Human Organization 24:277–287.
Toledo Blade
  1986   "FLOC Signs Contract with Campbell, Growers on Rights of
          Farm Workers." *Toledo Blade* (February 20):1.
U.S. Senate Subcommittee on Migratory Labor
  1970   *Migrant and Seasonal Farmworker Powerlessness.* U.S. Senate
          Subcommittee on Migratory Labor.
Valdés, Dennis Nodin
  1984   "From Following the Crops to Chasing the Corporations: The
          Farm Labor Organizing Committee, 1967–1983." In *The Chi-
          cano Struggle.* Guadalupe Luna, ed. Bilingual Press.
  1989   "The New Northern Borderlands: An Overview of Midwestern
          Chicano History." In *Perspectives in Mexican American Studies.
          Vol. 2, Mexicans in the Midwest.* Juan R. Garcia, ed. Mexican
          American Studies and Research Center, University of Arizona.
  1991   *Al Norte: Agricultural Workers in the Great Lakes Region,
          1917–1970.* University of Texas Press.
Village Voice
  1984   "Cesar Chavez's Fall From Grace." *Village Voice* (August 14):
          6–8; (August 19):12.
Wallace, Anthony F. C.
  1956   "Revitalization Movements." *American Anthropologist* 58:264–
          281.
  1970   *The Death and Rebirth of the Seneca.* Knopf.
Walsh, Edward J.
  1978   "On the Interaction Between a Movement and Its Environment."
          American Sociological Review 43(2):110–112.
Walsh, Edward J., and Charles Craypo
  1979   "Union Oligarchy and the Grass Roots: The Case of the Team-
          sters' Defeat in Farmworker Organizing." *Sociology and Social
          Research* 63:269–293.
Ware, George W.
  1978   *The Pesticide Book.* W. H. Freeman.
West, Irma
  1964   "Occupational Diseases of Farm Workers." *Archives of Environ-
          mental Health* 9(1):92–98.
West, Stanley A., and June Macklin
  1979   *The Chicano Experience.* Westview Press.
Wilk, Valerie A.
  1986   *The Occupational Health of Migrant and Seasonal Farmworkers
          in the United States.* Farmworker Justice Fund.
Williams, George C.
  1966   *Adaptation and Natural Selection: A Critique of Some Evolu-
          tionary Thought.* Princeton University Press.

Young, Jan
  1974   *The Migrant Workers and César Chávez.* Julian Messner.
Zald, Mayer N.
  1978   "On the Social Control of Industries." *Social Forces* 57(1):
          79–102.
Zald, Mayer N., and Roberta Ash
  1966   "Social Movement Organizations." *Social Forces* 44(3): 327–341.
Zald, Mayer N., and John D. McCarthy
  1979a   Introduction. In *The Dynamics of Social Movements.* Mayer N.
          Zald and John D. McCarthy, eds. Winthrop.
  1979b   Epilogue. In *The Dynamics of Social Movements.* Mayer N. Zald
          and John D. McCarthy, eds. Winthrop.

Index

Adaptation and social change: applied change, xv, 6; concept of, xi, xiii, 4–11, 98, 130, 139, 141, 174–175, 190, 192, 204–207; environmental challenges and external forces in change, xiii, 4, 12, 15, 92, 141, 175, 205; group-level change, 12; internal and external levels of change, 12–13; internal potentials and forces in change, 4, 13–15, 98, 130, 139, 175, 192, 194, 205; measures of adaptive change, 11–12, 174, 192, 198–199, 205; process of change, interaction of forces, and reorganization of the system in, xi, xiii, 11–18, 174, 190, 192, 197–198, 205–206; productive change, 206–207; social movements as an example of, 6–9, 18–19, 52; systems change, xiii, 9–11, 174–175, 190–192, 201, 205, 207; time frames in adaptive change, 17–18, 201

Agricultural Labor Relations Act (California), 47

Agricultural system, 23–26, 44, 174, 181; crew leaders in, 23–24, 40; and farmworkers, ix, 20–21, 23–26, 40–41, 63–65, 110, 114, 170, 182, 196; and food-processing corporations, 23–24, 35, 40–41, 44, 49–51, 58, 60–61, 63–65, 70, 75, 134, 168, 190; and growers/farmers, 23–25, 40–41, 58–61, 63–65, 73–74, 114, 134, 143–144, 170, 182–184. *See also* Corporations; Crew leaders; Farmworkers; Forces in the FLOC movement: external forces; Growers

American society and the farm labor movement, 5, 96–97, 173, 181, 187, 187–191, 200–204, 212

Anglos, local: reactions of, to FLOC movement, 58, 63, 69–70, 143–144, 170. *See also* Forces in the FLOC movement: external forces

Board of directors and union officers of FLOC, 54, 87, 89, 91–92, 99

Boycotts by farmworker organizations: effectiveness of, 50, 69–70, 78, 121, 148, 150, 153–154, 157–159, 164, 169, 172, 179, 197, 198; farmworkers' views about, 118, 119; FLOC boycott against Campbell Soup, 2, 4, 67–71, 77–79, 85, 103, 118, 119, 133–135, 147, 148, 156, 157, 193–196, 203; as a means for popular participation in social reform, 47,